CONTEM

AFRICA

M000204423

Contemporary States and Societies Series

This series provides lively and accessible introductions to key countries and regions of the world, conceived and designed to meet the needs of today's students. The authors are all experts with specialist knowledge of the country or region concerned and have been chosen also for their ability to communicate clearly to a non-specialist readership. Each text has been specially commissioned for the series and is structured according to a common format.

Published

Contemporary India
Katharine Adeney and Andrew Wyatt

Contemporary Russia (3rd edition)
Edwin Bacon

Contemporary China (3rd edition)
Kerry Brown

Contemporary South Africa (3rd edition)
Anthony Butler

Contemporary France
Helen Drake

Contemporary United States (5th edition)
Russell Duncan and Joseph Goddard

Contemporary Africa
Matthew Graham

Contemporary Japan (3rd edition)
Duncan McCargo

Contemporary Britain (4th edition)
John McCormick

Contemporary Latin America (3rd edition)
Ronaldo Munck

Contemporary Ireland
Eoin O'Malley

Forthcoming

Contemporary Russia (4th edition)
Edwin Bacon

Contemporary France (2nd edition)
Helen Drake

Contemporary Europe
Mikko Kuisma

Contemporary Asia
John McKay

CONTEMPORARY AFRICA

MATTHEW GRAHAM

First published 2019 by
RED GLOBE PRESS

Red Globe Press in the UK is an imprint of Springer Nature Limited, registered in England, company number 785998, of 4 Crinan Street, London, N1 9XW.

Red Globe Press® is a registered trademark in the United States, the United Kingdom, Europe and other countries.

ISBN 978–1–137–50034–2 hardback
ISBN 978–1–137–50033–5 paperback

A catalogue record for this book is available from the British Library.

A catalog record for this book is available from the Library of Congress.

CONTENTS

LIST OF ILLUSTRATIVE MATERIAL

Maps

Boxes

Tables

Images

Chart

PREFACE AND ACKNOWLEDEGMENTS

This book on Africa has been written as a relatively short and accessible introduction into this fascinating and regularly misunderstood continent. The book makes no assumptions about prior knowledge, and addresses themes concerning the entire continent by providing an introductory yet rigorous insight into a range of topics, including Africa's history, key political and economic developments, the emergence of social movements, the causes behind conflict, and popular culture. A core aim of the book is to challenge the misconceptions of the continent, and to move beyond the reductive and misleading popular perceptions that depict Africa through the prism of the 'single story'.

The challenge of writing such a book has been to distil a wide array of topics, and multiple case studies, into a readable, comprehensive, yet concise text. In doing so, I have had to be selective in my choice of examples. I could not include everything, but wherever possible I have sought to provide a range of examples that demonstrate Africa's diversity – I hope the reader takes this into account if something has been excluded. I have thoroughly enjoyed writing this book and expanding my own knowledge on a range of African topics, and I hope that by reading it you too will be enthused and encouraged to keep on finding out more about the continent.

I am extremely grateful to a lot of people who have been involved in the research and writing of this book, of which there are too many to mention here. I would like to thank Nandini Bhattacharya for her support, encouragement, and critical comments on the various drafts, the anonymous reviewers for their constructive and helpful comments on how to improve the final manuscript, Lloyd Langman and Lauren Ferreira for all their guidance throughout the project, and the team at Red Globe Press who have made this book a reality. I would like to thank the History programme, and my colleagues in the School of Humanities at the University of Dundee for making it a stimulating and enjoyable place to work, as well as to all the students who I have had the pleasure and privilege of teaching African and South African history to here. I would also like to acknowledge the International Studies Group at the University of the Free State, where I am a Research Associate, for their support in writing this book.

Finally, my utmost thanks to the invaluable encouragement and input from my family: Bill, Lorraine, Rachael, Ryan, Iris, Mary, and Clive. They have constantly supported my academic journey. Thank you.

Matt Graham
Dundee

1 WHAT IS AFRICA?

Africa is probably the most misunderstood region in the world. It is a continent that generates an enormous amount of interest and attention, yet is also subject to significant misrepresentation and generalisation that does little to account for its diversity or complexity. Africa is home to over 1 billion people (UN, 2017) and is the most linguistically varied place on earth with over two thousand languages spoken, but all too frequently, it is often viewed as a homogeneous, single entity. Nonetheless, in the west such a perception is commonly encountered and perpetuated. Owing to the sheer size of Africa, it can often be difficult to comprehend the vast differences, hence the resort to oversimplification. Furthermore, at first glance, certain developments that have occurred seem to have little consistency, or are simply regarded as uniquely 'African', such as authoritarianism, corruption, and the collapse of states. For those uninitiated in African affairs, trying to understand these trajectories can be overwhelming. In order to provide some coherence to this web of complexity, the stock response is to slip into reductive explanations that do little to explain *why* things have happened. The consequence is to simply look at the outcome, rather than to understand how and why they have occurred.

This book sets out to challenge and break down such simplistic perspectives, and to provide different ways of thinking about Africa. It seeks to highlight the diversity and multitude of differences that Africa offers. The continent provides a fascinating canvas from which to study a range of political, historical, economic, societal, and cultural themes. Although this book emphasises Africa's heterogeneity throughout, it does not posit that effective and intuitive comparisons cannot be made about it. In terms of historical and political trajectories there are a series of remarkable similarities, which include the experiences of European colonial rule; experiments with divergent forms of political and economic systems (often with varying degrees of success); the challenges and inhibitors associated with poor governance and conflict; and more recently, the consolidation of democratic structures, and rapid economic growth across the continent. The outcome is a rich tapestry of case studies that will allow the reader to develop a broader knowledge of Africa, and to critically investigate a range of ideas and issues.

The central aims of this book are to challenge easy and reductive assumptions, and to provide a short and clear introduction into contemporary Africa's social, economic, political, and cultural composition. It will offer a succinct, overarching assessment of Africa, with the primary purpose of explaining the reasons why the continent is where it is today. It will address broad themes such as modes of governance, economic systems, and culture, which will act as an introduction to the continent. This book makes the assumption of no prior knowledge when examining these topics. The overarching and broader points will be supported by a range of supplementary information in the form of specific boxed case studies, maps, graphs, and images that will add relevant detail to the narrative. This structure allows the reader to dip in and out of this book, quickly highlights some of the key points, and provides clear instruction for further enquiry. This is a relatively short book dealing with a huge subject matter, and it would be almost impossible to offer an all-encompassing assessment of such a large and complex continent. Understandably, not everything can be addressed or discussed, and carefully selected, pertinent examples that span the continent have been chosen in order to provide the most comprehensive picture. The choice of examples and subject matter in order to achieve this goal has naturally meant that the book has had to be selective. However, the purpose is to develop a broad yet detailed foundational introduction to the continent, rather than becoming embroiled in the finite detail, multiple examples, and the intricacies of the academic debates. The book will offer critical and thought-provoking assessments throughout, as well as the author's own opinions and judgements. This is not the final word on Africa, merely a starting point.

Before progressing on to the substantive topics of this book, which are outlined at the end of the chapter, the rest of this introduction will examine two important debates. The first section discusses in detail what actually constitutes Africa, traversing some of the ideas about the composition of the continent. This is a crucial starting point, as it provides a clear impression of what is meant by 'Africa' in this book, while highlighting the contested nature of the term. The second section will focus on the notion of the 'grand narrative' in the context of Africa. This section will seek to explain why labels such as 'Afro-pessimism' and 'Africa Rising' are so unhelpful and demonstrate why they do little to establish a more rounded understanding of Africa.

What is Africa?

This may seem like an unusual question to begin a book devoted to this continent, and one which at first glance has a fairly straightforward answer. Yet, depending on context, historical time frame, and personal perspective, the picture that emerges is far more complex than it might appear. In truth, there is no consensus to this question, and certainly no simple response. Ask different people from across the world and you will be given a variety of answers. A fundamental point to make is that 'Africa' does not necessarily mean, constitute, or represent the same thing for all people, including its inhabitants. Where does this confusion stem from, when the defined land mass of Africa is easily identifiable, stretching from the shores of the Mediterranean in the north, through to the convergence of the Atlantic and Indian Oceans in the south? In brief, the competing visions of Africa revolve around geographic, political, cultural, and academic interpretations. Importantly, it must be recognised that what is regarded as Africa has been a continually changing entity over time, but one which was irrevocably altered by the intervention of European colonialism. The current political map of Africa was, with a few exceptions, externally imposed upon the continent in the late nineteenth century, which bore little resemblance to the cultural, ethnic, linguistic, or even geographic realties on the ground. Ali Mazrui (2005, 70) has emphasised the newness of modern Africa, arguing that it took 'European conceptualization and cartography to turn Africa into a continent ... it was Europe that continentalized the African identity'. This artificial construction of nations and nationalities has profoundly affected the continent. It must be remembered that the political map of Africa in its current form is still a relatively recent phenomenon, and as such is still evolving and debated; for example, South Sudan became the most recent independent nation in 2011.

How should we try to conceptualise Africa? Before reaching a conclusion there are a number of problems that must be explored. The first dilemma is whether all the nations on the continent should be considered part of Africa. The North African states of Morocco, Tunisia, Algeria, Libya, and Egypt are quite clearly on the continental land mass, yet for many, including its citizens, these countries are regarded as distinct and separate from the rest of Africa. The received wisdom is that the North's affinities lie predominantly with the Arabic world, due to the prevalence of Islamic and Arabic influences. The Sahara is thus seen to mark the delineation between two very different worlds. The vast majority of academic studies of the continent adopt such an approach by solely focusing upon sub-Saharan Africa; there are many good reasons for doing so, particularly when seeking to draw direct comparisons. However, this book will argue that all these nations must be included in any analysis, and although they will not be the primary focus for attention, they certainly form a part of Africa.

Why should North Africa be included when so many choose to exclude it? First of all, despite the apparent differences, there are many historic and contemporary links between the north and south, including the spread of religion, the migration of peoples, and the interconnected economic systems, which criss-cross the Sahara Desert. There is also a direct contemporary relevance for incorporating North Africa into our considerations. By including the North African states in our framework it helps build a greater understanding and interpretation of distinctly modern issues such as rising religious conflict, the emergence of transnational terror groups such as al-Qaeda in the Islamic Maghreb, the collapse of state institutions in Libya, and the mounting numbers of sub-Saharan African migrants arriving in the region, seeking to depart for Europe. These developments have not occurred in isolation, and have a profound effect on the nations either side of the Sahara. Secondly, the European powers conceptualised the continent as a whole, and the scramble for colonies truly began after the crises in Egypt in the 1870s, when the nation's inability to repay its mounting debts to London and Paris resulted in the Anglo-French takeover of its treasury and infrastructure, undermining its sovereignty; this move subsequently led to the intensification of overseas territorial acquisition. These external powers most certainly did not see dividing lines as they carved up the continent (Sanderson, 1985, 96–100).

Thirdly, and perhaps more problematically, by establishing such an artificial division, it is doing so on the basis of race and religion: an Arabic, Muslim north standing in contrast to the Black, Christian south (Cooper, 2002, 11). There is, however, no neat split on the map, and these overarching assumptions and generalisations based on race and religion do not bear historical scrutiny. Moreover, categorising people on race, and using labels such as 'black Africa', does little to dispel the myths and unhelpful connotations that universalise the continent as one and the same thing. Fourthly, the African Union (AU), the continent's multilateral institution, includes all these states, and, in the past, both Algeria and Libya have played active and enthusiastic roles in pan-continental affairs. For example, following its independence in 1962, Algeria became a beacon for African liberation movements from across the continent, and actively sought to assist many of them. Furthermore, the former Libyan President Colonel Gaddafi was a keen advocate of Pan-Africanism, and he played a crucial role in pushing forward the idea of a transformed continental bloc in the shape of the new AU in the late 1990s, as well as actively interfering in the domestic politics of many sub-Saharan nations. The political elite in these two countries clearly identified with the rest of Africa.

A second geographic and political issue is the status of Africa's island nations. The land mass is fixed and easily identifiable, but do the island territories in the Atlantic and Indian Ocean form part of the continent? Maps of Africa will often include Madagascar, yet simultaneously ignore five other island nations (Cape Verde, Comoros, Mauritius, São Tomé and Príncipe, and Seychelles). Although there are distinct differences between these islands and the mainland, particularly those located in the Indian Ocean, these nations consciously joined the Organisation of African Unity (OAU), and thus politically tied themselves to the continent's development. These nations should be considered as an integral part of contemporary Africa, and must not be forgotten. However, it is worth noting that there are several islands and enclaves around Africa that are not part of the continent. For example, the French overseas departments of Réunion and Mayotte, direct legacies of colonial rule, are, despite their geographic location, regarded as being part of the French Republic, to the extent that they send MPs to Paris and even use the Euro. Likewise, another relic of European expansionism is found in North Africa, where Spain governs two city-states, Ceuta and Melilla, which lie geographically within Morocco. These are both disputed territories, and even though Morocco continues to petition for them to be returned on the basis that they are colonies, the enclaves have been governed by Spain since the sixteenth century, and thus Rabat's historical claims to territorial sovereignty are not that clear-cut.

A final issue that complicates the picture is that there is no definitive number of countries on the continent. The official number is in dispute, and the outcome depends entirely on context. For example, the United Nations (UN) recognises 54 countries and the AU 55. The discrepancy revolves around two countries: Morocco and the Sahrawi Arab Democratic Republic (an area of territory within the disputed Western Sahara). In 1984, Morocco withdrew from the OAU in protest at the inclusion of the Sahrawi Arab Democratic Republic, a region which Morocco claims sovereignty over. However, the Sahrawi Arab Democratic Republic is a partially recognised territory, which has not been accepted by the UN, or for that matter, some African governments (see Chapter 9). Another example of an unrecognised African state is Somaliland, a region in the northwest of Somalia, which declared independence in 1991. Although the territory has a functioning government, maintains a degree of stability, and even has its own currency in circulation, Somaliland is not recognised by any nation or multilateral organisation. In both cases, the matter has yet to be resolved. Ultimately, the question of which countries constitute Africa can vary wildly depending upon specific settings, and perspectives.

How can we answer the original question: 'What is Africa?' First of all, it is virtually impossible to identify a single Africa. The geographic and cultural diversity is simply staggering, while the multiplicity of political and economic systems dismantles the notion of a homogeneous continent. If the continent is so diverse, what then binds it? For the majority of the continent there is a shared colonial past, with all except Ethiopia and Liberia experiencing some form of European conquest and rule. Although European colonialism differed depending on the region, context, and the specific colonial power, many modern African states share this commonality, which had an enormous bearing upon their post-independence development. Secondly, the struggles for independence that gathered apace after Ghana was granted its freedom in 1957, had many similarities in tactics, demands, and outcomes, which helped to unite African leaders in their determination to be free of external subjugation; unsurprisingly, this sentiment remains highly influential. Thirdly, in the post-colonial era, many African nations have experienced remarkably similar trajectories in terms of economic and political influences and choices, and unfortunately conflict and instability. In this regard, it makes it easier to draw comparisons about what unites the continent because of the array of shared developmental paths. Finally, on a theoretical and romantic level, the binding ideal of a united Africa is articulated through the vision of Pan-Africanism, and from the historic diaspora. This will be discussed in more depth in Chapter 9, but this powerful idea argues that for the continent to progress there must be social, political, and economic unity to drive Africa forward. Indeed, this unity is premised upon a shared history and a shared future for all those of African descent, both on the continent and in the diaspora. The enduring legacy of Pan-Africanism is still visible, with the ultimate ideal of a united continent continuing to be upheld by the AU. While there are many practical problems associated with realising Pan-Africanism, it remains an important philosophical means of conceptualising the continent.

Although many observers may regard conceptualising Africa in its totality as problematic, there are also many good reasons for doing so. Africa is home to a staggering diversity of political systems, structures of governance, ideologies, and economic practices, as well as cultural, religious, and ethnic interactions, not found anywhere else. The 'newness' of the continent in its current form meant that after independence, leaders had a rich array of options open to them; in many ways contemporary Africa has acted as a laboratory for the modern state. African leaders have all had to grapple with big questions such as nationhood, the purpose of the state, the role of identity in politics, and issues of violence and instability. The many and varied approaches towards confronting these challenges have resulted in a multitude of outcomes – some have failed, while others have succeeded. Therefore the plurality of contemporary Africa makes the continent a fascinating case study for enquiry into the range of themes outlined in this book, allowing for intuitive comparisons to be made.

A crucial interlinked question to the theme of 'What is Africa?' is 'Who are Africans?'. This is an equally charged and problematic question, which continues to generate significant debate. Ali Mazrui (2009, xi) identified two groups: 'Africans of the blood' and 'Africans of the soil'. The main argument was that those who are Africans of the blood were categorised by racial and genealogical terms and are 'identified with the black race'. The Africans of the soil therefore can include the people of Arabic North Africa, Indians in Kenya, and Whites in South Africa who are defined in geographical terms and 'are identified with the African continent in nationality and ancestral location'. However, this explanation does not necessarily cover all the bases. Another way to conceptualise 'Who are Africans?' is through utilising different categories that address themes such as race, geography, and African consciousness linked through Pan-Africanism and the diaspora (Adibe, 2009, 16). While these two authors have tried to pin down this question, each of their definitions have their own inherent issues, which simplify a complex debate; there is clearly no easy answer. The main thing for you to recognise is that not all African people are black, identity can be fluid and evolutionary, while many in the diaspora (see Chapter 9) identify themselves as being African even if they were not born on the continent. Therefore, when considering 'Who are Africans?' it is once more a multifaceted question and one that has a range of interpretations and perspectives dependent on your setting and outlook.

To summarise, this book makes reference to the whole continent including North Africa and the island territories. However, to try and avoid the pitfalls of thinking about Africa as a single entity, it might be helpful to (re)imagine the continent as many Africas. This book asserts that this will help escape the all-encompassing narratives that so often accompany the continent, and allow for a more critical and analytical understanding about what makes 'Africa'. By deconstructing the continent, and viewing Africa not only along regional lines, but through cultural, political, and economic lenses, it provides a better sense of where comparisons can effectively be made, while powerfully demonstrating the differences and complexities.

The problem of the 'grand narrative'

As we have established, Africa is home to multiple and conflicting realities. However, the grand narrative has had a profound effect on perpetuating generalised, stereotypical, and often misleading views of the continent. All too frequently simplistic interpretations and images are popularised by the media, non-governmental organisations (NGOs), and academics that ultimately extrapolate specific developments across Africa.

The oversimplification is far from helpful. What occurs in one country or region does not necessarily apply to another, let alone the entire continent, be it positive or negative.

In the west, Africa often suffers from a terrible public image, and the general perception of the continent is resoundingly negative. For example, at the start of each new course I teach on African history, I ask my students to list five things that immediately spring to mind. The vast majority of responses revolve around images of conflict, poverty, economic collapse, famine, corruption, poor governance, dictatorships, and instability. Even when something positive is mentioned it is largely superficial along the lines of giraffes, open wilderness, or the Maasai tribes people. Such immediate characterisations of Africa are not accurate or useful and this negativity posits a continent seemingly teetering on the brink of disaster. For example, the Ebola crisis in West Africa in 2014 only reinforced such opinions. Unfortunately, all of these aspects have, and continue to, occur across the continent. They cannot be denied, and it would be disingenuous to pretend they did not take place. These unseemly parts of Africa's recent history have significantly shaped the continent, and this book will be addressing many of these themes.

Yet some of the misrepresentations of the continent are far-fetched. For example, historian Hugh Trevor-Roper (1964, 9) observed 'that perhaps, in the future, there will be some African History to teach. But at present, there is none: there is only the history of Europeans in Africa. The rest is darkness, and darkness is not the subject of History.' Robert Kaplan (1994), in an article for *Atlantic Monthly*, painted an apocalyptic picture of West Africa, arguing that state collapse, crime, poverty, and violence indicated a 'coming anarchy' that would threaten the very bedrock of civilisation. By May 2000, the narrative had still not changed when *The Economist* wrote off the entire continent as 'hopeless'. Although the specific examples used in both *The Economist* and the *Atlantic Monthly* did happen, the subsequent analysis was largely based upon selectively chosen events in Sierra Leone and Liberia, which were then used to portray an entire continent. If you take a step back and think about the irrationality of generalising in such a manner, such claims border on the ridiculous. Very few people would use examples of economic collapse in Greece, or civil war in Ukraine, to create an overarching judgement on the state of affairs across Europe. But when it comes to Africa, this is exactly what happens time and time again. The public's poor opinions of the continent are further hampered by the selective reporting from the mass media and the tear-inducing campaigns by NGOs. The overwhelming negativity concerning Africa has profoundly shaped perceptions of the continent's past, present, and future. Once you are caught in the trap of thinking in such a way, it is often very hard to break free from conceptualisations of the 'dark' or 'hopeless' continent.

On the other side of the spectrum, there has been a new trend to (re)emphasise the positive developments. In recent decades, Africa has begun to shake off some of the negative perceptions that cling to its image by posting encouraging economic growth rates and witnessing enhanced prospects for popular democracy. By 2011, *The Economist* had made a dramatic U-turn in its depiction of the continent, choosing instead to assert: 'Africa Rising.' The idea of Africa's steady emergence from its previous malaise had already begun to gain traction by the mid-2000s, and an increasing number of academic studies (Mahajan, 2008; Radelet, 2010; Robertson, 2012; Rotberg, 2013; Moghalu, 2014) have vociferously promoted the claim of an 'emerging' or 'rising' continent. It is not only academics, but also major multilateral organisations that have started to utilise such terminology. In May 2014, the International Monetary Fund (IMF) convened the 'Africa Rising' conference in Mozambique, where its delegates celebrated the steady economic growth and stability, and the newfound optimism for the future. According to data from organisations such as the IMF, World Bank, and the African Development Bank Group, since the mid-2000s, there has been rapid economic growth rates, diminishing poverty levels, and increased investment in human and physical infrastructure across Africa. Two of the most frequently cited examples to illustrate these positive changes are the emergence of growing and healthy middle classes (Chapter 5), and the uptake and usage of mobile phone technology, particularly internet-enabled devices (Chapter 10).

Aside from the positive economic and infrastructural gains, Africa has experienced a growing shift towards embracing multiparty democracy and political accountability. Since the turn of the millennium, the number of democratic states has risen, and there are decreasing incidents of political violence. Increasingly, heads of state are now stepping aside from power following election defeats, rather than obstinately clinging to power; for example, when Nigerian President Goodluck Jonathan lost the April 2015 election, he was the nation's first incumbent president to ever step down voluntarily. The emerging economic growth and political stability has also coincided with a sharp decrease in the number of violent conflicts that had scarred Africa during the 1990s. As a consequence, the growing stability and peace provides a firm platform for improved economic growth; investors from around the world are now more likely to be attracted to African nations in the knowledge that their outlay is more secure than in the past. It would be hard to deny that Africa's future is looking infinitely rosier than that of previous decades. There is a new sense that Africa has collectively turned a corner, and is optimistically moving towards a brighter future.

Do these grand narratives help develop our understanding of the continent? Not really. The more we know about Africa, the less persuasive the grand narrative becomes. Once again, the emphasis on multiple realities must be reiterated; we cannot generalise so abstractly about an entire continent. A few examples will illuminate this neatly. The economic data clearly does not lie, and a series of African nations have been growing at exponential rates for some time, including Côte d'Ivoire and Ethiopia. This is something that must be rightly celebrated. Yet two caveats must be raised. First, do gross domestic product (GDP) growth rates actually filter down to the material benefit of the general population? While there are middle classes emerging across Africa, there is, simultaneously, ever growing income inequality and poverty. The poorest Africans are currently getting poorer, accentuated by human development levels much lower than other parts of the world (African Economic Outlook, 2015, vii–viii). Secondly, the economic boom is highly uneven. Not every region is progressing in the same way, starkly indicated by the fact that real GDP growth in 2017 was 5.3% in East Africa compared to West Africa's 0.4% (African Economic Outlook, 2017, 5). When these figures are broken down further, for every individual success story there are plenty of countries such as South Sudan and Zimbabwe that are not developing in the same way.

Furthermore, while the advancement of democracy and free elections progresses at pace, the continent continues to endure a high degree of authoritarianism and instability, and a significant number of one-party states. For example, in 2017, the then three longest serving global heads of states were found in Africa, with each governing for at least 37 years. For every democratic exemplar such as Mauritius or Botswana there will be a series of counter-narratives, including Angola, the Central African Republic (CAR), and Sudan. Africa, like many other places around the world, can and does experience both positive and negative developments all at once. A grand narrative simply perpetuates unrepresentative portrayals of Africa, which do little to represent the complexity and diversity of the continent.

Thematic approaches

The book is divided into a series of chapters that address a specific subject matter, indicated below, with the purpose of providing the reader the necessary information and detail to familiarise themselves with it. The chapters can be read as standalone pieces, although there will obviously be common threads running through them all. For more information on every topic discussed in this book there will be a guide to further reading.

Chapter 2 provides the **geographic setting**, examining the physical, demographic, and social dimensions of the continent. The focus is on themes such as the impact that Africa's physical environment has on the political and economic prospects of its nation-states; it highlights the wealth of natural resources found on the continent, the distribution of these (which is far from even) and the ways in which they are exploited; and finally points to the demographic and social indicators that are present.

The **historical dimension** is addressed in Chapter 3, which surveys Africa's trajectory from the pre-colonial era up until the onset of independence. Focusing on three historical eras – pre-colonial Africa, colonialism, and decolonisation – this chapter explores themes that include pre-colonial societies and polities such as the Asante and the Zulus; explains the processes of colonial conquest by the European powers; demonstrates the ways in which this power was maintained; and examines the reasons behind its collapse.

Chapter 4 sketches out some of the core **political developments** and outlines the main systems of governance in Africa. It assesses the main systems that have characterised political rule such as one-party states, military rule, dictatorships, and parliamentary democracies. The chapter examines how and why these various systems emerged across Africa, and the outcomes of such differing styles.

Chapter 5 addresses the **economic state** of Africa and seeks to explain how a continent so well-endowed in terms of natural resources has historically performed so poorly economically. The main aspects of the continent's economic trajectory are all investigated, such as state-led development and nationalisation, the impact of neo-liberalism, the post-Cold War recovery, and the expanded role of China, which are placed in the necessary domestic and international context.

Unfortunately, the prevalence of widespread conflict has been a major impediment to continental development and stability in post-colonial Africa, and therefore Chapter 6 focuses on **political violence**. This chapter examines how and why there has been such susceptibility to violence and explores various reasons for conflict, including ethnic rivalry, religious sectarianism, weak states, control of resources, and the Cold War.

Chapter 7 focuses on the development of **social movements and civil society** across Africa. In order to encompass as many variations as possible, this section takes a broad sweep of movements and institutions, covering women's rights, NGOs, trade unions, religious denominations, traditional authorities, and specific issue campaigns. The chapter analyses the role these movements have on society and assesses how they shape and continue to influence modern Africa.

Although there is no single **African culture**, nor can one universalising notion be constructed, Chapter 8 assesses some of the continental variations. It covers broad cultural themes such as music, film, literature, and sport, with each of these sub-sections focusing on specific regional and national examples to illustrate Africa's diversity.

Chapter 9 provides a survey of **Africa beyond the nation-state**. It examines the role and influence of continental initiatives and ideologies such as Pan-Africanism and the African Renaissance, as well as the efforts at regional and continental integration. This chapter also looks at the diaspora, while assessing the reality behind African migration, beyond the western conceptualisation of large numbers of people fleeing the continent for Europe.

The final chapter **concludes** the main themes, further contextualises and discusses some of the main points discussed throughout the book, and offers some observations about Africa's future. It highlights some of the positive developments such as the importance and growth of technology, while examining the challenges that climate change poses. This chapter will reiterate the overarching arguments of difference and variation, while demonstrating areas of instructive comparison and similarity.

 Further reading

There are several useful starting points to explore the different ways in which Africa has been conceptualised and constructed, with Valentin Mudimbe's (1988) *The Invention of Africa: Gnosis, Philosophy, and the Idea of Knowledge* and *The Cambridge History of Africa* (1975–1986), an eight-volume history of the continent, both good places to start, as they provide philosophical and historical insights into this question. Several other resources which will prove useful include Frederick Cooper's (2002) *Africa Since 1940*, John Iliffe's (1995) *Africans: The History of the Continent*, and Stephen Ellis's (2002) article 'Writing histories of contemporary Africa'.

2 LAND AND PEOPLE

This chapter will set the physical, demographic, and social dimensions of the continent. While it is possible to identify many commonalities in terms of geographic and demographic trends, the size and diversity of Africa must be kept in mind. By exploring themes such as the natural environment of the continent, this chapter acts as an important starting point that will allow for other areas in the book to be properly contextualised. The chapter begins with an assessment of the main physical characteristics of Africa, followed by a brief discussion of their impact on animal, human, and economic development. The second section will investigate the political map of the continent, demonstrating the external imposition of nation-states, and the effect these have had on the fortunes of many countries. The chapter moves on to detail some of the natural resources available, and the effect these have had for those who have access to them. The penultimate section assesses the demography of the continent, and most importantly the high fertility rates and the growing youth bulge, highlighting the opportunities and challenges this may provide. Finally, the chapter concludes by looking at some of the core trends in social development, while comparing some of the main similarities and differences across Africa.

In a chapter which will discuss themes such as 'human development', it must be highlighted that the standard form of measurement through indicators such as GDP, which are grounded in economic perspectives (see Chapter 5), are problematic in providing a full picture of the reality for many Africans (for example, see Jerven, 2013a). Alternatives such as the Human Development Indicator are useful for offering a more holistic approach, yet questions still arise as to whether it is even possible to measure 'development' (Storey, 2009). Furthermore, it has been argued that applying such terms continues to exert western power and norms on other parts of the world (Sardar, 1999). The important point is to be cautious when using development indicators, and to think critically about what they can tell us about the continent and its people.

The physical setting

Africa is the second largest continent, covering an area of about 11.7 million square miles including its island nations. From the most northern point situated at Ras ben Sakka in Tunisia, down to the southernmost tip, Cape Agulhas in South Africa, the distance is around 5,000 miles. At its widest, the continental land mass stretches over an expanse of 4,600 miles from Senegal to Somalia. The enormity of Africa is startling. However, the actual size of the continent is often distorted in public perceptions because traditional world maps that utilise the Mercator projection (see Map 2.1) downplay its land mass, making North America and Europe appear far larger than they really are. In reality, the African continent could comfortably accommodate the USA, India, China, and much of Europe within its boundaries. The alternative Gall-Peters projection neatly illustrates the differences in cartography and perceptions, while demonstrating the real size of the continent (Table 2.1).

Table 2.1 Size of Africa in comparative terms

	Size (million sq. miles)
Asia	17.2
Africa	11.7
South America	6.8
Europe	3.9

Africa is almost entirely surrounded by the Indian Ocean, the Atlantic Ocean, the Mediterranean Sea, and the Red Sea. Despite its size, one of the geographic anomalies is that Africa's coastline is largely straight and relatively short compared with that of other continents. Furthermore, this lack of coastline is accentuated by a relatively 'smooth' outline, which means there are very few natural harbours, which consequently affects economic activity. Africa is home to some of the world's most impressive river systems, including the Nile, Congo, Niger, and Zambezi. These rivers are crucial to sustaining the flora, fauna, and human activity in the countries that they flow through (see Box 2.1). Yet, unlike many other of the world's major river systems, the vast majority in Africa are not fully navigable, nor do they provide effective access from the coastline to the interior for the transportation of goods. For example, the Congo River is impassable at its lower reaches, blocked by 32 cataracts, including the famous Inga Falls. However, these rivers still hold many advantages for the countries they flow through, including the more recent realisation of their potential for hydroelectric power. For example, large electricity-generating dams are

Map 2.1 The Mercator projection and the Gall–Peters projection

Source: NASA (for both projections).

found on most major rivers including the Great Inga Dam on the Congo River, and the Kariba and Cahora Bassa Dams on the Zambezi.

Box 2.1 The Nile River

The Nile, formed by two major tributaries – the Blue Nile from Ethiopia and the White Nile from Lake Victoria – flows for 4,238 miles, making it the longest river in the world. The Nile is vital to the development of North East Africa, and has played a fundamental role in sustaining human habitation in the region. Not only is it a key source of water for Sudan and Egypt, but annual rainfalls in Ethiopia used to mean the Nile burst its banks, depositing rich and fertile soils on either side, creating a narrow band of excellent farmland that supported human civilisation. The creation of the Aswan High Dam in 1970, and as a consequence the formation of Lake Nasser (the world's third largest reservoir), has controlled the annual floods, as well as supplying hydroelectric power for the region. The flood control mechanism has had a subsequent effect on farming practices in Egypt, with farmers having to switch to new techniques in order to maintain agricultural production and replace many of the nutrients no longer deposited by flooding.

The Nile is truly an international river, whose vital importance has an enormous impact on political and societal concerns in the region. Various disputes have broken out concerning access and control of this precious water resource from the nations in North East Africa; Ethiopia's construction of the Grand Ethiopian Renaissance Dam on the Blue Nile has caused international controversy, and Egypt has sought an injunction to prevent its creation, claiming it will disrupt water flow and have detrimental effects on all the nations downstream. The Ethiopian government has ignored the protests, claiming that Egypt does not have hegemony over the river; construction of the dam is still currently underway.

Africa's physical landscape is characterised by diversity (see Map 2.2), and the continent is shaped by several major regions and distinct geographic features. This section in very general terms will set out some of the core physical features of Africa. Divided almost equally by the equator, the north and south of the continent have remarkably similar characteristics in terms of deserts, semi-arid zones, savannas, and tropical forests. Starting from the north, there is a relatively small coastal plain, bounded

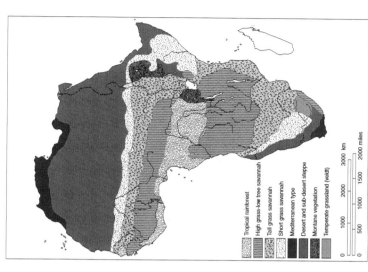

Tropical rainforest
High grass-low tree savannah
Tall grass savannah
Short grass savannah
Mediterranean type
Desert and sub-desert steppe
Montane vegetation
Temperate grassland (veldt)

0   1000   2000   3000 km
0   500   1000   1500   2000 miles

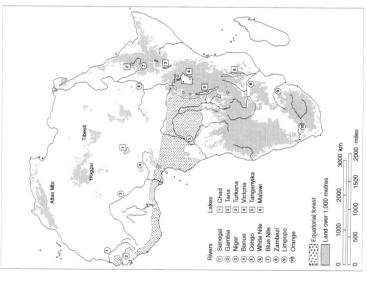

Tibesti

Hoggar

Atlas Mts

Rivers
① Senegal
② Gambia
③ Niger
④ Benue
⑤ Congo
⑥ White Nile
⑦ Blue Nile
⑧ Zambezi
⑨ Limpopo
⑩ Orange

Lakes
1 Chad
2 Tana
3 Turkana
4 Victoria
5 Tanganyika
6 Malawi

Equatorial forest
Land over 1,000 metres

0   1000   2000   3000 km
0   500   1000   1500   2000 miles

Map 2.2 Africa's geographic diversity

Source: Reid, Warfare in Africa *(Cambridge University Press, 2012).*

by the Atlas Mountains that stretch from Morocco through to Tunisia. This zone is often referred to as 'Mediterranean', due to the similarities in climate and soils with southern Europe. Regular amounts of rainfall, a temperate climate (at least compared to the region immediately below the Atlas Mountains), and good soils mean that this part of the continent can sustain diverse crops such as olives and citrus fruits. This fertile zone, however, cedes into desert conditions which is the dominant feature in the north of the continent. The Sahara Desert encompasses nations such as Algeria, Libya, Chad, Sudan, Niger, Mali, and Mauritania, and extends over 3.3 million square miles, making it the world's largest hot climatic desert. The Sahara is an inhospitable region, with very little vegetation in relation to its size, almost no rainfall, and extreme temperatures. Most of the population that does live there is confined to oases, the few areas of permanent water that can sustain human habitation. The desert climate is also replicated in the southern half of the continent in the Namib and Kalahari Deserts, which dominate the Atlantic seaboard of Angola, Namibia, and South Africa. This region extending to over 1,200 miles is also almost entirely uninhabited.

Stretching from Senegal to Sudan, the Sahel region extends east to west across the continent, acting as a transition between the deserts and the savanna terrain below. The climate in the closest margins to the Sahara is still hot and dry, with rainfall of less than 400 mm/year usually confined to a small window of around three months. Further south in the Sahel belt, the landscape transforms into steppe, an area of scrub, bush, short grasses, and acacia trees. Large parts of the Sahel region are supported by the enormous Niger and Benue Rivers, which proved crucial to sustaining early civilisations in West Africa. To the east, Lake Chad is similarly important in supporting vegetation and human life, although it has shrunk alarmingly in size in recent decades, due to the overuse of its water resources and climate change; since 1960, Lake Chad's size has reduced by a staggering 90%. The coastal regions of West Africa, as well as much of Central Africa, from Sierra Leone to the Democratic Republic of Congo (DRC), are dominated by the intertropical convergence zone, an area that experiences high levels of rainfall (over 1,400 mm/year), which in turn supports an abundance of tropical rainforests. It is of little surprise that this region was home to some of Africa's largest kingdoms and empires before the colonial conquest (see Chapter 3).

On the eastern side of the continent are the Ethiopian Highlands, a region of volcanic mountains, which has a relatively temperate climate, fertile soils, and abundant rainfall. It is these annual rains in the Ethiopian Highlands that resulted in the flooding of the Nile in its lower regions. However, in the lower sections of the eastern Horn of Africa, encompassing swathes of Ethiopia, Djibouti, and Somalia, the climate becomes increasingly arid and desert-like as the rain shadow effect and the prevailing winds prevent precipitation. Extending through the Highlands south to Lake Victoria, the region is home to the Rift Valley, a unique Y-shaped rock formation which is a long, deep fissure in the earth's surface. This geological phenomenon led to the creation of large, deep lakes in Central and Eastern Africa, a part of the continent known as the 'Great Lakes'. Encompassing seven major lakes including Lakes Victoria, Kivu, Malawi, and Tanganyika, this impressive system has been crucial to sustaining political and economic development. For example, areas of Kenya, Rwanda, and eastern DRC are extremely well provisioned by the Rift Valley and the Great Lakes, providing an excellent basis for agriculture. Furthermore, this region is one of the coolest in Africa, which made it a preferable area for European settlement in the imperial scramble (see Chapter 3), rather than the tropical, humid conditions found in West Africa. Further away from these water systems, much of southern and eastern Africa gives way to open expanses of savanna, covered by scrub and grasslands. This region has provided excellent conditions for grazing and pastoralism. Finally, the southern stretches of South Africa, especially in the Western Cape Province, neatly mirror the 'Mediterranean' conditions of North Africa, which means that there is a temperate climate here and the soils are able to support a wide range of crops and livestock.

The position of Africa between the Tropics of Cancer and Capricorn means that the vast majority of the continent experiences tropical climates characterised by hot summers and mild winters. Altitude in Africa has an important bearing on climate, and therefore areas such as the Ethiopian Highlands or the Drakensberg in South Africa get much cooler temperatures compared to 'low' Africa in the desert regions of the north and south-west of the continent. Africa experiences well-defined wet and dry seasons, with the rainfall following behind the sun's trajectory throughout the year; the result is that the wet season in the northern and southern hemispheres mark the start of summer. The key anomaly is the rainforests in the equatorial zone, which receive rainfall for much of the year. Importantly, large parts of the continent face the continued risk of severe drought conditions because the rainfall is unreliable, and what little there is quickly evaporates in the high temperatures (see Chapter 10). These wide discrepancies in annual rainfall clearly have serious consequences not only for the vegetation that can grow in these regions, but also for the ability to support human activity. Nations such as Niger and Somalia which are located in arid regions are far more susceptible to a lack of water, crop failures, and thus famines. Water security is an important concern for many nations, and with the effects of rapid climate change leading to desertification, soil erosion, and shrinking water sources, this will soon become an urgent challenge for the continent to tackle.

Aside from the geographic and climatic challenges, Africa also experiences some major challenges in terms of disease. Malaria is a debilitating threat to much of sub-Saharan Africa, with 21 nations severely affected by the disease. Globally, an estimated 3.3 billion people were at risk of being infected with and developing malaria (WHO, 2014a). The result is 429,000 annual deaths, of which 92% occur in Africa (WHO, 2016a). Global actions to combat malaria are progressing apace, but there is still some distance to go in reducing fatalities across Africa. Moreover, the tsetse fly, commonly associated with sleeping sickness and animal deaths, is another major parasitic challenge. Affecting much of the continent between the Sahara in the north and the Kalahari in the south, the tsetse fly is closely linked with poverty and hunger, especially as it has a dramatic effect on crops and livestock. Other major diseases that are found across Africa which affect humans include the waterborne bilharzia, tropical fevers, measles, and tuberculosis.

Box 2.2 The eradication of polio in Nigeria

In 2012, Nigeria accounted for more than half of the global incidents of polio, a debilitating disease that mainly affects children, resulting in paralysis. The Nigerian government declared polio a national health emergency and took drastic action to educate the population and put in place measures for eradication. Utilising the combined capabilities of government, civil society, religious groups, and health workers, Nigeria managed to eradicate polio in little more than two years. Over 200,000 health workers and volunteers embarked on a nationwide immunisation programme that reached 45 million children under five years old. Since the immunisation programme, there have been no new recorded cases of polio. As a consequence, in 2015 Nigeria was declared polio-free. Not only is this a major success for Nigeria, demonstrating the power of co-ordination action, it also made Africa a polio-free continent.

The physical realities of Africa have meant that the people living there are confronted by and have had to overcome some key challenges in terms of establishing societies and sustaining habitation (see Chapter 3). The serious effect of climate change, water scarcity, and environmental degradation are grave threats to many African governments, posing major questions regarding how they will be addressed in the future; some of these questions will be turned to more fully in Chapter 10. However, before moving on, it is worth reiterating what may seem a relatively obvious point: the physical features and climatic factors experienced across Africa have a huge effect on the opportunities and conditions for human and economic development.

Political geography

The political map of contemporary Africa is a very recent construction. Step back 150 years and the map would be totally unrecognisable, with few discernible states. The details of how the European powers partitioned the continent, and in doing so created 'contemporary Africa', are discussed more fully in Chapter 3. A crucial point is that these territorial boundaries were externally imposed on the continent, with no consideration for linguistic, ethnic, cultural, and geographic realities. The consequences of these borders have had a deeply felt impact across the continent. In global terms, the map of Africa is highly irregular. The most striking feature is the number of clean, straight lines demarcating boundaries; 44% of the continent's borders are straight (Alesina, 2011). Excellent examples of this phenomenon are seen in Mauritania, Western Sahara, and Namibia. No other continent experiences such a high concentration of 'unnatural' borders. The artificial imposition of colonial boundaries has had crucial legacies for the continent, including the separation of at least 177 linguistic and ethnic groups across two or more nations, while also confining competing or traditionally antagonistic groups within the same nation (Englebert, 2002, 1096). The impact this has had on societal harmony and political development will be assessed in greater detail in Chapters 3–6.

A quick glance at the political map (2.3) highlights the diversity in the size of countries, with Africa's 55 territories unevenly distributed in terms of dimension, geographic location, and physical features. For example, the two largest, Algeria (919,600 square miles) and the DRC (905,563 square miles), encompass vast sections of the continent. They are followed by Sudan, Libya, Chad, Angola, Mali, and South Africa, all of which have land masses of more than 450,000 square miles. In comparison, the smallest mainland nations, the Gambia (4,361 square miles), Swaziland (6,704 square miles), and Djibouti (8,958 square miles), are all very small, and even combined would not come close to the total area of North Kivu, the DRC's smallest province. The fragmented patchwork of countries means that some of the smallest are barely viable, suffering from a lack of resources, underdevelopment, and an inability to sustain mass economic activity. A good example is the Gambia, which is 300 miles long running alongside either bank of the Gambia River, and at its widest point is only 30 miles, diminishing to a mere 15 at its narrowest. Apart from the

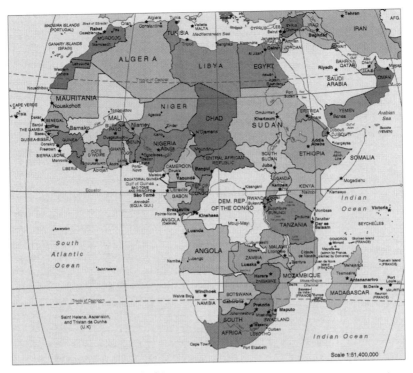

Map 2.3 Political map of Africa

uneven spatial distribution, the political map also reveals that Africa has a high concentration of landlocked nations: 16 in total, with 8 either side of the equator (Table 2.2).

Table 2.2 Landlocked nations

North of the Equator	South of the Equator
Burkina Faso	Botswana
Chad	Burundi
Central African Republic	Lesotho
Ethiopia	Malawi
Mali	Rwanda
Niger	Swaziland
South Sudan	Zambia
Uganda	Zimbabwe

Under colonial rule, many of these landlocked nations either had little purpose for the European powers or were situated in areas which were relatively inhospitable. These colonies were often kept for strategic or prestige purposes, or used to provide migrant labour to other territories in the empire; therefore states such as Chad and Mali were left relatively underdeveloped. Newly 'established' landlocked countries have emerged in the last decades: Ethiopia lost its direct access to the sea in 1993 after what is now Eritrea seceded and gained independence, and the creation of South Sudan established Africa's newest landlocked nation. In the post-colonial era, with the notable exceptions of diamond-rich Botswana and the recently booming Ethiopia, Africa's landlocked nations have generally suffered from poverty and low levels of development.

A key determining factor is that these nations are forced to rely on transporting goods via their neighbours, which is time-consuming, expensive, and reliant on political co-operation. The inability to access the sea means that it is nearly double the expense for landlocked nations to export goods and import essential items such as food and fuel in comparison to their neighbours with coastlines (World Bank, 2008). Furthermore, if neighbouring countries are themselves lacking in development opportunities, or they are stuck in a cycle of conflict and instability, then landlocked nations in Africa, such as Uganda, face some serious obstacles to growth (Collier, 2008, 55–57). Another example, South Sudan, which became independent in 2011, is still struggling to effectively export its vast oil reserves in order to kick-start the country's economy, due to the ongoing conflict with Sudan; the only alternative routes are via Kenya or Ethiopia, which will be expensive to establish and will take years to build. Quite clearly the size of a state, its location on the continent (i.e. the effect of the physical and climatic conditions) and the access to resources (see section below) has a major bearing on the opportunities for development.

Africa's natural resources

Africa is a rich continent, home to an abundance of raw materials and natural resources. However, the paradox that Africa faces is that despite the richness of resource deposits it is simultaneously poor (see Box 2.3). This section will sketch out some of the main resources that are found, their utilisation, and the potential for diversification, especially in terms of energy. It must be emphasised that Africa's raw materials are exported across the globe and are crucial to the economies of many nations. Furthermore, greater international competition to secure access to Africa's resources is underway, led by China's insatiable economic growth since the turn of the millennium; there is some debate about whether this constitutes a 'new scramble for Africa'.

Box 2.3 The resource curse?

A common perspective is that Africa suffers from a resource curse. For those countries that have reserves of oil, gold, diamonds, or any other mineral that is in demand, rather than acting as a vehicle for prosperity, they often bring poverty and underdevelopment (a theme that will be fleshed out further in Chapter 5). The problem has been that the dividends from these resources are regularly squandered. Why does this occur? There are several reasons. First, there is a focus on extraction rather than the processing and production of these materials into finished goods. The result is that other countries gain wealth through industrial production, instead of African nations. Furthermore, given the wealth these resources derive, it means that other sectors are neglected or become unprofitable, which creates an overreliance on one economic catalyst, and thus damages other industrial sectors – this is known as 'Dutch Disease'. Secondly, the value of raw materials is subject to price fluctuations, and at various times there are 'price shocks' as market values tumble. As the continent is dependent on exports, this can have an enormous impact on government finances. Thirdly, there is a lack of effective redistributive practices across the continent in which all too commonly the wealth derived from these resources is retained by a small elite, often connected to the ruling party. For example, a quick glance at Equatorial Guinea, a rapidly growing oil exporter, would show an average per capita income of around $23,000, yet the reality is that three-quarters of the population lives on less than $700 a year. Instead, President Teodoro Obiang's family has amassed a small fortune estimated at around $600 million, and acquired assets including aeroplanes, luxury cars, and houses, while the population remains in poverty (Blas, 2014; Human Rights Watch, 2015). Fourthly, many states remain institutionally weak, and there is a lack of transparency and oversight concerning these resources, providing opportunities for corruption, rent-seeking, and illegal flows of money away from Africa. The result is that tax earnings are lost, and the ability to invest in development projects is reduced. Finally, the access to and the control of resources have been accredited in sustaining conflicts across the continent, including Sierra Leone, Angola, and the DRC.

However, a notable exception is diamond-rich Botswana. In 1966, when it gained its independence, Botswana was a relatively impoverished and underdeveloped state. However, the government used the diamond income (worth roughly 40% of all revenues) to invest in infrastructure, health, education, and poverty reduction, which has meant it has economically been one of the world's fastest growing nations and has high per capita incomes. The example demonstrates that not all countries need face a resource curse, and if managed carefully and transparently resources can ensure transformative results.

Minerals and metals fundamental for many manufacturing processes are found and mined across Africa, and, as such, nations and multinational companies particularly in the developed world compete for access to these resources. Deposits of metals such as cobalt, uranium, platinum (Africa has the largest reserves in the world for these three), nickel, bauxite, copper, and iron ore are all found in enormous quantities in a number of nations. The industrial production of modern electronic devices such as smartphones, laptops, and tablets relies heavily on using Africa's raw materials; the DRC is crucial to this supply chain, providing core components including tungsten, tin, and tantalum. Furthermore, diamonds and gold are pivotal resources found across Africa which are extracted and sold in large quantities, and in terms of profits are the most valuable raw materials. The top four gold-exporting nations in order are South Africa (which is by far and away the largest), Ghana, Mali, and Tanzania, while the biggest diamond-producing countries are Botswana, South Africa, Namibia, Angola, and the DRC. It is important to note how important mining is to the economic well-being of many nations: Botswana is almost entirely reliant on diamond extraction. New discoveries of minerals across the continent bring billions of dollars' worth of investment and can be a major driving force towards greater development. Other natural resources, such as hardwoods, are found particularly across western and central Africa in the Congo Basin, and the commercial logging of the regions forests are an important aspect to economic activity; it is estimated that 6% of the continent's GDP derives from forestry.

Africa is home to large oil and gas reserves, and many governments are dependent on the extraction and production of them. As new sources are located in nations such as Tanzania, Ghana, and Mozambique, and old ones are exploited more extensively in Angola, Equatorial Guinea, Algeria, Nigeria, Congo-Brazzaville, and Libya, oil and gas continue to be a major economic dividend. The continent is responsible for 9.6% of world oil production, and holds 8% of the known untapped reserves (PWC, 2015). The continued exploration and extraction of oil and gas across the continent will continue to be important as G20 nations seek to move away from their dependency on the Middle East and Russia. However, access to large reserves of oil and gas has not been beneficial for establishing democracy or creating transparent norms in Africa. In repeated cases, the wealth derived from these reserves is frequently used to sustain autocratic governments in nations such as Angola, Equatorial Guinea, and Sudan. Other major non-renewable resources such as shale gas are found in various locations across the continent, with Libya reported to be sitting on the third largest reserves in the world. However, in comparison to other world regions, many of the resources mentioned above remain relatively underutilised due to a host of factors: geographic constraints, conflict, political instability, and corruption. These large deposits of minerals or fossil fuels found across the continent, which would be expected to generate wealth and development, are sometimes referred to as the 'resource curse', which is detailed in Box 2.3. Furthermore, these resources can contribute to conflict and instability, with access and control sometimes facilitating warfare. In numerous cases such as Angola, the DRC, and Sierra Leone, the control of oil and diamonds has sustained conflict; this theme will be discussed in more detail in Chapter 6.

Africa has enormous potential in terms of renewable energy, and this is likely to become increasingly important in terms of economic diversification and the need for alternative forms of cheap power. Opportunities arise with regards to solar energy, wind farms, biomass, geothermal energy, and hydroelectric power. For example, due to the high levels of daylight hours across the continent, solar energy is becoming an increasingly popular alternative, particularly in areas such as the Sahara. In Morocco, the potential of solar energy is being harnessed with the creation of a complex of four mega-solar plants near Ouarzazate, making it the largest of its kind in the world (Image 2.1). By 2020, when all the plants are online, solar energy from this complex alone will generate 580 MW of electricity, which will power over a million homes all year round (Neslen, 2015). Furthermore, there are also great opportunities for wind energy, and a number of wind farms are being established across the continent; one example is the Cookhouse wind farm in South Africa's Eastern Cape, which is the largest in southern Africa, with 66 turbines. Not only do these initiatives lessen the need to rely on non-renewable energies, they provide opportunities for economic diversification and employment, as new industries are required to create and sustain these developments. However, while there are clearly some positive changes underway in harnessing the potential of renewables, it must be stressed that these alternative energy sources still lag far behind the bonanza of oil and gas, which remain the bedrock for many nations' economies.

Image 2.1 Solar power complex near Ouarzazate, Morocco

Source: Philippe Petit/Paris Match via Getty Images.

Demographic trends

Until very recently, Africa's total population for a continent of its size has not been particularly large in comparison to the rest of the world. However, for the rest of the twenty-first century this is going to change dramatically. In 2010, the continent surpassed the 1 billion mark (of which half are under 20 years old), and Africa's population is now growing so rapidly that by 2050 there will be an estimated 2 billion people. To emphasise this figure, by 2050, approximately half of the world's population growth will occur in Africa. Notwithstanding some of the major challenges that affect African populations, such as physical geography, climatic factors, and diseases including malaria and HIV/AIDS, fertility rates across the continent now exceed all other regions, with the latest figures showing an average birth rate of 4.43 children per women; the current world average stands at 2.47, and is steadily falling (UN, 2017). Africa is bucking the global trend. The consequence is that family units in Africa remain large, while the average population is getting much younger. As a result, the emergent 'youth bulge' means that Africa has a greater proportion of people under 24 than anywhere else; 60% of people on the continent are under 24 years old (UN, 2017). For example, Niger has the youngest average population at 15.1 years old, closely followed by Mali at 16. In comparison to developed nations, the differential is huge: in the UK, it is 40.4; and in the USA, 37.6.

Table 2.3 Select African demographic statistics

| Country/region | Population (thousands) | | | | | | Population density (people per sq. km) |
	1950	1970	1990	2000	2010	2020 (projected)	
Algeria	8,872	14,550	25,912	31,184	36,036	43,008	15.1
Angola	4,355	6,301	11,128	15,059	21,220	29,245	17.0
Burkina Faso	4,284	5,625	8,811	11,608	15,632	20,861	57.1
Burundi	2,309	3,457	5,613	6,767	9,461	13,126	368.4
Cameroon	4,466	6,771	12,070	15,928	20,591	26,333	43.6
Cape Verde	178	270	341	439	490	553	121.7
Comoros	156	228	415	548	699	883	375.4
Democratic Republic of Congo	12,184	20,010	34,963	48,049	65,939	90,169	29.1
Egypt	20,897	34,809	56,397	68,335	82,041	100,518	82.4
Ethiopia	18,128	28,415	48,057	66,444	87,562	111,971	87.6
Ghana	4,981	8,597	14,628	18,825	24,318	30,530	106.9
Kenya	6,077	11,252	23,446	31,066	40,328	52,187	70.9
Lesotho	734	1,032	1,598	1,856	2,011	2,258	66.2

Country/ region	Population (thousands)						Population density (people per sq. km)
	1950	1970	1990	2000	2010	2020 (projected)	
Malawi	2,954	4,604	9,409	11,193	14,770	20,022	156.7
Mauritius	493	826	1,056	1,185	1,248	1,291	614.8
Mozambique	6,313	9,262	13,372	18,265	24,321	31,993	30.9
Nigeria	37,860	56,132	95,617	122,877	159,425	206,831	175.0
Rwanda	2,186	3,755	7,260	8,022	10,294	12,997	417.3
São Tomé and Príncipe	60	74	114	137	171	211	178.0
Seychelles	36	52	71	81	93	99	202.3
South Africa	13,683	22,503	36,793	44,897	51,622	56,669	42.6
Tanzania	7,650	13,606	25,458	33,992	45,649	62,267	51.5
Uganda	5,158	9,446	17,384	23,758	33,149	45,856	165.9

Source: Created using data from United Nations, Department of Economic and Social Affairs, Population Division (2015). World Population Prospects: The 2015 Revision.

The potential of these dynamic younger populations for Africa is both a blessing and a curse. Young populations could prove to be an excellent vehicle for growth and development, yet governments must enact policies to serve the needs of this demographic bulge, particularly in the spheres of education, skill provision, and most importantly employment. If these issues are not met, then many African nations could suffer serious consequences, with large, disaffected populations. Furthermore, there will be increased pressures on food production in order to feed these rapidly expanding populations, a feat that many countries are struggling to meet. For example, *The State of Food Insecurity in the World* report (FAO, IFAD & WFP, 2015) stated that 24 sub-Saharan Africa countries are already contending with serious food crises. This is an urgent predicament, which the continent as a whole will need to address.

The consequence of increased fertility, and the growing youth bulge, is that every country in Africa is experiencing rapid population growth. Table 2.3 sets out the historic and projected population growth rates, with some remarkable upward trends evident. There are obviously important variations between nations and regions, but without exception the population growth rates across the whole of Africa are rising. For example, Nigeria, a large nation already, will have grown from a population of 159.4 million in 2010 to 206.8 million by 2020, while in the same period even a small country such as Malawi will have experienced a population spurt of 6 million people. Although the population density across Africa is not particularly high overall at around 32 people per square kilometre, as Table 2.3 demonstrates, the rapid growth rates will have the greatest effect on the continent's smallest nations such as Cape Verde, Burundi, Rwanda, and Malawi, which are already the most densely populated on the continent.

With the surge in the continent's population, where are these people going to live? The consequence has been rapid urbanisation. According to the African Development Bank (2012) the urban population of the continent has been growing at 3.5% per year since the 1990s (making it the fastest growing in the developing world), and is projected to increase to 60% of the continent living in cities by 2050. The growth in some cities has been extraordinary. The numbers from the UN, set out in Table 2.4, illustrate the growth of the largest 12 African cities. In 2018, mega cities such as Cairo in Egypt, Lagos in Nigeria, and Kinshasa in the DRC all had populations of over 10 million people. The predicted growth rates are phenomenal; in the period 2010–2025, Luanda will see its population grow by 69%, Nairobi by 77%, and Dar es Salaam by 85%. The rise of Africa's cities stems from several factors. Each nation has at least one key urban centre, and due to their overwhelming dominance and proportionally larger populations, these receive the vast bulk of government investment into infrastructure, employment, and welfare spending. These 'hub' cities are key engines for productivity

Table 2.4 Growth of African cities – the continent's 12 largest

Rank	City	Country	2005	2010	2015	2020 (predicted)	2025 (predicted)	% Change (2010–2025)
1	Cairo	Egypt	10,565	11,001	11,663	12,540	13,531	23
2	Lagos	Nigeria	8,767	10,578	12,427	14,162	15,810	49.5
3	Kinshasa	Democratic Republic of Congo	7,106	8,754	10,668	12,788	15,041	71.8
4	Luanda	Angola	3,533	4,772	6,013	7,080	8,077	69.3
5	Alexandria	Egypt	3,973	4,387	4,791	5,201	5,648	28.7
6	Abidjan	Côte d'Ivoire	3,564	4,125	4,788	5,500	6,321	53.2
7	Johannesburg	South Africa	3,263	3,670	3,867	3,996	4,127	12.5
8	Nairobi	Kenya	2,814	3,523	4,303	5,192	6,246	77.3
9	Cape Town	South Africa	3,091	3,405	3,579	3,701	3,824	12.3
10	Kano	Nigeria	2,993	3,395	3,922	4,495	5,060	49
11	Dar es Salaam	Tanzania	2,680	3,349	4,153	5,103	6,202	85.2
12	Casablanca	Morocco	3,138	3,284	3,537	3,816	4,065	23.8

Source: Created using data from UN-HABITAT (2010), The State of African Cities 2010: Governance, Inequalities and Urban Land Markets.

and growth, providing numerous benefits for economic development. However, despite the opportunities that arise from large urban areas, the rapid growth of cities is posing some serious challenges to African governments (see Box 2.4). One result of urbanisation is that the already overstretched services, and the scarcity of available jobs and dwellings, are put under further pressure as people are drawn in large numbers from rural areas to major centres such as Kinshasa or Johannesburg on the perceived notion of greater access to prosperity. However, Africa's urbanisation, unlike other parts of the world, has not been driven by comparable industrialisation, which impacts on the availability of jobs and exacerbates economic inequality. One consequence has been the rapid rise in the number of slum dwellers across the continent, which many cities are simply unable to deal with effectively, creating understandable implications for quality of life.

Box 2.4 Lagos

Lagos is the commercial hub of Nigeria, and is emerging as a global powerhouse of a city in its own right. For example, it was reported by *The Economist* (2013) that the GDP of the city alone was larger than that of all neighbouring countries in West Africa, as well as major nations such as Kenya. Situated in the oil-producing Gulf of Guinea in the south-west of Nigeria, the city's fortunes are closely linked to the extraction and refinement of crude oil. With a population of around 12.5 million people, the city has been experiencing an unprecedented rise in the number of dwellers, putting it among the world's most populous places. This rapid growth has had several consequences for Lagos, with rapid urban sprawl, overpopulation, and emerging slum dwellings as incomers seek places to live. This had put enormous pressure on the city's infrastructure, creating problems of access to services. However, things are changing rapidly in Lagos, where, increasingly, improvements have been made and strategies implemented to deal with the challenges. The city has managed to increase the level of tax revenues through improved collection mechanisms, and has spent these receipts on upgrading the city's infrastructure. Clearly aware of the anticipated growth rates, the city leaders are planning ahead. For example, in 2008, a rapid bus transportation network was established, and a light railway system has also been constructed, both of which have eased congestion and helped the movement of people. There are still many challenges to overcome, but a far-sighted transformative commitment designed to deal with Lagos's continued growth rates and urban sprawl is beginning to make a difference.

While the 'Africa rising' perspective depicts the continent's rapid urbanisation as potentially beneficial, it obscures the fact that most Africans continue to live in rural communities. The urban population might have doubled from 19% to 39% in the last 50 years, but Africa's rural population has increased rapidly too, albeit with significant variations across the continent. Over half of the continent's countries remain predominantly rural societies: Burundi, Malawi, and Niger are more than 80% rural. As a consequence, African nations will stay overwhelmingly rural societies until the mid-2030s. However, categorisations of urban and rural can differ depending on the context and country in question; for example, Nigeria defines a town at 20,000 people, while Mali's benchmark is 40,000. Therefore, it should be recognised that there is no single, catch-all image of how Africans live, encompassing everything from sizeable, dynamic cities to isolated rural communities. The challenge for policy makers will be to promote both urban and rural strategies, in order to provide sufficient employment, welfare, and infrastructure to cope with the expected urban and rural population growth, and to provide opportunities for the emerging youth bulge within these settings.

Societal trends

Given the opportunities, challenges, and constraints facing the continent, what are the prospects for social development? This section presents a quick overview of social development indicators, which are quantifiable measures of social progress outlined by the detailed data from the UN (2016) Population Division's Department of Economic and Social Affairs. Life expectancy is a way of reflecting 'quality of life', and in those countries with lower figures they are generally poorer and less developed. There is a considerable degree of difference between nations across the continent. You are far more likely to live longer if you are born in a North African nation or an island country such as Cape Verde, Mauritius, and the Seychelles, all of which have life expectancy at comfortably over 70 years of age. However, in contrast, as a citizen of Angola, Chad, Central African Republic (CAR), Lesotho, and a host of other countries you will be lucky to live to your 60th birthday. It goes without saying that these figures mask enormous discrepancies within each country; for example, South Africa's white population are statistically more likely to live far longer than the migrant black labourers that work in the country's mining sector. Major causes of death across Africa such as HIV/AIDS (see Box 2.5), tuberculosis, and malaria continue to affect life expectancy, but encouragingly rates across the continent are improving rapidly. Since 1950, average life expectancy in Africa has risen from 37 to 58 years of age by 2011, and by 2060 this will have risen again to 71; these figures are extremely positive, demonstrating the major improvements being made in health care and quality of life (AfDB, 2014).

An emerging health challenge across the continent is the rapid rise in obesity levels, which is partially linked to growing wealth, urbanisation, and changing lifestyles. Although malnutrition coexists alongside obesity in many African nations, the increased consumption of high-fat or sugary products, often from fast-food chains such as KFC, McDonald's, and Wimpy, has led to a surge in the proportion of overweight people. For example, since 1980, Ghana's obesity rates have leapt from 2% to 13.6% of the population, while over half of women in Botswana are obese (*The Lancet*, 2014). The consequence of rising obesity levels is an increasing number of people suffering from Type 2 diabetes, high blood pressure, heart attacks, and a variety of cancers.

Box 2.5 HIV/AIDs

One of the greatest challenges facing African societies is the HIV/AIDs epidemic, a health crisis which has killed approximately 15 million people on the continent, with a further 25.5 million people, predominantly in eastern and southern Africa, currently living with the disease (UNAIDS, 2016). The high infection rates have lowered life expectancy; disrupted family structures, creating a large number of AIDs orphans; and had a huge impact on welfare budgets, as governments have struggled to contain the disease. Despite the deleterious effects on the socio-economic well-being of millions of sub-Saharan Africans, enormous progress is being made in reducing and managing infection rates. By 2015, more than 12 million Africans were on the world's biggest antiretroviral (ARV) treatment programme; in South Africa, 3.4 million people are receiving ARV. In order to achieve reduced infection rates, governments have sought to make ARV treatment easier to access, negotiated cheap drug deals with pharmaceutical companies, and expanded prevention, testing, and sex education programmes in a bid to halt HIV/AIDs spreading further. While steady, positive changes are being achieved in fighting the disease across Africa, HIV/AIDs remains a significant cause of death, as the continent continues to account for two-thirds of all new infections. Therefore continuing efforts by governments and international agencies are required to raise awareness, treat suffers, and reduce HIV/AIDS infection rates.

Infant mortality rates can be used as a means of identifying the quality of a nation's healthcare system, welfare provision, and more broadly the level of social development. There is often a close correlation between GDP and socio-economic development, and lower infant mortality. A positive, yet often unreported occurrence has been the rapid drop in infant deaths across Africa with almost all countries experiencing sharp declines; Ghana, Kenya, Senegal, Rwanda, and Uganda have witnessed extremely large reductions in mortality rates of more than 6% per year. However, the differences across the continent are stark: richer countries such as Mauritius, Tunisia, and Cape Verde have very low infant mortality, while in poorer nations including Angola, Guinea-Bissau, and South Sudan rates remain unacceptably high. The uneven nature illustrates that not all positive developments are realised by all Africans, and variations in lived experience differ not only within a country, but between them too.

Adult literacy is another crucial determinant of a nation's social development. The figures are often closely linked to government spending on welfare provision and the educational opportunities available to the population. Mirroring the points outlined previously, there is a close connection between the wealth of a nation, its ability to dedicate spending to welfare provision, and overall literacy rates. Since the early 2000s, enormous strides have been made in improving education levels across Africa, which has seen unprecedented numbers of children now accessing school (Chapter 10). Several countries do have shockingly low levels of literacy such as the CAR and Niger, but on the whole access to education and thus literacy rates is steadily improving. However, there are serious challenges remaining, with 34 million children never going to school, while the continental average for enrolment in secondary education is 43% and by the tertiary stage only 8% (UNDP, 2016, 232–233). With the rapid rise in the youth population, African governments must take the opportunities to increase educational spending and invest in their nations' and peoples' future.

Gender equality statistics are another useful tool for illustrating the opportunities available for women, and the extent to which a nation has implemented policies to achieve equality. The statistics are comprised of an amalgamation of factors including the ability for women to access education, their representation in parliament, chances of employment, and the likelihood of enduring gender-based violence. Those nations with a low score (closer to 0) are generally indicative of more progressive, developed, and liberal nations. The African continent has enormous variations in the status of women, and equality of opportunity. Several nations such as Burkina Faso, Chad, and the DRC have alarmingly low levels of equality for women. In contrast, South Africa and Rwanda have made encouraging steps towards greater gender equality, especially in terms of political representation and the number of female parliamentarians; since the election of Ellen Johnson

Sirleaf as Liberia's president in 2006, three women have led African nations. However, in comparison to the world leader Norway with a rating of 0.068, France with 0.080, or the UK with 0.068, there is still a lot to be done to overcome patriarchal attitudes and practices across the continent.

Finally, the Human Development Index (HDI), published by the United Nations, is a measure of life expectancy, education, gross national income, and quality of life across the world. This is a tool which is an attempt to gauge the standards of living for people and their opportunities in life. In comparative world terms the statistics do not make for comfortable reading for many African nations. Not one nation on the continent is characterised as having 'Very High Human Development'. Only four African nations make it into the top 100 (high human development), with Seychelles the highest ranked at 63rd in the world, followed by Mauritius in 64th place, Algeria 83rd, and Tunisia 97th. Unfortunately, African nations dominate the bottom of the HDI list: of the 188 nations that the UN has recorded data for, 19 of the 20 worst performing nations are African; in ascending order CAR is ranked last, followed by Niger, Chad, Burkina Faso, Burundi, and Guinea.

This chapter has outlined some of the details behind Africa's land and peoples, providing a platform from which other themes can be discussed in more depth later on. In addressing the variations in physical and climatic features on the continent, the imposition of the modern state, the availability of resources in different regions, and the impact of population growth and human development, this chapter provides a sense of the variation and complexity of contemporary Africa. Clearly the dimensions addressed here indicate some of the different circumstances that African people experience, and the consequent effects that these have on human activity. While many challenges abound, there is an enormous amount of potential for the future, and plenty of positive developments are apparent throughout the continent.

 ## Further reading

Two books that offer an accessible introduction to various aspects of Africa's geography are Alfred Grove's (1993) *The Changing Geography of Africa* and the edited collection *The Physical Geography of Africa* (Adams, Goudie, & Orme, 1999). For more detail on African urbanisation and the changing nature of cities' development, see Susan Parnell and Edgar Pieterse's (2014) *Africa's Urban Revolution* and Bill Freund's (2007) *The African City: A History*. A detailed and comprehensive overview of Africa's demographic developments can be found in Hans Groth and John May's (2017) *Africa's Population: In Search of a Demographic Dividend* which assesses a wide range of factors including disease, mortality, and migration.

3 HISTORY

In order to fully understand contemporary Africa we need to examine how it got where it is today, by examining the historic developments that have influenced and shaped the present. The history of Africa, from the pre-colonial era through to the age of independence in the 1960s, is one characterised by layers of change and evolution. There have been some major junctures in Africa's past, which brought about enormous disruption and modification to its states and societies, such as the rise of kingdoms like the Asante in West Africa, or the imposition of white minority rule in southern Africa. While history is often written around such major turning points, it is crucial to note that Africa's past is predominantly about evolution and flexibility, especially in terms of societal composition, political norms, and ethnic identity. For example, European colonialism, which lasted a relatively short time in the continent's historical trajectory, did not totally rupture or transform African societies; many political and cultural practices of the pre-colonial era remained unaffected by imperial rule, with profound effects on post-colonial polities.

The weight of recent history continues to loom large over contemporary Africa. Key issues such as artificial territorial boundaries, the ethnic composition of nation-states, styles of political governance, and economic inheritance all continue to affect Africa's present. This chapter does not wish to claim that all of modern Africa's difficulties can be attributed to the past, as this is demonstrably untrue, but the spectre of colonialism has proved a useful cover for many politicians since independence. In order to truly get to grips with the nuances of the contemporary state, and the paths taken by many nations, this chapter will identify some core historic themes that have indelibly shaped the continent.

Most of the contemporary histories written about the continent tend to focus on the role of external influences in shaping Africa: for example, they examine Islamic and Ottoman rule in the north, or more commonly, the arrival of Europeans, associated mainly with territorial occupation of the continent. Undoubtedly, the intrusion of foreign rule, the religious conversion of African societies, the introduction of 'alien' political ideologies, and the establishment of international economic trading links all had an enormous impact on the continent. However, viewing Africa through the eyes of outsiders creates a historical prism with two fundamental problems. The first is that it generates the impression that Africa's past is something that simply happened to it, which ultimately denies African agency in events. The second is that Africa's history often 'begins' in the nineteenth century, which fundamentally neglects its complex and distinct past that existed in the pre-colonial era. Indeed, such a Eurocentric approach has frequently written Africans out of their own history, depicting them as bystanders to the ebb and flow of external interventions. Such a narrow view of history fails to provide a more complete picture of how Africans influenced many political and socio-economic developments, both positively and negatively. For example, the slave trade, which had deleterious effects on the continent, was not a new phenomenon, and there had been an active domestic market before the Europeans arrived and started transporting people to the Americas. It was local leaders and traders who captured and sold slaves to Europeans (Rodney, 1966; Fage, 1969; Lovejoy, 2012). This is not to negate in any way the barbarity and complicity of European's in organising the Atlantic slave trade, but simply to point out that history has often provided an account that has depicted these despicable events as happening to Africa without its peoples' involvement. The reality is far more complicated.

This chapter offers a brief review of African history, assessing some of the core themes within three main epochs: pre-colonialism, colonialism, and the advent of decolonisation. The pre-colonial section will examine how different political entities were formed, survived, and interacted across the continent. Importantly, it will look at several powerful kingdoms and empires, including the Zulus, the Asante, and the Sokoto Caliphate, and assess the impact they had. The second section will focus on the era of European colonialism (which lasted in most cases less than 80 years). Crucial themes such as the reasons behind the imperial conquest of Africa, the creation of new territorial 'nations', how rule was implemented and maintained by different powers, and the divergent impact that external interventions had in different locations will be addressed. Importantly, it will highlight that despite some profound changes, the different European powers were unable to 'successfully' engineer or alter all dimensions of African societies; the result was many important continuities survived from the pre-colonial period into the post-colonial era. These continuities are fundamental to understanding some of the complexities that have since shaped contemporary states and societies, as colonial political and institutional practices were fused with earlier customs and traditions. The final section will look at the rise of African nationalism, the challenges that this brought to European rule, and some of the reasons behind the decolonisation process which accelerated after World War II.

Given the sheer scale of the continent, and the multidimensional ways in which people experience or understand the past, this chapter will understandably generalise. It will therefore seek to demonstrate the most important concepts and developments across Africa's history, while highlighting where significant debate has occurred in the academic literature, and how this has affected our understanding of the continent.

Africa before 1850

When assessing African societies before the arrival of European colonialism in the nineteenth century there was an apparent absence of formal, demarcated states. There were a number of major political entities such as Abyssinia, Asante, Dahomey, ancient Egypt, Hausa, and Mali, clustered largely in the western and eastern regions of the continent, but these are often seen as exceptions to the rule. For the rest of the pre-colonial African map, large tracts of it were seemingly 'empty', devoid of almost anything resembling modern nation-states or formal institutions of political governance. It prompted Robert Jackson (1993, 67) to observe that Africa was a continent of 'loosely defined political systems and societies rather than states' (Map 3.1).

However, to equate a lack of territorial boundaries with being ungoverned would be frankly misleading. Indeed, the historic and archaeological evidence indicates an entirely different picture, pointing instead towards a plurality of systems for political control, and societal organisation across the continent. Much like other world regions, kingdoms and empires came and went, while state formation continued to evolve and adapt over time. By the time Europeans began to actively interfere in continental affairs in the 1800s, there had come into existence a number of increasingly powerful and sophisticated entities such as the Sokoto Caliphate and Buganda, which had many similarities to modern conceptualisations of state power. Although not wanting to overgeneralise about thousands of years of history, it is best to consider pre-colonial African societies as falling into one of two camps: centralised polities or stateless societies – although there were obviously many that were somewhere in between.

Without overlapping too much on the themes set out in Chapter 2, several points concerning Africa's geography and environment must be reiterated. I do not want to push the argument for geographic determinism too far, but undoubtedly the natural environment had a major impact on human, cultural, and consequently political and economic development, which is often ignored. It cannot be emphasised enough just how large Africa is, and the diverse, yet often extreme, physical conditions that can be

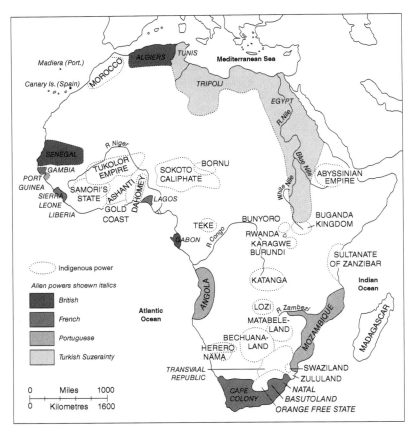

Map 3.1 Selected African kingdoms in 1876

experienced across the continent. Africa's geographic setting is, with a few notable exceptions, unforgiving – irregular rains, poor soils for agriculture, diseases, challenging climates, and transport difficulties, to name just a few, meant that particular regions were far less suited for supporting widespread human activity. The continent has, by and large, been dealt a bad ecological hand (Davidson, 1992, 216). It is therefore no surprise that most, but not all, major political entities emerged only in western and eastern regions where conditions were far more conducive to sustaining humans. As a consequence, the entire continent was characterised by relatively low population densities, which had a profound effect on the ability to establish larger political entities, and to sustain economic activities. Many people clearly appreciated the difficulties of establishing formal, territorial fixed states in such conditions, and thus concluded that they could live without them.

The vast majority of people therefore lived in small, localised groups or settlements, often no bigger than villages, usually under the governance of a council of elders, or a 'big man', who could control economic flows, distribute patronage, dispense power, and provide protection. These groups like the Tiv, Igbo, and Maasai were largely self-sufficient, and were organised in such a way as to adapt to and work with the physical conditions around them; as a consequence, it was often community or ethnic kinship that was far more important to these societies surviving or flourishing than any preconceived notion of loyalty to a state or monarch. Even after colonial rule was implemented, these communities were left largely unaffected by the new dispensations, with traditional forms of governance continuing. This close affiliation to family and ethnicity remains an extremely important part of contemporary African society, and is a theme that will be returned to later in this book (see, for example, Chapters 4 and 6).

Another key geographic factor was the availability of land, which is closely tied to low population densities. A point of comparison is mainland Europe, where land was at a premium, and thus competing kingdoms quickly realised the need to demarcate territorial boundaries and defend these in order to project their power. The modern conceptualisation of the state is based on the premise of exerting control over territory, and exercising sovereignty over it, which was enshrined in the Treaty of Westphalia in 1648. However, pre-colonial Africa was entirely different. Ownership of land was not an overriding concern because there was plenty of it available. In fact, the core problem facing African leaders was the scarcity of people. Therefore, power in Africa was based not on territory but on the ability to control people (Vansina, 1990). Crucial to establishing any form of powerful polity was the ability to exert authority over as many people as possible. This could be done in several ways: through coercion and punitive measures (illustrated dramatically by the Zulus under Shaka); incentives such as offering protection, or access to resources and food (for example, the Buganda); or boosting economically productive populations, often through slavery (such as the Dahomey).

Yet this posed an enduring dilemma for leaders across the continent. Jeffery Herbst (2000, 35) argues that pre-colonial leaders frequently struggled to extend and project their power in any meaningful fashion over long distances. The inhospitable environment and poor transportation meant that when centralised political entities did emerge they found it very difficult to exert any form of control over people beyond a specific point. The further away from the centre of power, the harder it was to exact loyalty or tribute, and thus territorial boundaries were often rather fluid. The result was often a complex form of devolved governance, where local leaders and communities would pledge allegiance to stronger power(s), while simultaneously enjoying relative autonomy under its auspices.

For example, the Sokoto Caliphate was a confederation of city-states, each ruled by an emir, who owed their position entirely to the sultan who acted as the overarching authority (Asante, 2015, 135). However, for many states this lack of formal control over territory became ever more problematic as distances increased, opening up possibilities for resistance in outlying regions. As a consequence, the inability to exert total control or reach by formal political institutions, combined with the abundance of land available, meant that disaffected populations could simply up sticks and move if they felt subjugated or wished to avoid conflict. The result has been a high level of mobility across the continent, which impacted not only on the creation of 'modern' states but also on forming cohesive overarching 'national' identities that encompassed different groups; individuals were far more likely to identify with their local community or kin. The number of African languages, often found in relatively small geographic locations, is one such legacy of this mobility of people.

These factors are fundamental to keep in mind, as they underpin and shaped much of Africa's historic trajectory. Communities were hamstrung by the conditions around them, which affected the creation of 'modern' bureaucratic institutions. One striking feature of the pre-colonial era is the rapid rise, and subsequent fall, of many major entities like Ghana and Kongo. However, African societies before colonialism should be considered differently, and certainly not against a Eurocentric model. Do not mistake the lack of visible 'states' in the European understanding of the term with there being no laws, representation, or hierarchical lines of power or social control in this era, as it would fundamentally skew the picture and mask the reality of unique and complex forms of societal organisation. The rest of this section will briefly comment on several broader themes of pre-colonial Africa: the rise and influence of Islam; early European interventions and the Atlantic slave trade; and the rise of African powers during the eighteenth century.

One of the most significant developments in pre-colonial Africa was the rise and spread of Islam across the north of the continent, which in turn opened up this region to new external influences, cultures, and ideas. The widespread adoption of Islam began in 641 with the Umayyad invasion of Egypt, after which the empire rapidly expanded across North Africa; by the early eighth century, the whole region had been brought under Umayyad control. The subsequent spread of Islam across the Sahara, through into West Africa and the Sudanic belt over the proceeding centuries, was largely driven by traders and merchants, who proved vital to the dissemination of Islamic religious and cultural ideas. The cross-Saharan trade and communication networks thus played a crucial role in the widespread adoption of Islam, while simultaneously assisting the formation of some major political kingdoms (see Box 3.1). It would

Box 3.1 The Songhai Empire

The Songhai Empire, founded by Sunni Ali, rose to prominence in the fifteenth and sixteenth centuries, dominating the western Sahel region. The Songhai Empire, expanding outwards from the city of Gao in 1464, replaced Mali as the paramount power in the region, whose authority was based on its control of the Niger River bend and the domination of the West African salt and gold trade (Asante, 2015, 76–77, 122–125). These revenues allowed for a standing army to be retained, which not only protected its economic position but also allowed for the empire's expansionism throughout the region. The empire rose to a state of international importance, with Timbuktu becoming a key city in the promotion of Islamic scholarship, which further aided the spread and adoption of Muslim practices across the Sahel. The city became famed not only for its scholarship but also for the impressiveness of its buildings including its mosques and courts. However, from its height in the early 1500s the empire fell into decline, as it began to lose control over the Saharan gold trade, which was undermined by European traders and new emergent powers such as the Hausa. This economic decline prompted a sustained political crisis for the Songhai Empire, fuelled by civil war and problems of succession. The final collapse of Songhai was a result of an invasion by Morocco in 1591, whose better equipped army destroyed the empire and took control of its territories. However, despite Morocco's conquest of the vast Songhai Empire, it failed to effectively implement hegemony over the territory, ultimately abandoning total control, which saw the remnants of this once grand medieval empire disintegrate into smaller communities and kingdoms.

not be an understatement to claim that this was a transformative process. From the fifteenth century onwards, the outcome was that most political entities that emerged across the Sahara were influenced, at least in part, by Islamic tradition. However, it must be noted that Islam in Africa was not homogenised, and remained highly flexible and adaptable, with indigenous practices and traditions incorporated into the religion; the outcome was a series of hybrid forms of the religion (see Chapter 7). The Islamic influence in North Africa was reinforced with the arrival of the Ottoman Empire, which, by 1550, had expanded across the region, with the exception of Morocco. The Ottomans proved to be an important economic, cultural, and religious authority, and proved a remarkably durable power, surviving (by and large) until the early nineteenth century (Map 3.2).

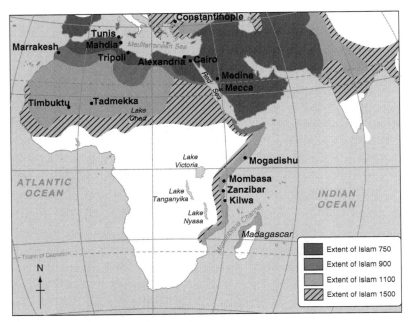

Map 3.2 The spread of Islam in Africa

A dramatic historical development in the late seventeenth century that had lasting repercussions across Islamic Africa, triggering instability and upheaval, was the emergent division within Islamic practice. The cleric Nasir al-Din demanded the introduction of a purer form of Islam (to expunge the hybrid practices that had emerged), and called for all secular leaders to abdicate their power to clerical authority (Curtin, 1971). In 1673, in what is modern-day Mauritania, Nasir al-Din declared a jihad against those leaders that refused to cooperate. The call to jihad by the Fulani had profound consequences for future generations as it offered a legitimate tool to either challenge or coalesce power. A century on, in the early 1800s, a new era of successful jihads began, which shook the political order, prompting the fall and emergence of new kingdoms. In 1804, Usman dan Fodio led his followers in a holy war against the Hausa city-states (present-day Nigeria), with his armies capturing important cities such as Gobir, Kano, and Daura by 1808. From the remnants of the Hausa state, these campaigns saw the formation and rapid expansion of the Sokoto Caliphate, which became one of the most powerful entities in Africa. Even after the British conquest, many of the caliphate's structures were maintained when governing northern Nigeria (see the discussion on indirect rule in the section on p. 50, 'The colonial era'). The expansion and consolidation of Islamic power, tradition, and culture were crucial historical developments. Islam opened up northern Africa to external influences and cultures, promoted widespread conversion to the religion, helped drive economic trade across the Sahara, and played an integral part in the rise and fall of political entities.

Another important development was the arrival of European traders by the mid-fifteenth century. Before then, much of the continent away from the Islamic north had been relatively isolated from wider international ebbs and flows. This general isolation meant that medieval 'Africa was still mostly moving to its own rhythms, followings its own procedures and seeking its own paths, channels and routes' (Oliver, 2001, 9). However, aided by great leaps in maritime technology, European ships could now travel further than ever before. For example, by the early 1500s, Portuguese sailors had journeyed around the Cape of Good Hope, and travelled much of the Indian Ocean coastline. The outcome of these technological changes marked the beginning of greater interactions between African communities and Europeans, bringing in their wake economic links, through the trade in gold, copper, spices, beads, cloth, and later people in coastal areas. Europeans did not penetrate far into the interior, checked by powerful African kingdoms and the inability to travel great distances as well as extremely high mortality rates through diseases such as malaria. It was therefore far easier to deal with local leaders and communities close to shore; an array of forts and small trading stations were constructed along the coastline to facilitate trade. The result was the emergence of powerful mercantile states such as the Sultanate of Zanzibar, which, via the control of trade routes, used their commercial advantages to extend their military and political power over large swathes of East and Central Africa.

Following Portugal's forays around the African coastline, other European nations such as France, Britain, the Netherlands, and Spain established connections. However, these trade links became less benign with ever-increasing European demands for indentured labour, fuelling the growth of the Atlantic slave trade. Three contextual points must be made before developing this theme further. First, as has been mentioned earlier, slavery was not a new phenomenon to Africa, with states such as the Mali Empire and Kongo utilising those captured into servitude to plug specific gaps and roles in communities, sometimes refusing to resell them. The sale of slaves provided the means to purchase firearms and support armies, which in turn meant that warfare and violence radiated out from those states which were engaged in the trade, illustrated by the militarism of the Dahomey and Ndongo. However, these internal slaving networks are often overlooked because African history is often written from an external perspective. Second, while the Atlantic slave trade is the most well-known, there was an active trade in north and eastern regions by Arab slavers, which saw millions of Africans transported across the Red Sea and Indian Ocean into the Middle East (Nunn, 2008, 141; Lovejoy, 2012, 15–18). Finally, the slave trade was uneven and did not affect the whole continent, with southern Africa and sections of Central Africa experiencing virtually none of the deleterious effects that other regions did (Manning, 1983, 839).

The emergence of the 'New World' as a centre for large-scale sugar plantations, a labour-intensive agricultural activity that relied almost exclusively on indentured labour, was a major catalyst for the expansion of slavery. Starting in the sixteenth century, and lasting until the mid-nineteenth century, the flow of slaves to the Americas, bought by European traders along the African coastline, became an important component of a global trade network linking three continents, commonly referred to as 'triangular trade'. The exact number of Africans sold into slavery is unknown, although various efforts have been made to quantify it. The current estimates for the Atlantic slave trade are around 12.5 million people (Nunn, 2008, 142; Trans-Atlantic Slave Trade Database), while another 6 million were transported in the Saharan, Red Sea, and Indian Ocean trades (Map 3.3).

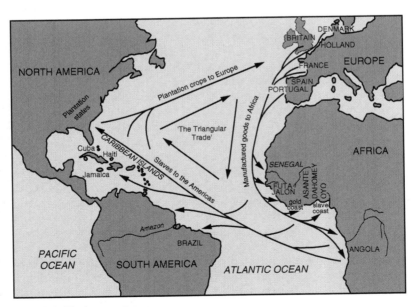

Map 3.3 Slaving routes

Source: Shillington (2012), History of Africa, *Palgrave Macmillan.*

There has been a lively academic debate about the effects of the slave trade on African economies, politics, and societies, with some polarity in opinions. The obvious argument is that it was catastrophic, and its legacy is one of underdevelopment, extraction, and exploitation of African resources. Scholars such as Walter Rodney (1972), Nathan Nunn (2008), and Joseph Inikori (1994) argue that it weakened state structures, and made some economies reliant on slavery, rather than alternative forms of production. Others assert that it changed the political dynamics in those areas involved, resulting in insecurity and instability, with warfare and raiding becoming key features of society. Several major kingdoms such as the Asante, Oyo, and Dahomey owed their power to the slave trade, waging wars and raids against neighbouring regions and selling the captives to European traders in return for goods (Lovejoy, 2012, 4–5). Both Martin Klein (1992) and Andrew Hubbell (2001, 27) have referred to this as the predatory state; in the western Sudan region, they demonstrate how states used a cycle of warfare and violence for the express purpose of enslaving local populations, which became a fundamental part of their economic life. As a consequence, surrounding communities reverted to violence and slavery to protect themselves, only deepening the crisis. There are, however, a few historians such as John Thornton who insist that slavery was only one part of the wider economic and societal picture, and that it was not as damaging as has been emphasised elsewhere. Thornton (1998, 125) also highlighted that African elites made decisions about who was captured and sold, arguing that 'Europeans possessed no means, either economic or military, to compel African leaders to sell slaves. The willingness of Africa's political and commercial elite to supply slaves should be located in their own internal dynamics and history.'

Following growing moral public uproar across Europe, Britain outlawed the slave trade in 1807 (although not slavery, which was banned in 1833), and began utilising its navy to prevent others from maintaining it. Although there was a marked decline in slavery after 1807, abolition did not bring an immediate end to the African slave trade, which stubbornly persisted for a further 50 years. The abolition of slavery clearly impacted on the interests of those states that were orientated towards the trade, prompting Dike (1956) to call it a 'crisis of adaptation', where states collapsed or struggled to recover; yet other scholars (Lovejoy & Richardson, 2002) have offered a more nuanced assessment of this development demonstrating how states such as the Asante started using their slaves internally to shift towards more 'legitimate' forms of commerce such as palm oil and kola nuts.

A significant continental exception was South Africa, where the Dutch East India Company founded the Cape Colony in 1652. Here a relatively sizeable European community settled, which rapidly began to extend the territorial boundaries of the colony northwards, bringing them into contact, and conflict, with indigenous peoples such as the Koi and Xhosa. After the British took control of the colony and imposed new rules, particularly abolishing slavery, the Boer population, incensed by the encroachment on their way of life, departed on the Great Trek in 1834; this migration of people resulted in the establishment of two new 'white' republics in southern Africa: the Orange Free State and the Transvaal. The other early European colonial intrusion in the nineteenth century was the French conquest of Algeria in 1830. By 1848, the Mediterranean region of Algeria was regarded as a fundamental part of France, which resulted in hundreds of thousands of Europeans arriving in the colony, one calibrated solely for the benefit of the white settlers. However, before the onset of full-scale imperial ambitions in the late nineteenth century, the settlement by white Europeans and their descendants was an anomaly.

By the early nineteenth century, before the onset of colonial acquisition in Africa, the continent saw the emergence and consolidation of several major political entities (Box 3.2). There were still many stateless

Box 3.2 The rise of the Zulu nation

The emergence of the Zulus as a significant power in southern Africa was nothing short of remarkable. Before 1819, the Zulus were a relatively minor clan within the broader Nguni people, but they rose to prominence through the military prowess of Shaka. In the late eighteenth century, the Nguni had started to coalesce as a series of larger entities, each of which faced the combined pressures of land shortages, access to cattle herds, and the encroachment of the Boer Republics into their territory. These pressures ultimately led to war between the clans, and it was during these conflicts that Shaka, fighting for the clan leader Dingiswayo, demonstrated his military ingenuity and intelligence. When Dingiswayo died, Shaka rose to clan leader, where he set about extensive military training for his armies, introducing age-based regiments while revolutionising weaponry (with short-handled spears) and tactics (the bull-horn formation). The Zulus defeated their main rival the Ndwandwe in 1820 and 1823, which cemented Shaka's authority over the Nguni clans. Out of the continued warfare a highly centralised and military orientated state was established. Lacking any major opposition, the Zulus set about the imperial conquest and incorporation of surrounding peoples and territory; by 1825, the Zulus controlled an extensive swathe of the eastern regions of modern-day South Africa. When smaller kingdoms were brought to heel, traditional forms of Nguni clan leadership were maintained, allowing some semblance of autonomy, although leaders had to pay tribute to Shaka, while offering loyalty and soldiers to the central polity. The rapid expansion and military ambitions of the Zulus, along with continual raiding, caused chaos in southern Africa, bringing unprecedented societal dislocation, the mass movement of people (known as the *mfecane*, or annihilation), ecological crisis, and cyclical violence. Shaka was not a popular leader – he was known for cruelty and arbitrary decision making – and he was assassinated in 1828 by his half-brother, Dingane. However, the legacy of Shaka's military and political leadership survived, and substantial mythology surrounds his life and accomplishments. The rapid rise of the Zulu nation was an astonishing feat of nation building in pre-colonial Africa.

societies in existence, but gradually across west, east, and, increasingly, parts of southern Africa, centralised, powerful states were on the rise. Kingdoms such as Buganda in Eastern Africa had many of the features of 'modern' states such as bureaucracies and nascent infrastructure. Different powers across the continent reached this level of centralised authority through different means, characterised by the role of Islam in acting as a consolidating force in state formation, seen with the Sokoto Caliphate; by the ability of centralised kingdoms such as Buganda to gain a monopoly over resources, trade, and agriculture, and then exact tribute from neighbouring regions; and by the creation of highly militarised states such as the Zulus, who revolutionised tactics and warfare in southern Africa, utilising violence as a predatory force to secure people and resources.

By the mid-nineteenth century, Africa was experiencing the intrusion of external powers from Europe and the Middle East, while witnessing political and economic expansion and amplification from new, powerful entities. The formation of political states centred on commercial control of resources and trade, a unifying religious message, or military prowess became the dominant feature of this era. It must be emphasised that the emergence of these African states was as 'modern' formations: for example, the Zulus had a powerful nationalist ideology, linked closely to advancement and reform in military techniques and societal organisation.

The colonial era

There is no specific, catch-all reason as to why European powers began to colonise Africa, but the consequences reverberated well into the twentieth century. The shadow and impact of colonial rule over Africa hides the fact that compared to other continents such as South America and Asia, the process of territorial occupation in the late nineteenth century was not only very late but also spanned a relatively short period – in most cases around 80 years. What makes the 'Scramble for Africa' surprising is that European leaders in the decades before 1884 (the symbolic start of the partition) had almost no inclination to extend authority and power into the unknown hinterland. What changed? Primarily, without some enormous technological advances in medicine and communication, conquest by Europeans would not have been possible. A crucial scientific discovery was quinine, which dramatically reduced malaria deaths, allowing explorers to venture out from the coasts into the interior. This scientific advance was complemented by the advent of steamships, railways, and the telegraph, ensuring swifter communication of messages and people to, and within, Africa. Finally, the invention of the Maxim gun allowed small invading armies to easily defeat much larger forces, with little loss of life. Yet the combination of these advances does not explain the motivations for Europe's partition of Africa.

There is no overarching explanation for colonialism. Multiple hypotheses have been mooted, with different suggestion(s) working in different locations, and for different colonisers. The historiographical debate is fiercely contested and fascinating (Hobson, 1902; Robinson & Gallagher, 1961; Mazrui, 1969; Fieldhouse, 1973; Oliver & Sanderson, 1985; Stoecker, 1986; Darwin, 1997; Flint, 1999; Cain & Hopkins, 2002; Ferguson, 2004; Chamberlain, 2010) but in brief, the suggestions include the defence of global interests; a response to crises on the periphery of empire; to derive economic benefits; the influence of 'gentlemanly capital'; national prestige; great power rivalries; the influence and role of 'men on the spot'; an ideological mission; European racism; and public pressure. There is no single point of causality, and certainly no universal explanation for the imperial conquest of Africa, but the motivations can be categorised broadly under the headings of economic, political, and cultural. Therefore, in order to develop a better understanding of the reasons for imperialism, answers should be sought in specific locales, dependent on the impetus of that European power.

The speed of European conquest was remarkably swift and all-encompassing in scope. By 1914, the map of Africa had been transformed, and all but two states, Liberia and Abyssinia (Ethiopia), were under external domination (see Map 3.4). The 1884 Berlin Conference is often

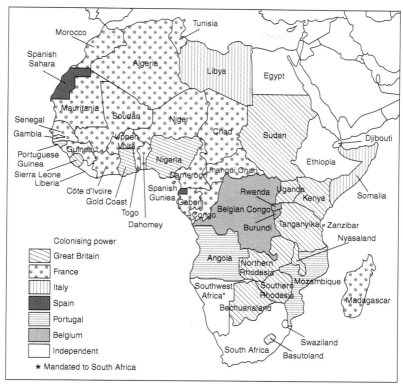

Map 3.4 Colonial map of Africa

Source: Nugent (2012), Africa Since Independence, *Palgrave Macmillan.*

seen as representing the beginning of the 'scramble', but it obscures the previous encroachment of European powers into African affairs well before this date. By the 1880s, several nations had 'staked their claims' by carving out spheres of influences, exemplified by the British across southern Africa and the French in West Africa. Aside from the established European nations, several leaders, not wanting to miss out, entered the fray. In this regard, the personal ambitions of King Leopold II of Belgium would notoriously represent the worst excesses of colonial brutality. Leopold, who did not have the backing of the Belgian state, had in the 1870s turned his attention to the Congo Basin, and the 'void' in the map. He established a private organisation, the International Association, designed ostensibly to administer the region on behalf of the people, but in reality was a personal tool for wealth extraction. With the help of Henry Stanley, Leopold staked his claim to the gigantic land mass at the centre of the continent, which would later become the Congo Free State (also known as the Belgian Congo, Zaire, and today as the Democratic Republic of Congo). The brazen land grab acted as a starting pistol for Britain, France, Italy, Portugal, and Germany to accelerate their claims to the continent.

In order to prevent competition escalating, the Berlin Conference, held between November 1884 and February 1885, was convened by German Chancellor Otto von Bismarck. The task of the conference was to mediate the growing conflicts between the rival European demands, deal with the competing claims over the Congo and Niger River basins, secure free trade in Africa, and discuss the 'rules' for future annexations. It must be stressed that not one African leader was invited, despite the obvious presence of several powerful states in this era. One of the core stipulations of the conference was that European powers must provide evidence of 'effective occupation' in a territory, via a physical presence or treaties with local leaders. The outcome was an initial, rough paper partition of Africa, followed only later by actual occupation. However, a major problem was that the cartography of much of the continent was unknown to European statesmen. Therefore in keeping with Westphalian ideas of sovereignty, nation-statehood, and formal territorial boundaries, the European powers imposed 'order' on the map, and created their own new borders (see Chapter 2). Often in straight lines, these bore little resemblance to the reality on the ground, with no appreciation for ethnic and linguistic boundaries. The result was Europe riding rough-shod over existing African states and governance structures. A cynical evaluation of the partition came from Lord Salisbury, who stated 'we have been giving away mountains, and rivers and lakes to each other, only hindered by the small impediment that we never knew exactly where they were' (Meredith, 2005, 2). The significance of the artificial boundaries imposed on Africa, and the inability to acknowledge existing structures, is one of the most important and long-lasting legacies, with enormous ramifications for state and societal evolution. The Berlin Conference was therefore a crucial moment in the continent's historical development. However, it did not start the partition of Africa, nor did it solve the question of translating abstract notions of control into reality. Initially at least, Africans had some agency in the process of establishing the boundaries agreed on at Berlin as 'Africans were hardly passive. They influenced the initial demarcation, [and] created new trading systems across borders' (Howard, 2010, 22).

The theoretical annexation of Africa may have occurred in Europe, but once negotiated, the thorny issue of how best to cement their claims on the ground arose. A core concern for the colonisers was to achieve this as inexpensively as possible, with limited administration costs. Perhaps an indication as to the motivations behind Africa's annexation was that once 'authority' had been established, there appeared to be very little appetite to do much with the territories, as most colonies received negligible investment or resources from the metropole until after World War I. While colonial rule was underpinned by violence, brutality, and coercion, outright military intervention was the last resort in attempting to secure territorial claims. The preferred option was always diplomatic, under a fragile veneer of legalism, albeit with the threat of violence lurking in the background. After 1884, administrators, army generals, and profiteers set out across the continent to find local leaders to convince, or co-opt, into signing treaties that effectively gave Europeans authority over resources and territory. Many African leaders did not understand or appreciate the details of these treaties that were being signed, and often it was too late by the time they had realised the enormity of them; King Lobengula of the Ndebele even wrote to Queen Victoria complaining about British activities in his kingdom. An alternative way of initially securing colonialism on the cheap was through the use of chartered companies, favoured particularly by Britain. It meant that the cost of conquering and administering territory could be passed from the responsibility of the treasury on to a private company, which would deal with the running of the colony; notable examples were the Royal Niger Company, and the British South Africa Company led by Cecil Rhodes. However, many of these proved unsustainable in the long run and by 1924 all were incorporated into the control of the government (Image 3.1).

While it may appear that the colonial conquest of Africa was relatively easy, backed by technological superiority and a sense of European supremacy, there were significant acts of resistance to the imposition of external rule. Several examples serve to illustrate this point. The French from 1882 onwards faced tough and sustained resistance in what is now Mali and Guinea, in its attempts to subdue the Wassoulou Empire, led by Samory Touré (Vandervort, 1998). Touré's armies, spread across West Africa, engaged the French in conventional and guerrilla warfare over many years in a bid to prevent the loss of their power and land. The resistance only ended in 1898, when Touré was finally captured, but it was a bruising and costly effort to impose French colonial authority in the region. In East Africa, Ethiopia successfully repelled Italian efforts to colonise the territory in 1896, at the battle of Adwa, which resulted in a peace treaty that recognised the independence of the territory, under Emperor Menelik II. In southern Africa, the British faced several testing confrontations, first with the Zulus and then the Boer Republics (Meredith, 2007; Nasson, 2011; Judd, 2013). The British endured its heaviest

Image 3.1 The Rhodes Colossus Striding from Cape Town to Cairo

Source: Punch, 10 December 1892.

imperial defeat at the battle of Isandlwana in 1879, where over 1,300 soldiers were killed by the Zulus, who sought to prevent the invasion and annexation of Zululand. Another far more costly conflict broke out in 1899, with the Transvaal and the Orange Free State, known as the Anglo-Boer War. The Boer Republics, enraged by the aggression and attempted annexation of their territory, launched a pre-emptive attack against the British army in a bid to head off the threat. The Anglo-Boer War was a protracted and bloody conflict, which saw thousands of people die, and nearly constituted a crisis of empire for Britain. In the course of repressing the rebellion, the British resorted to scorched earth tactics, and the internment of women and children in concentration camps, many of whom died. These brutal tactics stoked fierce resentment and hostility among the Boer population, which had long-lasting consequences in South Africa.

A final example of resistance, followed by bloody reprisals, is from South West Africa (Namibia), where the first genocide of the twentieth century occurred (Zimmerer & Zeller, 2008; Sarkin, 2011). The German settlers had increasingly come into conflict with the Herero and Nama people, who were rebelling against the confiscation of their land and livestock. The German army defeated the Herero uprising in battle in 1904, but the survivors were systematically driven into the Kalahari Desert, where the water holes were either guarded or poisoned; those that did survive were sent to labour camps. The estimate is that 75,000 people died. Scholars including Zimmerman (2001, 245) have explicitly linked the brutality of colonial rule with the final solution by the Nazis, arguing that 'the holocaust brought to Europe practices developed in colonial Africa as the genocidal war against the Herero ... make all too clear.' While there was clearly active and courageous African opposition across the continent to colonialism, the technological and military might of the colonisers made the outcomes predictably one-sided.

Once territory had been secured through diplomacy or warfare, the question of how to extend authority became an important question. Here the continuities with pre-colonial forms of governance become increasingly apparent. In many colonies, authority and power were confined to the major urban centres. With few white administrators, relatively small police or security forces, and little infrastructure, it meant the reach of European officials did not extend very far. When infrastructure was introduced it was mainly focused on serving the needs of the white minority, the educated African urban elites, and any useful centre of economic productivity, rather than the majority of the population. The only exceptions to this norm were in Algeria, Kenya, Rhodesia, and South Africa, where attempts to construct 'modern' state machinery and infrastructure occurred, due entirely to the large number of whites that settled in these colonies. The lack of state capacity, and the inability to broadcast power, was a major weakness of colonial rule. Furthermore, those people in stateless societies, or those that remained mobile like the Saharan nomads, proved to be an enigma for colonial rulers, and like previous generations of African leaders, they struggled to find a solution to exert control over them.

It must be noted that colonialism itself is a rather generic, catch-all term, which hides a multitude of differences and experiences in control, collaboration, and mind-set, varying enormously between colonies and colonial power. Each European power took different approaches, vigorously debating the merits of their preferred form of rule. In broad terms, there were three main styles: indirect rule, direct rule, and settler society.

An uncomfortable reality is that colonialism could not have been sustained or perpetuated without the active collaboration of African rulers to maintain rule or order. To secure authority, a conscious policy developed to identify existing leaders and monarchs, or promote ethnic groups, for positions of power. For example, after the British had quelled the resistance of the Sokoto Caliphate in northern Nigeria in 1903, the pre-colonial system of governance was retained. The British acted as the overarching authority, but the day-to-day control was left to the newly appointed sultan and the various emirs, who maintained a significant degree of autonomy and power. With only a few administrators, the British could take a back seat in proceedings; this low-cost form of governance, utilising pre-colonial structures, is known as **indirect rule**, (see Box 3.3) often accredited to its architect, General Frederick Lugard. The result was that different ethnic groups could be pitted against each other by the British, while no efforts were made in trying to establish a common 'national' identity among their subjects. In fact, none of the European powers were able to broadcast total power, or gain legitimacy from their subjects, and as such they all had to utilise a form of indirect rule; however, what worked in Nigeria did not necessarily work in Nyasaland, which meant that there was often significant degrees of interpretation, flexibility, and non-conformity in approach and governance, even by a single colonial power.

Box 3.3 Frederick Lugard: The architect of indirect rule

Indirect rule was a form of colonial control devised by the British governor of northern Nigeria, Lord Frederick Lugard. The system was a simple means of establishing control over a territory without the expense and personnel required to maintain it. In the case of northern Nigeria, once the resistance of the emirs of the Sokoto Caliphate had been subdued, the protectorate was to be ruled as before by the defeated leaders that were willing to accept ultimate British authority; the pre-colonial systems of governance in the region were simply retained under indirect rule. The emirs kept some of their original power and authority, especially over the day-to-day governance of affairs, helping to enforce colonial policies, but they lost control over tax and security matters. These leaders were advised by British officials, who instructed them on the aims of colonial policy. The result was that only a small number of white officials was required to govern a region that extended over thousands of square miles. Those leaders who refused to adhere to British ideals and policies were simply removed, which ensured some semblance of loyalty. Indirect rule proved to be an effective form of British colonial control, in that it was cheap and easy, saving the need for centralised bureaucracy.

In contrast, France, Belgium, Germany, and Portugal all favoured a form of centralised bureaucracy and administration as a governing tool, with previous ruling structures subordinate to the higher authority of external power. Under this model of **direct rule**, existing authorities were subjugated, and a policy of divide and rule among African groups emerged to weaken any potential challenge to colonial rule; for example, in Rwanda, the Tutsi were given preferential status over the Hutu, based on class divisions. Unlike the British, who offered no pretence that its colonial peoples were inferior, the other European powers instead preached that their African subjects, could, at some unspecified date, assimilate into full citizenship. Imbued with notions of superiority and racism, the French in particular argued that by bestowing the benefits of civilisation, egalitarianism, and culture, the subjects could 'evolve' into being French. Indigenous populations were encouraged to renounce their own heritage and embrace the colonisers' language, culture, and educational values, which might result in them becoming citizens. However, the chance of achieving full citizenship rights was rare, and most colonial peoples were not treated as equals. The fact that the possession of colonies violated all of the much vaunted principles of egalitarianism in almost every way was conveniently ignored. Such an approach morphed into the nebulous idea of the 'civilising mission', adopted in part by all colonial powers, in which Africans would 'benefit' from the benign rule of Europe. Yet many people did adopt such ideals, with several first-generation post-independence leaders such as Léopold Senghor maintaining close links with France. Although assimilation did not extend across the whole empire, by 1848 the French did implement citizenship rights, including the right to vote, in the four communes of Senegal (Saint-Louis, Dakar, Gorée, and Rufisque), which were its oldest colonial settlements in West Africa; by 1914, there was African representation in the French National Assembly.

In the vast majority of African colonies very few Europeans ever settled, but in those places that saw an influx of migrants, most notably Algeria, Angola, Kenya, Rhodesia, and South Africa, the scenario was entirely different. The structure and emphasis of these **settler colonies** were orientated towards the white minority, with the state designed to protect their interests in all walks of life; in order to maintain and extend power, these forms of colony adopted aspects of indirect rule. In settler colonies, there was usually a premium based on the control of land, as they had more temperate climates and better soils for agriculture. The result was that large numbers of Africans not only lost their access to land but were often forcibly resettled to 'native reserves', which were by and large unsuitable for sustaining the populations. These colonies were far more conservative in outlook, and the white populations had closely held ideas of racial superiority, which impacted directly, and negatively, on Africans' day-to-day experiences; most notably through systematic fear, intimidation, and brutality. With the onset of nationalist challenges to colonial rule, it was in these colonies where the greatest resistance from white minorities occurred.

By 1914, the reality was that colonial rule across the continent was still fragile and incomplete, with only a few exceptions. Africa's contribution in World War I is often a forgotten chapter in the continent's history, which was acutely highlighted during the 2014 centenary celebrations. Yet the colonies were a vital component to the war effort, and European powers exploited them for all that they could (Lunn, 1999; Strachan, 2004; Liebau, 2010; Samson, 2012). Millions of people and large amounts of resources were utilised by Britain and France, while Paris was even accused of 'breaching the rules of civilisation' by transporting colonial soldiers, the Tirailleurs Sénégalais (from across North and West Africa, based on martial race theory), for use on European battlefields. Furthermore, the German army in East Africa under Paul von Lettow-Vorbeck remained undefeated, despite a significant number of Allied forces pursuing them across the region.

Once the war was over, there was a concerted effort by the European powers to exploit their territories, while Germany's colonies were divided among the victors in the Treaty of Versailles. Throughout the 1920s, there was a greater focus on investment not only to make the colonies pay for themselves but to recoup some of the losses during the war. The continent saw widespread investment in roads, railways, and ports, to assist in the extraction of resources to Europe. Yet not all communities were passive or receptive to external intrusions, demonstrating a level of African agency and resistance; for example, the Sefwi in Ghana had demanded input into decision-making processes, and regularly opposed colonial infrastructural developments that disrupted their interests (Boni, 1999, 70).

Simultaneously, a number of key reforms, in accordance with pretensions of a civilising mission, were introduced focusing on social provision and education. For example, the Belgian Congo witnessed an enormous investment in the economic and societal development of the country, with funds dedicated to the expansion of health and education services. This apparently benign form of colonialism sought to co-opt subjects into European rule, who could subsequently assist with colonial development. The nascent education system was usually run by the church, which ensured a form of cheap schooling and the opportunity for missionaries to facilitate widespread conversion to Christianity. The result was the rise of educated African elites, who grasped the opportunities afforded by colonialism, with many future nationalist leaders such as Hastings Banda and Léopold Senghor studying at universities abroad.

However, let us not pretend that the increased developments in infrastructure and education were designed to benefit the majority, nor grounded in anything but a means of economic exploitation shrouded under a cloak of paternalistic racism. The colonial powers annexed the continent based on economic and political interests, yet tried to justify occupation through the notion of a civilising mission. The premise was that Europeans were only ever temporary custodians, allowing those that embraced ideas of 'civilisation', Christianity, commerce, and education to transform African society. There was always the promise that when indigenous populations were 'ready' they would reap the benefits and be able to gain full independence. In the early stages of colonialism, many Africans bought into these ideas, believing that they and their newly created states would flourish from this input, acting as a vehicle towards modernity. But, herein lay the fundamental contradiction of colonialism. The European powers wanted to extract and exploit what they could, therefore any moves towards 'modernity' or independence could not happen too fast. Indeed, the timescale for change by colonial administrations was unhurried, few resources were allocated to aid progress, and many policies explicitly held back African society. The gulf between promises and reality only widened. The veneer of a civilising mission soon began to slip. Those that had benefited most from educational opportunities became increasingly frustrated and started to agitate for what had been promised: independence. There was a realisation that colonialism was in fact acting as a barrier to progress, inhibiting opportunities for Africans to take control of their own affairs.

Decolonisation: The road to independence

The process of decolonisation was one of the most significant political developments of the twentieth century, which ultimately saw the granting of freedom to millions of Africans. From the end of 1945 through to the mid-1960s, the vast majority of African colonies received their independence as the European powers withdrew direct control; the notable exceptions were the Portuguese colonies, and the white minority states of Rhodesia, Namibia, and South Africa. The general stereotype of decolonisation is one of violence and intransigence of ruling minorities in states such as Algeria, Belgian Congo, and Kenya; yet, in reality, the process was undertaken remarkably swiftly, and in a largely peaceful, negotiated fashion. However, what is clear is that decolonisation was most certainly a struggle against continued European rule.

The academic debate concerning decolonisation is multifaceted, with many different arguments assessing the reasons and motivations behind the process. The narrative for decolonisation traditionally starts with World War II, which is often regarded as the beginning of the end for colonial rule and the catalyst for African independence. It is easy to see why. The conflict brought about enormous changes to the established world order and fundamentally weakened the power and superiority of the main colonial powers. Old international structures were irrevocably altered, with two new superpowers emerging from the chaos, combined with a growing appetite for independence from emboldened African nationalists. The strength of the European powers was undermined by the significant early defeats of France and Belgium. The German invasion of France in 1940 saw the Free French flee to Equatorial Africa, making Congo-Brazzaville (also known as the Republic of the Congo) the capital of the resistance, while the Belgian government relocated to the Congo. This was a major shock to their prestige and ingrained sense of dominance. More humiliatingly, the French relied heavily on African support in order to defeat the Vichy regime, demonstrated by the governor of Chad Félix Éboué's efforts to organise the colonies behind the Gaullists. From then on, the colonial relationship was permanently altered (Image 3.2).

Image 3.2 Algerian infantrymen in the liberation of France, victory parade in Paris, 8 May 1945, France, World War II

Source: Photo12/UIG/Getty Images.

Throughout the conflict, the European empires relied heavily on the continent to sustain the war effort, with huge numbers of Africans recruited into colonial armies or involved in military production; over 1 million Africans served in the British military during the course of the war (Table 3.1).

Table 3.1 Number of African soldiers fighting in World War II

Colonial power	African colonial troops	Troop numbers
Britain	South Africa	334,000
	King's African Rifles (Kenya, Tanzania, Uganda, Malawi)	289,530
	Royal West Africa Frontier Force (Nigeria, Ghana, Sierra Leone, Gambia)	243,550
	Egypt	100,000
	Southern Africa (Lesotho, Botswana, Swaziland, Zambia, Zimbabwe)	77,767
	Mauritius, Seychelles	6,500
France (Vichy & Free French)	Algeria, Senegal, Mali, Burkina Faso, Benin, Chad, Guinea, Côte d'Ivoire, Niger, Republic of Congo	190,000
Italy	Eritrea	60,000
Belgium	Congo	24,000

Source: Created using data from D. Killingray and M. Plaut (2012), Fighting for Britain: African Soldiers in the Second World War.

Yet this mass recruitment had several unintended consequences for the long-term sustainability of empire. It cannot be underestimated how crucial the cross-cultural experience of serving away from the continent was for African soldiers. Not only did they gain new skills and knowledge but the exposure to troops from India in particular, a colony that was agitating for independence, was an extremely significant factor in fostering African nationalism. In turn, when many of the troops returned home, especially in Kenya, they felt neglected and unappreciated in the post-war dispensation, which only hardened demands for change. Finally, the war had raised expectations of reform and change: why else would so many have joined the war effort if they were not rewarded in some way?

However, the promises made by European nations were never intended to be fulfilled. Such cynicism was exemplified by the Atlantic Charter, signed in 1941, and agreed to by all the Allied nations. This document explicitly set out the main aims of the war, one of which was the right to self-determination – the antithesis of colonialism. Winston Churchill strenuously insisted that self-determination was not applicable to the colonies, yet the Charter became a beacon for nationalist leaders, offering confidence and inspiration to challenge European rule. World War II was therefore an important first step in unmasking the contradictions of colonialism, and for providing the impetus for future African resistance.

With the mounting pressures arrayed against the colonial powers, the immediate post-war era could easily be regarded as a 'crisis of empire'. Assumptions of imperial superiority had crumbled, European states were ravaged by the costs of war, and the growing demands for colonial reforms had put the very concept of colonialism in question. However, for the colonial powers the notion of the empire coming to an end was unthinkable. Although there was a clear realisation that post-war reforms had to be implemented to ensure Africa's economic and social development, these were designed to maintain power, not hasten its demise. Indeed, for Britain, the loss of its Asian colonies had repositioned its African territories' importance within imperial considerations; the African colonies were 'to be given a shot in the arm rather than in the head' (Cain & Hopkins, 2002, 630). The immediate post-war era witnessed a revival of colonial interests that lasted until the mid-1950s; African colonies provided vital resources to kick-start battered economies, as well as supplied a useful source of revenue for European recovery. For example, by 1952, Africa was the source of 20% of Britain's sterling reserves (Hargreaves, 1988, 101).

Political calculations were also at work, demonstrated by Britain establishing the Central African Federation in 1953, which incorporated Nyasaland, Northern Rhodesia, and Southern Rhodesia (present-day Malawi, Zambia, and Zimbabwe, respectively) into a new political entity (Cohen, 2017). This example of creating new colonial structures did not represent British moves towards loosening its grip on power. Likewise, France had little inclination of conceding its territories, demonstrated by the restructuring of the colonies into the French Union, as part of the 1946 Constitution; the result was that overseas territories were regarded as part of 'one France', much in accordance with earlier ideas of assimilation. Yet the new scheme was fictitious, especially in regard to notions of equality; the new constitution gave only limited rights and representation to Africans, with all substantial power residing with the French parliament (Thomas et al., 2015, 129–131). However, the dispensation did allow for the continuation of African deputies in parliament. There emerged a number of influential African leaders, such as Félix Houphouët-Boigny and Léopold Senghor, who used their position to demand the French government to uphold the ideals of the Union. Ultimately, most of the post-war reforms were merely window dressing to mask the continued imperative of political domination and economic extraction. These were not the actions of nations considering the dissolution of empire.

What changed and how did African decolonisation proceed? First of all, decolonisation was a loose, uneven process, with no overarching explanation, but it was broadly characterised by voluntary (or according to one line of argument planned) retreat by the metropole; violent liberation struggles; or negotiation with nationalist leaders. By 1945, there were four independent nations – Egypt, Ethiopia, Liberia, and South Africa – but within two decades the vast majority of the continent was free. It should be noted that although Britain declared Egypt independent in 1922, there was only nominal freedom for Egyptians, with the British retaining significant influence over the country until 1956, demonstrating the ambiguities and informalities of colonialism. The symbolic date for the onset of continental liberation is 1957, when Ghana was awarded its independence. However, the watershed moment for independence was 1960, when 17 nations were granted freedom. It must be noted, though, that North Africa, with the exception of Algeria, was the first region to be free of colonial rule. The tradition of imperial control in North Africa was slightly different compared to sub-Saharan Africa, and along with the active fighting there in World War II had created opportunities for nationalist challenges to the status quo; indeed, this region never 'conformed' to European ideals of colonialism. Libya was the first North African nation to gain independence in 1951, after the UN decreed it should be free of British administration; it was followed by Morocco and Tunisia, both in 1956, where violent resistance prompted France to withdraw, albeit with Paris's main intention to focus on the retention of Algeria. The broader influence of North African decolonisation had an impact across the continent and was enormously important; the artificial division and conceptualisation of Africa should not cloud our judgement as to how influential this was. The complex nature of the decolonisation process and the causalities specific to each state are beyond the scope of this book, yet a few broad points help capture the move towards African independence (Map 3.5).

First of all, the steady rise of African nationalism (Chapter 7) was an important factor in the rebellion against European rule. Post-war colonial reforms had only enacted limited social changes, and impatience was growing among the emerging band of nationalist leaders about the slow timescale for hypothetical independence. The social structure of the colonies had also changed before the war, and there was rapid urbanisation and a growing working class, with accompanied poor social, living, and material conditions; World War II only exacerbated these problems. Riots in Accra in 1948, and strikes in Dakar and St Louis in 1945–6, were

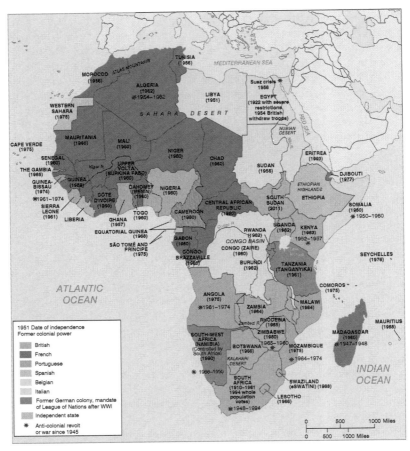

Map 3.5 Decolonisation by date

indicative of the growing dissatisfaction and unrest among colonial populations. Connected to these developments was the rise of trade union organisations, which acted as an important vehicle to articulate some of the demands for change (see Chapter 7); from this milieu, it provided a platform for nationalists such as Sékou Touré in Guinea, or the Kikuyu Central Association in Kenya, to connect material underdevelopment with demands for independence. In some colonies like Ghana, political parties had been legalised, and they became an important mobilising tool (Box 3.4). Nationalist leaders, utilising the message of self-determination that had featured so prominently during World War II, were able to highlight the hypocrisy of colonialism, while continually pushing for

Box 3.4 Kwame Nkrumah and Ghanaian independence

In the Gold Coast colony, often regarded as an exemplary territory by colonial officials, the British administration rapidly lost the initiative in the post-war era in the face of well-organised nationalist protest. Growing social discontent escalated and rioting broke out in Accra in 1948, which did little to challenge colonial authority but prompted British authorities to act. In a bid to halt a perceived communist uprising, the United Gold Coast Convention (UGGC) leadership were arrested, including Kwame Nkrumah, a young, well-educated, and ambitious leader. Following a review of colonial rule in the colony, the British offered vague promises of reform, but did agree to start a gradual move towards self-rule under the close guidance of imperial officials; in doing so, they released all the UGGC leadership, except Nkrumah, who was regarded as a revolutionary threat. Nkrumah quit the UGGC after his release and created the Convention People's Party (CPP) in 1949, bringing together a wide range of political interests. The CPP established a sophisticated political machinery (including a youth wing and a newspaper) to generate popular support across the country: the key campaign slogan was 'self-government NOW'. The demand starkly highlighted the ambiguity of Britain's gradualist proposals for autonomy. Nkrumah was arrested again in 1950, yet despite this impediment, the CPP won the 1951 National Assembly elections with some ease. British Governor Charles Arden-Clarke perceptively chose to release Nkrumah, rather than alienate his supporters, hoping to act as a guide to the CPP. From there on in, the British worked closely with the CPP, attempting to nurture and influence Nkrumah's political activities; in reality, it set in motion a six-year transition process from colonialism to independence. In his position of power, albeit under British 'supervision', Nkrumah steadily worked to erode the justifications for continued colonial rule, and by 1956, following another election victory, London had no reason to cling to power. Britain agreed to withdraw, and Ghana received its independence on 6 March 1957.

greater and far-reaching changes. With little they could do to appease or stem the tidal swell of demands, the European powers were on the back foot, and every concession simply undermined the edifice of colonialism, further encouraging nationalists to push harder. By the start of the 1960s, there was little reason for the European powers to resist the onset of independence in the majority of colonies; there certainly was no desire

Image 3.3 President Kwame Nkrumah of Ghana

Source: Underwood Archives/Getty Images.

to engage in conflict to maintain the dying embers of empire. Another vital mobilising influence in the push towards decolonisation was Pan-Africanism (Chapter 9). This ideology became the lodestar for a number of African leaders, especially Kwame Nkrumah, who used its message to make demands for independence, call for continental unity, and to assert for a more confident world view for the continent (Image 3.3).

The picture of decolonisation was far more complicated where there existed large concentrations of white settlers. In fact, decolonisation in these colonies was characterised by white intransigency and violence, with little consideration for the legitimate concerns of the populous. In states such as Algeria and Kenya, which experienced the earliest challenges to colonial rule, rebellions were brutally suppressed. The consequence of such stubbornness was long-lasting conflict between security forces and liberation movements. In Algeria and Kenya, the excesses of colonial rule came to the fore, with the use of counter-revolutionary strategies to quell unrest, such as mass internment, torture, resettling of communities in 'protected' villages, and disproportionate brutality (see Box 3.5). For example, during the Mau Mau rebellion (1952–1960), more than 1 million people were forcibly resettled (Anderson 2006, 294). The endemic violence by the British against the Mau Mau led to extensive official cover-ups; the sheer magnitude of this brutality was finally brought to light when former combatants took the British government to court, culminating in a compensation payout in 2013. The violence enacted by the colonial powers once again demonstrated the brutality of, and lack of legitimacy for, minority rule.

Box 3.5 The Algerian Revolution, 1954–1962

Before the onset of the Algerian Revolution, there had been several instances of unrest and resistance against French rule, exemplified by the Setif Uprising in 1945. Frustrated by the lack of reforms, the National Liberation Front (FLN) emerged in 1954 under the leadership of Ahmed Ben Bella, a movement that embarked on a revolutionary guerrilla strategy designed to make the colony ungovernable. In November 1954, a series of attacks against symbols of colonial power marked the beginning of the conflict. The French response was swift and brutal, characterised by repression, indiscriminate violence, collective punishment, and mass arrests. A cycle of violence erupted as massacres of settlers were followed by reprisals against Algerians. France refused to accept any possibility of compromise or independence, motivated by the 1 million *pied noirs* (white settlers) living in Algeria, combined with the army's refusal to suffer another humiliating defeat, following the Suez Crisis and its withdrawal from Indo-China. By 1956, France had 500,000 soldiers permanently stationed in Algeria to quell the resistance, and both they and the FLN resorted to ever more violent tactics. In 1957, the city of Algiers was effectively handed over to military rule, where General Jacques Massu implemented a counter-revolutionary strategy across the city to defeat the FLN, which ultimately broke the liberation movement, forcing it in to exile. France may have won the war, but they did not win the hearts and minds of Algerians, who harboured a continuing resentment. However, the impetus for African decolonisation was accelerating, and Charles de Gaulle began negotiations with the FLN;

a ceasefire was agreed in 1959, which was followed up by a promise of independence. The *pied noirs* and the army, feeling betrayed by the rapprochement, set about their own campaign of violence, with several revolts, mutinies, and assassination attempts on de Gaulle's life. However, the revolt was crushed, and a referendum was held in July 1962, in which Algerians voted overwhelmingly for independence. The French granted independence on 3 July, with the FLN assuming power, prompting nearly all the *pied noirs* to flee Algeria en masse. The conflict was enormously costly, an estimated 1 million people died, and the legacy of violence cast a shadow over Algeria's post-colonial settlement, especially towards the Harkis who were regarded as colonial collaborators.

While efforts for decolonisation accelerated elsewhere across the continent, the 1960s did not bring independence to other white minority states, which continued to obstinately cling to power. The desperate attempts to maintain power was because settlers in those territories had the most to lose, and given their ideological and racist assumptions of superiority, were unwilling to broach the possibility of compromise. One of the consequence of long-lasting violent liberation struggles (particularly in Portuguese Africa) was the emergence of revolutionary movements coming to power. The Portuguese colonies of Angola, Mozambique, Cape Verde, Guinea-Bissau, and São Tomé and Príncipe remained under European domination despite the wider continental shift to independence, consequently triggering protracted wars of independence in these territories from 1961 to 1974. Independence was only granted after the cost of continuous warfare and growing unpopularity initiated the Lisbon Coup in 1974, which led to the swift retreat of Portugal from its colonial empire. Elsewhere, the apartheid regime in South Africa had entrenched legalised racial oppression, following the National Party's election victory in 1948. The white minority refused to cede their racial hierarchy, and despite significant pressures at home and abroad, the apartheid state resisted demands for genuine change until the 1990s. A final example was Rhodesia, which had its own 'independence' in 1965, but only for the white minority, which sought to cement their power through a Unilateral Declaration of Independence (UDI) from Britain; the consequence of which was a vicious war of liberation that only brought about true independence in 1980.

It is important not to underestimate the influential effects of wider continental and international events as a motivation for decolonisation.

The fiasco of the botched efforts by France and Britain to retake the Suez Canal in 1956 was an indication that neither power was able to operate as an effective imperial force, especially without the support of the USA. It was a clear indication that the international order had changed. Harold Macmillan's 'winds of change' speech in 1960 was a belated acknowledgement that the game was up. Furthermore, by the end of the 1950s, economic imperatives had changed; the colonial powers had a greater interest in American and inter-European trade networks. The colonies were no longer important to post-war recoveries, and instead were becoming increasingly costly due to the need for developmental reforms (Cooper, 1996a). Moreover, by the end of the 1950s, the futility of military action in Algeria and Kenya, and the dramatic failure of Belgian decolonisation in the Congo in 1960, was a stark warning of how not to proceed; it was hard to legitimise the cost in lives and resources. Peaceful, organised, and 'planned' retreats were preferable outcomes. Ghana's long transition to independence, achieved in 1957, meant it was increasingly difficult to justify continued colonial rule elsewhere, particularly in West Africa. The main colonial powers watched each other's progress, and prescient of wider developments did not want to be outdone. Indeed, the contagion effect encouraged different nationalist leaders to point to precedents and question why they had not been granted their demands. The outcome was that an array of factors paved the way for independence.

An interesting debate concerns whether decolonisation was a planned process or whether it was a haphazard retreat lacking coherence. There is a line of argument that asserts that British decolonisation was a dignified and planned process, which successfully wrapped up the imperial project (Flint, 1983; Pearce, 1984). This triumphant, self-aggrandising perspective can be summarised as such: '[Britain] fulfilled their duties as trustees … The British Empire thus realised its long-cherished ideal of becoming … "a self-liquidating concern"' (Brendon, 2008, xix). However, such a perspective is nonsense. There was certainly no official plan and the rewriting of the historical record to cast colonial retreat in the best possible light is simply misleading (Shepard, 2006). France, Britain, and Belgium had all strenuously tried to maintain power as best they could, and only when it became apparent that their empires were no longer viable, due to the pressures from the colonies, the metropoles, and the international community, did they seek ways to extricate themselves. It was only when the writing was on the wall was there a move to implement an 'orderly' retreat. As late as 1958, France held a Yes/No referendum in West Africa, in a bid to bind its territories closer to the mainland, with the promise of limited autonomy for each; only Guinea, led by Sékou Touré, voted no in the referendum, suffering severe reprisals as a vindictive French government withdrew, taking everything with them. As a consequence, Guinea also refused to join the newly established French Community in 1958, which was designed to maintain French influence over its colonies.

The example of Congo's independence from Belgium in 1960 only served to underline the consequences of a hasty, unprepared withdrawal; Belgian Congo became the byword for how not to decolonise. One of the most significant legacies of this process is that the European powers hastily left the trappings of parliamentary democracy, without the necessary tools or mechanisms for it to be maintained. Colonial states had limited administrative structures or reach; were non-hegemonic; had prevented legitimate political opposition; dominated the distribution of economic resources; and ruled through violence and intimidation. These were characteristics of authoritarian states, not democratic governments. Yet it is of no surprise that many of these aspects featured prominently in post-colonial Africa. The enduring legacies of pre-colonial governance and societal formation, overlaid by the structures imposed by colonialism, soon became apparent in post-colonial states.

After power was transferred to African leaders and political parties, they inherited some major challenges that had a profound effect on the political and economic development of the continent. A whole host of issues left by European colonialism meant that a remarkably similar set of challenges confronted every independent leader. A quick overview of the key problems include a lack of economic development, combined with a dependency on one resource or cash crop, geared entirely towards the demands of the former colonial power (see Chapter 5); an insufficient infrastructure network, designed either to extract resources as quickly as possible or to simply support the needs of a white minority, thus not serving the majority; poor levels of education (estimates are that only 20% of Africans were literate in 1960), which had an impact on the management and function of newly inherited state institutions and economies; a 'democratic deficit' which meant that the ideals of liberal democracy hastily left by the former colonisers (which had been consistently withheld from all Africans) consequently had weak foundations (see Chapter 4), which were exacerbated by the experiences of strong centralised bureaucracies but weak state institutions that had little popular legitimacy; and finally, the imposition of arbitrary borders, which created divisions and disunity, dividing cultural and linguistic groups within and across territories, creating tensions, suspicions, and conflict (see Chapter 6). The consequence was that independent Africa was hamstrung by a series of deep-rooted historic legacies that were difficult to revoke. Therefore across the continent there was a pressing need to establish unified 'nations' where one might not have previously existed, and to seek ways of generating swift economic development in order to match the expectations of newly liberated peoples.

It must not be forgotten that the era of independence was a period of genuine hope, excitement, and optimism for the future of Africa. Many of the new leaders came to power on the back of popular goodwill, armed with bold and ambitious visions for the futures of their nations. There was a sense that Africa could move into a new age and confidently assert itself on the world stage. It was only after the dust of independence had settled that the legacies and inheritance outlined in this chapter became more noticeable. It is this complex history of the continent that provides the necessary context for an analysis of contemporary Africa.

 ## Further reading

In a chapter that addresses such an extensive time period, there is an array of literature that can be consulted on each and every aspect of the continent's historical trajectory. The following suggestions are just a snapshot of what is available on a continental level, but for further in-depth enquiry, individual nations should be consulted. Useful starting points for an overview of pre-colonial African history would be Molefi Kete Asante's (2015) *The History of Africa*; Roland Oliver's (2001) *Medieval Africa, 1250–1800*; Toyin Falola's (2008) *Key Events in African History*; Christopher Ehret's (2016) *The Civilizations of Africa: A History to 1800*; and the relevant volumes of the *Cambridge History of Africa*. For more on the implementation, extension, and impact of colonial rule see Crawford Young's (1994) *The African Colonial State in Comparative Perspective*; Walter Rodney's (1972) *How Europe Underdeveloped Africa*; and Frederick Cooper's (2005) *Colonialism in Question*. For the different dimensions of decolonisation, consult Martin Shipway's (2007) *Decolonization and Its Impact*; Ali Mazrui and Michael Tidy's (1984) *Nationalism and New States in Africa*; Todd Shepard's (2006) *The Invention of Decolonization*; and John Hargreaves's (1988) *Decolonization in Africa*.

4 POLITICAL SYSTEMS

At face value democracy is establishing a footing across Africa at a pace unlike any other period since independence. Since the early 1990s, following the end of the Cold War, the continent has increasingly abandoned poor governance practices and moved towards greater political plurality and freedom in what Samuel Huntington (1991) termed as the 'third-wave of democratisation'. However, this transition from authoritarianism towards democracy remains far from complete. While African nations continue to make significant progress towards achieving greater democratisation, it is highly uneven. Elections are regularly held across the continent, albeit with varying outcomes. Crucially, in several notable cases incumbent presidents defeated at the polls chose to step aside rather than cling to power. The example of Nigeria is a case in point, where in a moment of genuine optimism following decades of military rule, and civilian maladministration, President Goodluck Jonathan handed power to Muhammadu Buhari after electoral defeat in 2015, prompting an unprecedented peaceful transfer of power. Electoral politics is now firmly entrenched across much of the continent.

Yet, for all the prevailing positivity, many nations remain stubbornly immune from democratic trends, with over half of the continent still considered authoritarian, while even the perceived better performers, such as Botswana, are regressing in their levels of freedom (Economic Intelligence Unit, 2016; Freedom House, 2017). Africa's political trajectory is now split, divided between a small band of democratic states such as Mauritius and Ghana, a larger cluster of flawed or hybrid democracies which include Tanzania, and a wide tranche of states that are authoritarian, encompassing regimes in the CAR, Chad, and Angola. In reality, parliamentary democracies, one-party states, presidents-for-life, and military governments all currently coexist simultaneously in Africa. Your perspective on the state of African politics will largely depend on which case studies are utilised, and whether elections alone should be viewed as a barometer of success; bear in mind that for every choice there will be always be a counter-point, providing a totally different point of view. The notion of multiple realities is never more important when considering modern African politics. What is apparent is that African political development since independence has undergone several major evolutions that have had a marked effect on the different forms of governance and control found across the continent today.

When considering African politics, the governance indices mentioned above will be utilised to help frame the different styles of government. They are a useful way to examine the topic, yet it must be recognised that terms such as 'democracy' or 'authoritarianism' hide a multitude of different forms of governance. For instance, a country such as Zimbabwe might hold elections, a hallmark of democracy, yet until 2017 was ruled by a dictator through the power of a domineering one-party state. Therefore, it is worth looking closely at individual African nations to understand their various political characteristics, which may not fit neatly into a single overarching label. Although democracy will be used as a benchmark for Africa's political development and is regarded as a good thing for the continent (despite its many flaws), this is only one perspective. Many people do not believe democracy is an ideal form of governance; for example, an Afrobarometer (2016) survey found that 32.4% of Africans *did not* believe 'democracy is preferable to any other kind of government'.

This chapter will be split into two broad parts in order to best assess Africa's trajectory: the post-colonial era (1952–1990) and democratisation (1990–present). It will sketch out the evolution in political developments and highlight the main forms of governance, while illustrating how the broader changes have created the divergence in approaches currently practised across Africa.

Politics in the post-colonial era (1952–1990)

The rise of the one-party state

The first point to make is that in the immediate post-colonial era (1950s–1990), African states followed a remarkably similar trajectory to one another, in that they jettisoned fragile democratic structures left by the former colonial powers in favour of establishing one-party states. The one-party state soon became the de facto form of African politics, albeit with several variants (such as military rule or dictatorships) and different contextual motivations for pursuing this form of governance. In short, this style of government is characterised by a single ruling party, often authoritarian in nature, with all opposition in the form of political parties, trade unions, civil society, and student activism either co-opted or banned. Only a handful of multiparty states such as Botswana, the Gambia, and

Senegal survived, although they could hardly be described as full democracies given that the incumbent always won. As a consequence, not one African state changed government or president via the ballot box until 1990. Demands for reform and democratisation were only taken seriously following a combination of mounting domestic pressures; growing protest from dissatisfied populations; widespread economic collapse; and an altered international climate following the end of the Cold War. This long stretch of continental-wide undemocratic practices, combined with some heinous examples of misgovernance characterised by the idiosyncrasies of personal rule by presidents such as Jean-Bédel Bokassa (CAR), Mobutu Sese Seko (Zaire, now the DRC), and Teodoro Obiang Nguema Mbasogo (Equatorial Guinea), tarnished the reputation of African politics. Importantly, the one-party state system was not monolithic with a wide variety of approaches, forms, and popularity.

It is crucial at this point to re-acknowledge some of the colonial legacies outlined at the end of Chapter 3, which had a pronounced effect on the shift towards autocratic governance across the continent. It must be remembered that democratic institutions were established only as colonialism crumbled. These governance structures were weak as they were externally imposed, and accentuated by the profound lack of democratic traditions under colonial rule. Moreover, the new constitutions often lacked wider legitimacy, nor did they have the full backing of nationalist politicians. Furthermore, at independence the former colonial state structures were largely appropriated wholesale by new political elites; indeed, with so many challenges facing independent nations, why alter the structures of power? However, these colonial institutions and structures had many intrinsic problems that prevented democracy from taking root. Importantly, they were never devised for democratic purposes, but rather to serve the needs of a minority; were built on a strong centralised bureaucracy; provided limited wider access to the levers of power and economic wealth; while autarchy, backed by violence, was deeply embedded within the system of rule. The outcome was a small elite that held centralised control over all levers of the state, who monopolised the political and economic spheres, and held the power to neutralise any opposition through co-option or coercion. Therefore, from the very start of the independence era, elites had the mechanisms to impose one-party states, often centred on a powerful leader, characterised by overtones of authoritarianism, and modelled precisely on what they had inherited (Zolberg, 1966). This widespread centralisation and monopolisation of power is crucial to understanding the political trajectory of the continent.

In the 1960s, the one-party state was in vogue, and contemporary observers and nationalist leaders such as Kwame Nkrumah (Ghana), Julius Nyerere (Tanzania), and Jomo Kenyatta (Kenya) offered several justifications for their creation (see Box 4.1). The first overriding argument was that of national unity. The premise of African unity was a helpful myth in the anti-colonial struggle, yet given the diverse nature of the ethnic groups ensconced within the newly created nations, it had never been a reality; elites were fully aware that their citizens were divided by ethnicity, region, religion, and wealth. These divisions were a major cause for concern. There was a widely held belief that competing political parties representing these divergent constituents would cause internal ruptures, sow the seeds of state weaknesses, and provide opportunities for nefarious international interests to take advantage of independent states. The rapid collapse of the Belgian Congo into chaos in 1960, spurred on by political and ethnic rivalries, and exacerbated by self-interested western powers, was a prime example used by many new leaders of what would happen if such divisions were left unchecked. Therefore, what better way to overcome ethnic or regional factions than a disciplined party, exerting centralised control. A further challenge facing African leaders was that of creating 'new' nations that would supersede any of the aforementioned internal divisions. The departing colonialists had never instilled a sense of nationhood among colonised peoples, actively fostering ethnic or religious competition rather than unity. In order to create a sense of nationhood and purpose, the argument was that only through an undivided and strong central party could a sense of national unity and belonging be forged.

Box 4.1 Nkrumah's one-party state in Ghana

While the one-party state in Africa is often viewed through the lens of military rule and dictatorships, which admittedly many clearly were, several had some de facto legitimacy given that they were backed by huge majorities in elections. Perhaps the most instructive example is the trajectory of Ghana under Kwame Nkrumah's leadership, whose Convention People's Party (CPP) won a landslide victory in 1956. However, facing political opposition, Nkrumah began to dismantle the multiparty system. He immediately banned regional and ethnic organisations, followed by legislation that manipulated the constitution, allowing for political critics to be arrested, who could be tried in special courts which circumnavigated the official judiciary. As a result, opposition in Ghana was effectively nullified. In 1964, Nkrumah held a referendum on whether a one-party state should be established in Ghana, although there was in fact no formal opposition to speak of. As a consequence the referendum won easily and Ghana became a formally constituted one-party state.

Another major draw towards the one-party state lay in the need for economic and social development. Africa's newly independent nations all required serious work to kick-start their economies, develop national infrastructure, and to fulfil the promises made during elections. Time was of the essence, yet parliamentary democracy by its very nature creates opposition and can slow progress through debates and constitutional wrangling; Félix Houphouët-Boigny, the former president of Côte d'Ivoire, described opposition parties as an 'unnecessary luxury' (Thompson, 1964, 275). Multiparty democracy was regarded as inhibiting the path to rapid development, which could simply be avoided by the implementation of a one-party state, where decisions could be made and implemented quickly without dissent or obstruction. It must also be remembered that the 1960s were the zenith of state socialism and planned economies, with the one-party state offering a modern and appealing alternative to western democracy. The speed at which the Soviet Union and later China modernised offered clear examples that nations could achieve their own 'leap forward' through the one-party. Given the choice of either jobs and material uplift or the chance to cast a democratic vote, it was argued that there was only one winner. Who cares about democracy when you have little money or food? In the quest to achieve their ambitions development goals many African leaders regarded democracy as a needless distraction. Similar arguments concerning democracy verses development are still being made today in Ethiopia by the ruling government, the Ethiopian People's Revolutionary Democratic Front (EPRDF). Since the mid-2000s, ambitious modernisation plans and strident efforts to alleviate poverty, aided by staggeringly high GDP growth rates of around 10% for more than a decade, have been at the expense of democracy, free speech, and human rights.

In the various guises of the one-party state in Africa there were some leaders who genuinely believed that true democracy and mass participatory politics could only be achieved through this governance style. Influential leaders such as the Zambian President Kenneth Kaunda (1974) and Tanzanian President Julius Nyerere (1968) argued that, based on the communal nature of African society, all citizens would be engaged through 'One Party Participatory Democracy' enabling free and open debates, which would provide the opportunity for everyone to be involved in shaping the direction of the party, and therefore the national direction of the state. For example, in Tanzania, Nyerere (1968) called for the implementation of Ujamaa, a form of African socialism, in which consensual politics, under the remit of village democracy, would provide the mechanism for popular participation and debate within the national framework of the Tanzanian African National Union (TANU). Nyerere's vision of African socialism was replicated elsewhere, particularly in

Senegal, where President Senghor believed that the organisational principles of African societies meant the needs of the individual must be sacrificed for the greater good; under the direction of the state, embracing both traditional and modern outlooks, a new 'African' route to socialism could be achieved.

In Kenya, the approach to popular participation was slightly different. The country had been a de facto one-party state since independence, but it was formally mandated in 1982 after the Kenyan African National Union (KANU) banned opposition parties. However, President Kenyatta allowed for competition and debate within the confines of KANU, and through a process of national elections all MPs required the support of local associations to stand for appointment. The result was a semblance of democracy, which ensured that MPs had to work hard locally for their ticket (although this led to corruption and patronage), while providing the space for discontent to be expressed in a way that did not damage the leadership of KANU (Widner, 1993, 60).

However, many of these civilian one-party states encountered problems of lengthy incumbency, the rise of factionalism and rivalries, and a glaring inability to meet the needs and expectations of the populace, despite the promises of mass participation. For almost every one-party state, maintaining political control proved problematic. With so many nations experiencing societal divisions, and in many cases an absence of legitimacy, power and influence had to be secured through neo-patrimonialism (see Box 4.2). While neo-patrimonialism ensured some semblance of stability (hence the initial justifications), it was highly flawed, establishing intrinsic structural weaknesses. Across Africa, the one-party state in its various guises has generally performed badly.

Box 4.2 Neo-patrimonialism

The main form of exerting political control in contemporary Africa is through what is termed neo-patrimonialism. This form of governance sees the fusion of the modern state with traditional forms of patrimonial or traditional authority (Hyden, 2000, 19), in which elites utilise resources for their own purposes to secure the loyalty of clients, often characterised by nepotism, patronage, rent-seeking (i.e. siphoning off money or resources without reinvestment or development; often labelled as the predatory state), and corruption. Elites in charge of centralised states used their personal, ethnic, religious, or regional networks to dispense opportunities for power and economic gain, in return for authority and control. With little or no opposition, elites were able to abuse their position of power. However, this shaky form of control is centred on access and control of state resources; once this diminishes (see the discussion on economics in Chapter 5) the loyalty towards elites rapidly dissipated. A key characteristic in post-colonial Africa was the party's dominance over the civil service and parastatal organisations, which acted as a quick way of providing opportunities and resources for supporters. Civil services swelled across the continent swallowing large chunks of national budgets, and as a consequence putting government finances under enormous strain. However, retaining power became a paramount concern. Indeed, it became the be-all and end-all because once power was lost it was highly unlikely it would ever be regained; therefore leaders accumulated as much wealth and power as possible, and guarded this jealously. Further issues with neopatrimonialism are that it is fundamentally unstable, leading to corruption; undermines political authority and official state structures, leading to the decay of those institutions; is inefficient in that the focus is on elite enrichment and not national development; and creates disillusionment, factions, and rivalries as the system excludes more people than it includes. With opposition parties banned, the only form of recourse to enact political change was through either internal party purges and rebellions or more commonly the military coup.

Personal rule

In many cases, the system of neo-patrimonial rule provided the conditions for leaders to take leave of the one-party and enact individual control of the state. In what was referred to by Jackson and Rosberg (1982a) as personal rule, they identified how powerful leaders such as Mobutu, Houphouët-Boigny, and Idi Amin seized power. These leaders subsequently established a form of governance 'shaped less by institutions or impersonal social forces than by personal authorities and power' (Jackson & Rosberg, 1984, 438). The result was that a single leader could dominate and influence the proceedings of the state, bypassing any notional laws, while ruling by decree. Personal rule is the epitome of authoritarianism, delusion, egotism, and state inefficiency, with little interest in the nation or people beyond the leader's own immediate interests. Many such leaders, of which there is a startling number, rose to power through the initial anti-colonial struggles ('fathers'/'guardians' of the nation) or through military coups. Given that many leaders lacked legitimacy or popular support, their power was maintained by coercion and violence, a network of patronage, and the Machiavellian manipulation of followers through arbitrary decision making, and the regular shuffling of ministers. Mobutu enlisted all of these tactics in maintaining his power in Zaire, but he was an especially keen advocate of manipulating his cabinet ministers by stoking factionalism and rivalry, aided by indiscriminately elevating or redeploying people to contain potential opposition and challenges to his presidency (see Box 4.3).

The outcome of personal rule in Africa has been a form of oligarchy, in which leaders maintain political power for as long as possible. As a consequence, personal rule has dominated the continent's political system with a host of presidents remaining in power for more than 30 years (see Table 4.1). Notwithstanding the list in Table 4.1, there is another tranche of current leaders who have held power for well over 20 years, including presidents such as Omar al-Bashir (Sudan), Idriss Déby (Chad), Isaias Afewerki (Eritrea), and Denis Sassou Nguesso (Republic of Congo).

Table 4.1 List of the longest serving presidents in Africa (as of 2018)

Name	Country	Number of consecutive years in power (* indicates still in office at time of writing)
Muammar Gaddafi	Libya	41
Omar Bongo	Gabon	41
Gnassingbé Eyadéma	Togo	39
Teodoro Obiang Nguema	Equatorial Guinea	39*
José Eduardo dos Santos	Angola	38
Robert Mugabe	Zimbabwe	37
Paul Biya	Cameroon	35*
Félix Houphouët-Boigny	Côte d'Ivoire	33
Dawda Jawara	The Gambia	32
Mobutu Sese Seko	Zaire (now DRC)	32
Yoweri Museveni	Uganda	32*
Habib Bourguiba	Tunisia	31

Box 4.3 Mobutu's kleptocracy in Zaire

One extreme example of personal rule was Mobutu Sese Seko (1965–1997) who took power through a military coup in the Congo, which he later renamed Zaire in 1971. A centralised form of power in Zaire became all-encompassing as Mobutu circumvented parliamentary control, surrounded himself with a cortege of sycophants via an extensive network of patronage, and later established the personality cult of 'Mobutuism'. Any opposition to his rule was removed through regular purges of the political elite, military, and civil service to ensure that no challengers could emerge. Mobutu was able to amass a vast fortune, much of which was gained through the exploitation of state resources, corrupt activities, and control over Zaire's enormous natural resource deposits. Mobutu's kleptocratic behaviour meant that state resources were utilised entirely for the Zairian elites' own enrichment, with little regard for the well-being of the country. The mass nationalisation of key businesses ensured patronage opportunities for his family, ethnic group, and supporters, who looted assets and siphoned off profits; however, the outcome was inflation and economic decline, plunging the vast majority of Zairians into poverty. Two instances highlight the scale of Mobutu's looting: during his reign an estimated $5 billion was deposited outside the country in his personal bank accounts in Switzerland, while he also had built his own version of Versailles in the remote location of Gbadolite, which included among other things an international airport so he could charter Concorde flights for shopping trips to Paris. As part of the Cold War, Mobutu's excesses and human rights abuses were tolerated by the USA and western organisations in return for his anti-communist stance (Image 4.1).

Image 4.1 Zairean president, Mobutu Sese Seko and Queen Elizabeth II en route to Buckingham Palace

Source: Keystone/Getty Images.

Personal rule is often associated with the worst excesses of African leadership, and as such there have been several grandiose examples of personal enrichment, combined with the violent retention of power; the following three presidents discussed below all came to power via the military. One extreme example of the rapacious looting of the state is that of Jean-Bédel Bokassa (1966–1979). In the CAR, Bokassa set about establishing a state that revolved around him, with 'the distinction between Bokassa's personal accounts and those of the state ceas[ing] to exist' (O'Toole, 1986, 52). On top of looting state coffers, he maintained power through a cult of personality, extreme violence and terror, the elimination of any challengers to his rule, and by maintaining a close relationship with the French government, which tacitly tolerated his behaviour for 14 years. The moment that highlighted the sheer scale of his self-aggrandisement was when he declared himself emperor in 1977, in a ceremony that cost more than £20 million (Image 4.2).

In Uganda, Idi Amin seized power from Milton Obote through a military coup in 1971, to preserve his own privileged position that was under threat. Amin's rule (1971–1979) quickly spiralled into chaos and violence as he suspended Uganda's constitution to govern by decree; enacted brutal repression against his opponents, real or imagined; while overseeing the collapse of the economy through corruption, self-enrichment, and a disastrous nationalisation policy in which the Asian population was expelled. Despite Amin's relatively short presidency, it was characterised by violence

Image 4.2 Jean-Bédel Bokassa coronation

Source: Photo 12/UIG via Getty Images.

and delusion, in which his highly personalised style of decision making had disastrous consequences for Uganda (Decalo, 1990, 177).

Enter the military

Since independence, the military has played a prominent and influential role in African politics. In the immediate post-colonial era military personnel began to utilise their position of power and monopoly over violence by leading coup d'états against civilian politicians. North Africa experienced its first coup in 1952, when General Nasser led the overthrow of the Egyptian monarchy, while sub-Saharan Africa soon witnessed a rapid spate of military takeovers starting in the Congo (1960), and then encompassing nations including Benin (1963), Congo-Brazzaville (1963), Togo (1963), Burkina Faso (1966), CAR (1966), and Ghana (1966). By the mid-1990s, and the onset of democratisation, over two-thirds of the continent had experienced some form of military rule; 41 sub-Saharan African states (85.4%) had either had a successful or attempted coup, while every North African country, with the exception of Morocco, had witnessed the military seize power. Of the nations that gained their independence before 1990, only Botswana, Cape Verde, and Mauritius had survived without any form of military intervention (McGowan, 2003, 345). The result has been the military becoming a permanent fixture in African political life.

Why has military rule been so prevalent across Africa? With over 60 years of coups, there are clearly different contextual reasons as to why the military has felt emboldened to seize power, but there are several common themes. First of all, given the preponderance of one-party states and neo-patrimonial leaders, most African nations lacked the mechanisms for political change. Without formal opposition parties the most common solution was through military intervention. Most coup leaders were equipped with a standardised list of grievances to legitimise their actions, including the unpopularity of the incumbent government; the incompetence and failings of civilian politicians; widespread corrupt behaviour; economic stagnation or decline; and societal discontent. Utilising these concerns, military leaders often claimed they would instil organisation, efficiency, and discipline to governance structures, and establish an effective 'new' direction for the nation. Only after 'order' had been imposed or the necessary changes implemented would political power be returned to civilian politicians.

In the early 1960s, when coups were less prevalent, a series of military interventions did result in power returning to civilian leadership. For example, in Togo, the president Sylvanus Olympio was assassinated in 1963 by resentful members of the armed forces who used his unpopular establishment of a one-party state to justify their actions. After overthrowing Olympio, the coup leaders returned power to new civilian politicians under the remit of a national coalition. However, in this instance, the military's attitude soon changed as they chose to overthrow the new political elite in 1967 after declaring that civilians had once again demonstrated their inability to govern Togo effectively. Other examples of the military returning power after coups include the Congo (1960), Benin (1963), and Ghana (1979), yet much like in Togo, each of these nations saw permanent military rule reintroduced after brief periods of 'failed' civilian rule.

Military leaders had appreciated that with its monopoly over violence, and with very few people willing to support or die for unpopular regimes, the successful seizure of power was not that difficult. All would-be coup leaders needed was to capture key state infrastructure (usually the presidency, airport, and radio station), imprison the president, and utilise the threat of violence to quell potential opposition. As public dissatisfaction grew throughout the 1960s, there was very little domestic opposition to the first wave of military takeovers; for example, Amin's coup in 1971 was greeted by public celebrations across Uganda. Furthermore, there was rarely any international consequences for coup leaders. The geopolitical nature of the Cold War ensured that the superpowers were often willing to tolerate the seizure of power by the military as long as there was no radical ideological reorientation. Only France acted decisively when its interests were threatened, especially as it retained military bases across West Africa. Examples of French interventionism occurred in Gabon in 1964, when they prevented a military coup from toppling Léon M'ba, while in 1979 the CAR was invaded to overthrow Bokassa's regime. However, Table 4.2 clearly shows that once one coup had occurred a precedent was set, with the likelihood that it would trigger a series of further coup attempts.

Although public dissatisfaction and poor governance were clearly valid reasons for some military interventions, this does not tell the whole story. In reality, many coups were prompted by self-interest or 'corporate' grievances (Decalo, 1990). The reasons for military takeovers are multifaceted encompassing financial, political, ethnic, and personal concerns. One motivation for military intervention was army elites essentially seeking to gain access to resources and patronage opportunities. In other cases, such as Ghana (1966), attempts by civilian institutions to limit the power and influence of the army, including the formation of alternative security structures such as 'elite' presidential guards, were viewed as a threat to entrenched military interests. Moreover, when political and military leaders' interests clashed, usually concerning budgets, the army intervened to protect their own privileged status. Alternative factors centred on ethnic, regional, and religious concerns within either the army itself or society at large. For example, attempts to establish a more representative and ethnically balanced armed force in Nigeria was challenged by Yoruba and Igbo generals who seized power in 1966 (see Box 4.4).

Table 4.2 Successful coups in Africa, 1952–1990

Country	Year
Egypt	1952
Sudan	1958, 1969, 1985, 1989
Congo	1960, 1965
Togo	1963, 1967, 1967
Congo-Brazzaville	1963, 1968
Benin	1963, 1965, 1965, 1967, 1969, 1972
Central African Republic	1966, 1979, 1981
Burkina Faso	1966, 1974, 1980, 1982, 1983, 1987
Nigeria	1966, 1966, 1975, 1983, 1985
Uganda	1966, 1971, 1980, 1985
Ghana	1966, 1972, 1978, 1979, 1981
Burundi	1966, 1966, 1976, 1987
Sierra Leone	1967, 1968
Mali	1968
Libya	1969
Somalia	1969
Madagascar	1972
Swaziland	1973
Rwanda	1973
Niger	1974
Ethiopia	1974
Chad	1975
Seychelles	1977
Comoros	1978, 1989
Mauritania	1978, 1980, 1984
Equatorial Guinea	1979
Liberia	1980
Guinea-Bissau	1980
Guinea	1984
Lesotho	1986
Tunisia	1987

*Source: Created using data from P. McGowan (2003), 'African military coup d'état, 1956–2001',
363–364.*

Box 4.4 The military in Nigeria

Nigeria experienced almost permanent involvement of the military in post-colonial politics. The first of two military coups in 1966 was prompted by civilian politicians' maladministration, who had presided over an economic decline and the exacerbation of ethnic tensions. Yet these coups occurred largely due to ethnic splits within the military, with Igbos resenting the dominance of Hausa/Fulani officers from the north; the divisions within the army thus contributed to a broader struggle for power in Nigeria, which allowed General Yakubu Gowon to gain power in the second coup of 1966. A consequence of this second coup was the Igbo-dominated region of Biafra declaring independence from Nigeria in 1967, sparking a vicious civil war. After the civil war ended in 1970, Gowan maintained military rule by overseeing post-war reconstruction efforts (aided by huge oil receipts) and emphasising the need to unify Nigeria's ethnic divides behind an all-encompassing national identity. Gowan had promised a return to civilian rule by 1976, but he recanted on this decision in 1974, declaring an indefinite delay. Gowan was subsequently deposed by Murtala Mohammed in July 1975, although his rule was short-lived, assassinated less than a year afterwards in a failed coup in 1976. These incidents clearly demonstrated that once one coup had been successful, the chances of further attempts multiplied.

Olusegun Obasanjo succeeded Mohammed, who governed Nigeria until 1979 with the aid of the Supreme Military Council. Power was transferred back to civilians following a transition in which parties were unbanned and elections held, as well as an explicit effort to decouple the military from the political process: the constitution even stated that military coups were illegal. In the 1979 election, Shehu Shagari, backed largely by northern constituents, become president. However, Shagari's rule was characterised by extensive corruption, economic decline, and political squabbling, which prompted the military to end this brief interlude with democracy in 1983 through another coup led by Muhammadu Buhari (incidentally Nigeria's current civilian president). Yet, in a depressingly familiar pattern, Buhari was toppled in 1985 by Ibrahim Babangida. Previous military leaders had all, at least rhetorically, promised to re-implement democracy after their coups, yet Babangida and his successor Sani Abacha (who seized power in 1993) governed Nigeria in a far more personalised and autocratic manner, overseeing corruption, nepotism, and human rights abuses. It was only in 1999, when

Obasanjo became president once more, that Nigeria became a multiparty democracy. However, former military generals Obasanjo and Buhari have both been president in the democratic era, highlighting the enduring influence of the army in Nigerian politics.

Finally, there were instances where military conquest was simply a cloak for personal advancement and power, including Moussa Traoré in Mali (1968), Teodoro Obiang Nguema of Equatorial Guinea (1979), and Samuel Doe in Liberia (1980).

During the Cold War, an interesting dimension was the emergence of Marxist-Leninist military states. Lacking some of the justifications for the seizure of power outlined previously, several militaries, including Congo-Brazzaville, Benin, Somalia, and Ethiopia, adopted Marxism as the official state ideology. Marxism proved a useful legitimising tool that established international links with the Soviet bloc, and ensured financial aid and ideological support while neutering potential political opposition from leftist groups. Furthermore, a key characteristic of Marxist-Leninist states is a sizeable security infrastructure, allowing for violence and coercion to be 'legitimately' incorporated into the governance structure. However, the adherence to Marxist ideology was often a pragmatic choice, and there is significant doubt as to the depth of the ideological purity of these military states. The only exception was the Derg in Ethiopia, which took power in 1974, formally adopted Marxism in 1975, and immediately began an extensive reorientation of the state, with its attempts at implementing collectivisation and nationalisation backed by the Soviet Union and Cuba.

The military became an important political actor throughout post-colonial Africa, and powerful nations such as Algeria, Zaire, and Nigeria all succumbed to the loss of civilian governance by the mid-1960s. However, African militaries were unable to resolve the challenges that had bedevilled their civilian counterparts, and many generals capitulated to the privileges and excesses of office. In fact, some of the worst examples of governance were under military rule. Military leaders proved just as unpopular, and many failed to unite divergent ethnic and religious tensions; presided over economic stagnation and decline; were no less corrupt or unprincipled; oversaw political decay; and, importantly, prevented opportunities for democracy to be implemented. The legacies for contemporary African political systems are still being felt today.

Fragile democracy

Democratic consolidation across the African continent was not particularly successful in the post-colonial era. As has already been discussed, multiparty parliamentary democracies were swept away in favour of more autocratic rule. The vast majority of African leaders had legislated against opposition parties, neutering potential avenues for dissent. However, several nations aptly demonstrated that the overall lack of democracy in Africa was by no means inevitable. During the post-colonial era, Botswana, Mauritius, the Gambia, and Senegal all retained a form of multi-party democracy.

The most commonly referred to case study of entrenched multiparty politics in Africa is Botswana. Since the first election in 1965, Botswana has held regular elections, with active opposition parties contesting each ballot. It must be noted that the Botswana Democratic Party (BDP) has won every election so far, and the power of its incumbency must not be underestimated in overwhelming any opposition at the polls. Unlike many of its neighbours, a crucial component of maintaining Botswanan democracy is that the BDP has continued to oversee impressive economic growth rates, and under the first president Seretse Khama successfully decoupled the civil service from party politics, providing it with a degree of autonomy. Another example of a state entrenching democratic norms was Senegal. Although initially a one-party state under the leadership of Léopold Senghor, opposition parties were first legalised in 1974, and the constitution then rewritten to allow for a limited number of political movements to stand in elections. While this liberalisation of Senegalese politics was a stage-managed process, it did provide a greater degree of freedom than most African nations. Only after Senghor willingly ceded his presidency in 1980 did his successor Abdou Diouf legalise all political opposition in Senegal and begin the process of greater democratic participation and freedom.

Although democracy was never fully entrenched across Africa, except in only a handful of cases, it did not totally disappear as a popular ideal. It must be noted that democracy was frequently demanded by populations, in spite of the actions taken by political leaders to the contrary. For example, despite the permanence of military rule in Nigeria, democracy remained an overarching ambition; indeed, as Diamond (1997) highlighted, successive military juntas in Nigeria were only able to claim some semblance of legitimacy based on the claim that they were overseeing the transition (albeit a prolonged one over 30 years) to democracy.

Democratisation?

The second 'wind of change' in the 1990s

The shift towards a greater degree of political freedom and democracy that emerged across the African continent in the 1990s was a momentous process after decades of authoritarianism and one-party rule. The continental change began in Algeria in 1988, when rioting broke out over declining living standards. The riots prompted a loss of political legitimacy for the incumbent National Liberation Front (FLN) government, whose declining power resulted in democratic reforms and the adoption of a new constitution. The next key transition towards democracy was in the island nation of São Tomé and Príncipe in 1989; the abandonment of socialism led to economic and political reforms, which culminated in a national constitutional conference, whose delegates agreed to implement a multiparty electoral system and hold elections. The precedent for democratic reforms was set, and within a few years much of the continent had experienced some form of political change, albeit highly uneven in depth and commitment. The ideals of liberal democracy (at least rhetorically) became increasingly normalised as life presidents, military rulers, and one-party states were forced into conceding demands for popular change as a series of interlinked domestic and international factors coalesced to make political reform possible across Africa.

What prompted the start of democratisation that swept Africa in the 1990s? Internationally, the world had changed dramatically in a short space of time, with the collapse of the Cold War altering mentalities and undermining previous political certainties. The Cold War had created a framework in which repressive leaders were effectively given unwavering support to act how they pleased from their superpower allies, with almost no repercussions for poor governance or autocratic rule. Moreover, the superpowers had provided crucial material and military aid, which ensured that ailing leaders could continue to maintain power. However, the demise of the Soviet Union meant that socialist nations such as Ethiopia, Benin, and Congo-Brazzaville suddenly lost their external patrons, while those affiliated to the USA were expected to adhere to the tenets of liberal democracy which included free opposition parties, parliamentary elections, and basic human rights. It was increasingly difficult to justify or maintain unpopular regimes based on Cold War logic or external backing. For example, the 1989 peace agreement in the Angolan Civil War, a striking example of Cold War interventionism in Africa (see Chapter 6), was premised on Cuban and South African soldiers withdrawing from the conflict, as well as the end of Pretoria's ongoing occupation of Namibia; as a consequence, Namibia was granted independence in 1990.

These wider political changes were explicitly linked with economics and, importantly, aid budgets. Perhaps the most telling sign of this altered international mindset was through the actions of the World Bank (1989), which in a comprehensive report unambiguously tied aid with political conditionalities (see Chapter 5); in particular, the report emphasised the need for good governance and democratic reform. Furthermore, this was followed by a range of measures taken by Britain and France from 1990 onwards, and then the European Union (EU) in 1991, which link economic aid with good governance. In the 1990s, the EU aid budget to Africa amounted to more than half the continental total (Olsen, 1998), prompting the realisation that domestic political changes would have to be enacted or external funds would cease. Against a backdrop of widespread economic decline and the altered international context, many African governments simply had no choice but to concede to multiparty elections.

On the domestic front, seemingly well-entrenched elites were under increased pressure to reform (see Box 4.5). By the 1980s, many leaders' political legitimacy was under scrutiny, with trust in government at a low point. The aforementioned economic crisis meant that previous neo-patrimonial networks were crumbling, with supporters' loyalty no longer guaranteed to prop up ailing leaders. With increasing unpopularity, declining living standards, and a broader economic malaise, numerous governments found their authority undermined, leaving very few positives to 'sell' to their nations amid a maelstrom of issues. With the inability to dispense patronage, the previous utilisation of violence and coercion to maintain authority had also lost its potency; fear can only work for so long as a tool for survival. Increasingly dissatisfied populations turned to sustained popular protest across Africa. The rejuvenation of civil society (Chapter 7), particularly in the form of religious groups, trade unions, and student activism, led the way in coalescing opposition to incumbent governments, with the final demand often being democratic elections. For example, churches began to make public their vocal opposition to Hasting Banda in Malawi, while in Zambia Frederick Chiluba's trade union movement morphed into the Movement for Multi-Party Democracy (MMD) which challenged, and later defeated, incumbent Kenneth Kaunda in 1991. These demands for democratic reforms were often backed by the emergence of an increasingly critical independent press, who were able to support opposition groups through their journalism; Benin's president Mathieu Kerekou argued it was through the power and influence of the press that he lost the 1991 elections, claiming 'it was because of journalists that everything has turned out so badly' (The Sowetan, 1992). It is of little surprise that in the 1990s African leaders in countries such as Cameroon, Ethiopia, Swaziland, and Zambia all sought to harass and restrict the freedom of the press.

The move towards democratisation was not always welcomed, and several incumbent leaders sought to utilise their position to manipulate nascent reformist processes in order to retain power. In several cases the continental shift towards democratisation proved unsuccessful as successive leaders managed to weather the wind of change. Examples include Togo's president Eyadema and Zaire's Mobutu, both of whom conceded to demands for national conferences to negotiate an alternative dispensation,

Box 4.5 The francophone model of reform

Across francophone West Africa the model for change was based on the constitutional conference in which incumbent leaders met with opposition groups to discuss future options; in almost every case the final demand was for political reform and elections. The template was set in 1990 when the embattled Benin president Mathieu Kerekou, appreciating his loss of authority through mounting domestic protest and a lack of international finance, arranged a national conference with civil society groups in a bid to stave off his demise. However, the delegates seized this opportunity by declaring sovereignty over the conference, stripping the governing party of power, and implementing a transitional government; soon after, a new constitution was adopted and elections held in 1991, in which Kerekou was defeated. A subsequent election in 1996 saw the transition to democracy take root in Benin as power was peacefully transferred between presidents, starting the cycle of electoral competition in the country. Benin provided a solution to democratisation, and national conferences were later called in nations such as Chad, Gabon, and Niger.

and even permitted opposition parties to form and elections to be held; however, they still managed to subvert the process to such an extent that they consolidated their power. In other cases, the national conference formula was rejected by sitting presidents because it was 'uncontrollable', choosing instead to seize the initiative by rapidly unbanning opposition groups, providing the semblance of democratic reforms, and then calling snap elections, with the odds heavily stacked against any potential challengers; examples included Cameroon's Paul Biya, Guinea's Lansana Conte, Kenya's Daniel arap Moi, and Burkina Faso's Blaise Compaoré. In some extreme cases the political changes that occurred during this period led to internecine violence (see Chapter 6), most notably in the Rwandan genocide (1994) and the Sierra Leone civil war (1991–2002).

Even if presidents did maintain power, two important developments emerged from the wave of reform in the 1990s. The first was that for much of the continent multiparty elections were held for the first time (18 alone in 1996), which began the process of entrenching democratic norms. National elections now occur as a matter of course across the continent. While there are clearly multiple problems with simply viewing elections as equating to democracy, especially given the number of leaders/one-parties that retained power, you do need to start somewhere to normalise and reinforce the functions of competitive politics (Lindberg, 2006). The second most significant development was the adoption of new constitutions across Africa, which enshrined many fundamental political rights, the most important of which was the widespread introduction of two-term presidential limits. Over 33 nations implemented this provision in the 1990s, which were designed to undermine clientist networks, strengthen democratic trends, and ensure that leaders could not cling to power (Vencovsky, 2007, 15–16). The reforms, pushed by domestic and international pressures, altered the landscape of African political governance and set in motion an ongoing transition away from the practices of the past.

Perhaps the case that encapsulated the democratisation process most in the 1990s, at least from afar, was South Africa. After decades of oppressive white minority rule, the National Party in 1990 unbanned the African National Congress (ANC), and released Nelson Mandela from prison, setting in motion a four-year transition towards majority government. This was no easy process, with negotiators forced to grapple with the social, economic, and political legacies of apartheid and chart an acceptable compromise for all sides, against the backdrop of a low-level civil war, as ethnic violence and racial unrest erupted. Yet the transition proved largely successful, a new interim constitution was finally agreed, and the first democratic elections were held in April 1994, which saw the ANC emerge victorious, heralding a moment of genuine optimism for the continent.

The contemporary outcomes of democratisation

Since the onset of the 'third wave of democracy' in the 1990s (Huntington, 1991), what is the state of African politics today? The first observation is that electoral political systems are now firmly established across the continent and significant steps have been made to create the framework to support this. The wave of elections since 2015 could be regarded as the breakthrough for African democracy in which Nigeria and Burkina Faso experienced successful outcomes that saw power peacefully transferred between presidents, without contestation. However, as Table 4.3 indicates, the transition away from authoritarianism has been highly uneven.

Clearly there are wide discrepancies between nations and within Africa's sub-regions, as to the commitment to political freedoms outlined by Freedom House (2018); 10 nations are regarded as 'free', but a further 22 are deemed as 'not free'. Furthermore, these generalisations of freedom mask enormous variations in the levels of democratic commitment

Table 4.3 Freedom in Africa, 2018

Free	Partly Free	Not Free
Cape Verde (90)	Seychelles (71)	Algeria (35)
Mauritius (89)	Sierra Leone (66)	Mauritania (30)
Ghana (83)	Lesotho (64)	Zimbabwe (30)
Benin (82)	Malawi (63)	Angola (26)
São Tomé and Príncipe (82)	Liberia (62)	Djibouti (26)
South Africa (78)	Burkina Faso (60)	Egypt (26)
Namibia (77)	Madagascar (56)	Gabon (23)
Senegal (75)	Comoros (55)	Rwanda (23)
Botswana (72)	Zambia (55)	Cameroon (22)
Tunisia (70)	Mozambique (52)	Rep. of Congo (21)
	Tanzania (52)	Burundi (18)
	Côte d'Ivoire (51)	Chad (18)
	Nigeria (50)	DRC (17)
	Niger (49)	Swaziland (16)
	Kenya (48)	Ethiopia (12)
	Togo (47)	CAR (9)
	Mali (45)	Libya (9)
	The Gambia (41)	Sudan (8)
	Guinea (41)	Equatorial Guinea (7)
	Guinea-Bissau (41)	Somalia (7)
	Morocco (39)	Eritrea (3)
	Uganda (37)	South Sudan (2)

* The number in brackets represents the overall Freedom Score (100 = best and 0 = worst), comprised of categories covering Political Rights, Civil Liberties, and Political Freedom.

Source: Created using data from Freedom House, https://freedomhouse.org/report/freedom-world-2018-table-country-scores.

exercised by leaders and governments across Africa. This section will sketch out some of the key developments since the 1990s.

On a continent not regarded positively for its commitment to democratic ideals, only a smattering of nations could be considered as being democratic – for example, Cape Verde and Botswana. These nations have democratic constitutions and practices, and protect political freedom for their citizens. However, one stands alone as the leader for democratic ideals and for the strength of the institutional framework that exists to support it in Africa: Mauritius. Since independence, Mauritius, a series of small islands in the Indian Ocean, has consolidated democracy, strengthened by strong economic growth and the avoidance of neo-patrimonialism; this is despite the country inheriting many of the shared historical legacies experienced by much of the continent. The post-colonial government rapidly implemented astute policies to support the welfare of islanders and promote stable economic growth, which allowed for bureaucratic independence. Furthermore, through responsible political leadership, especially focused on consensual decision making, democratic practices were inculcated. The result has been 11 free and fair democratic general elections since 1967, and most importantly the regular alternation of power, shared among three main political parties: the Militant Socialist Movement (MSM), the Labour Party, and the Mauritian Militant Movement (MMM). The December 2014 election saw Ameenah Gurib-Fakim appointed as Mauritius's first female president in 2015, and the third (Liberian Ellen Johnson Sirleaf (see Box 4.6) and Malawian Joyce Banda were the other two presidents) on a continent that is overwhelmingly dominated by male heads of state (Table 4.4). Mauritius is widely considered the only full democracy in Africa because of the rotation of political power among the nation's leaders and parties.

Box 4.6 Ellen Johnson Sirleaf's legacy

In January 2018, Africa's first female president Ellen Johnson Sirleaf oversaw the first democratic transfer of power in Liberia after reaching her two-term constitutional limit. During Liberia's 14-year civil war (1989–2003), in which 250,000 people were killed, women across the country endured endemic levels of sexual violence; an estimated 70% of all Liberian females over the age of 14 were raped during the conflict. Yet through the concerted actions of women's organisations (see Chapter 7) not only was peace achieved, but they also successfully mobilised behind Sirleaf's presidential election campaign. In a deeply patriarchal society, it was a shining example of the power women could exert in the political arena.

The initial policies of the Sirleaf administration were testament to the goal of achieving gender equality in Liberia by implementing strident anti-rape legislation; a court for gender-based violence; and a national programme for women's education. In acknowledgement of her work she was awarded the Nobel Peace Prize in 2011 along with Leymah Gbowee and Tawakkul Karman. However, Sirleaf's popularity and international recognition were undermined domestically by mixed political outcomes and increasing criticism of her record in office. Moreover, in terms of women's emancipation, critics believe she fell short in dismantling patriarchal structures and encouraging greater participation in politics. For example, during Sirleaf's presidency the total number of women in parliament actually fell.

Yet Sirleaf made history by demonstrating that women could achieve the highest political office in Africa. Facing numerous challenges and pressures, her presidency successfully maintained peace after the civil war, enshrined human rights legislation, and fought to protect women's interests. In 2018, Sirleaf was bestowed with the prestigious Mo Ibrahim Prize for Achievement in African Leadership for her 'exceptional and transformative leadership'. Ultimately, Sirleaf's achievements will ensure that she will be viewed as an international inspiration who broke the glass ceiling for women in African politics.

Outside of the small band of democratic states, one of the main observations is that the democratisation process of the 1990s was never fully completed. The result has been an outward projection of democracy across the continent, but beneath the surface a number of underlying

Table 4.4 Women in African politics

Global rank	Country	% women in parliament
1	Rwanda	61.3
5	Namibia	46.2
10	South Africa	42.4
12	Senegal	41.8
14	Mozambique	39.6
18	Ethiopia	38.8
25	Tanzania	37.2
27	Burundi	36.4
34	Uganda	34.3

Source: Created using data from the Inter-Parliamentary Union, correct as of June 2018, http://archive.ipu.org/wmn-e/classif.htm.

continuities have persisted. A useful way to characterise the majority of African governments is under three main categories: 'flawed', 'hybrid', and 'authoritarian' versions of democracy (Economist Intelligence Unit, 2017). Such broad categorisations encompass a sweep of governance styles from nations that are to all intents and purposes democratic to others which are inherently authoritarian but utilise a minimal adherence to democratic practices to legitimise their power. It is clear that although the democratisation of the 1990s may have inculcated regular elections across the continent, the process did not imply that all those nations are democratic; perfect examples are Burundi, Sudan, and Zimbabwe.

Across Africa there is a wide divergence in governance approaches and styles. On one side there are a group of nations such as South Africa and Senegal that have many of the trappings of democracy, such as regular elections, permitting opposition parties, a largely independent judiciary, the non-interference of the military, and the existence of a free press. However, even the continent's better performing governments exhibit some remarkably illiberal tendencies, more akin to their authoritarian counterparts. On the other extreme, there are a number of deeply entrenched authoritarian countries such as Egypt, Eritrea, and Angola. They do hold elections (which are fundamentally compromised), but simultaneously utilise coercion and violence to maintain power; suppress or harass opposition parties; restrict the freedom of the press; and exploit the levers of the state in their favour, including altering constitutional arrangements. Almost every African nation is located within the 'flawed', 'hybrid', and 'authoritarian' categories, but these are by no means fixed positions, with a range of variations that incorporate multiparty systems, personal rulers, and dominant party states.

However, in a number of countries there is a clear sense that multiparty democracy is taking hold, demonstrated by Ghana and Senegal. Although these nations have incumbent governments that utilise their position to maximum effect, there is still a significant chance that opposition parties can win a democratic election, and power will be peacefully transferred as institutions and practices are accepted by all political actors. Crucially, where an incumbent leader respects the presidential term limit and does not re-stand for office, the likelihood of political power changing hands dramatically increases (Cheeseman, 2010), exemplified by Benin's election in 2016. Similar to US politics, a common political feature is a duopoly of parties, where power repeatedly switches between the two. In Ghana, the former military leader Jerry Rawlings pre-empted the emerging democratisation process by unbanning opposition parties and holding elections in 1992. Rawlings and his National Democratic Congress (NDC) won the first election and the subsequent 1996 election. However, with growing criticism of the NDC, its candidate John Atta

Mills was defeated in 2000 by the more effective opposition, the New Patriotic Party (NPP) led by John Kufour; Kufour also won in 2004. However, by 2008, John Atta Mills led the NDC to the narrowest of victories over the NPP's Nana Akufo-Addo (an election accused of systematic fraud), which was repeated again in 2011, with the NDC's incumbent president John Mahama emerging victorious, who was then defeated in 2016 and replaced by Akufo-Addo. After decades of military rule, the repeated exchange of political power in Ghana indicates a commitment to democratic consolidation and public political engagement.

While it would be hard to claim that Nigeria has become a beacon of multiparty democracy, the 2015 election, which saw the first ever change of political leadership via the ballot box, has been regarded as a moment of optimism after military dictatorships and political instability. With the incumbent Goodluck Jonathan and his People's Democratic Party (PDP) acknowledging electoral defeat and peacefully transferring the presidency to Muhammadu Buhari and the All Progressives Congress (APC), there is the hope that this has set a precedent for future elections. Staffan Lindberg (2006) has argued that African nations can move beyond their autocratic political histories and entrench democratic norms through a commitment to a series of election cycles. The important characteristic must be the *possibility* of a leadership change, in which an election process is devoid of significant manipulation or conflict. Although Lindberg's thesis holds some merit, democratic consolidation can only occur when a level of equality enters the political system through the reform of authoritarian structures and the removal of incumbency advantages, rather than simply transferring power between leaders. There must be the creation and maintenance of strong democratic institutions, including opposition parties and civil society actors, as well as an adherence to democratic norms, for change to become inculcated. Little in the way of democracy is gained if presidents such as Chiluba (Zambia) or Banda (Malawi) take power democratically, yet maintain systems that mirror the previous politically autocratic incarnations (Gyimah-Boadi, 2015).

A common governance form found across Africa is the dominant party system, although it must be recognised there are several dimensions to it which range from hybrid democracies through to authoritarian states. The first strand is epitomised by countries such as Botswana, South Africa, and Tanzania, which are clearly multiparty democracies that hold regular elections with opposition parties contesting them. However, the patrimonial nature of African politics, the fragility of state institutions, the weakness of opposition parties, and the personalised nature of power mean that incumbent presidents are highly unlikely to lose, gaining such large majorities that they can govern almost as they please (Maltz, 2007; Cheeseman, 2010); as such these can be characterised as either flawed or hybrid states. The danger of this form of governance is that the incumbent government can descend into semi-authoritarian practices, which stunt the opportunities for democratic progress and the possible transfer of power (see Box 4.7). These nations are typified by a strong president backed by a large and usually subservient majority in parliament. The result is the blurring of the party and the state, in which the interests of the party take precedent. As a consequence decision making, particularly fiscally, can escape the oversight of parliament, resulting in excessive spending or corrupt activities. In South Africa, the 1999 Arms Deal was highly circumspect with evidence of impropriety, fraud, and corruption by ANC MPs and their associates, while more recently the state-sanctioned spending on former president Jacob Zuma's private residency, Nkandla, was approved by the Department of Public Works. Importantly, the vocal criticism and objections from opposition parties, the mass media, and the

Box 4.7 Tanzania's dominant party

Tanzania offers a good example of a dominant party state in which the ruling party Chama Cha Mapinduzi (CCM) has remained in power and retained its majority since the restoration of multiparty democracy in 1992. There is an active opposition movement in Tanzania, and the rule of law is largely respected. In 2015, incumbent president Jakaya Kikwete stepped down after his second term ended (a limit which is observed in Tanzania, which is an exception to the norm) and was succeeded by John Magufuli, who won 58% of the vote in the run-off against Chadema's Edward Lowassa. The 2015 election was the closest ever held in Tanzania, and the CCM faced stiff competition from opposition parties, which gained significant numbers of seats in parliament; after 54 years in power, the CCM experienced a drastic decline in votes after a high point of an 80% share in 2005. The new president Magufuli immediately embarked on an anti-corruption and waste campaign in Tanzania by cancelling independence day celebrations, banning unnecessary foreign travel for MPs, and even firing the managers of Arusha's main hospital after he witnessed patients sleeping on the floor; his actions, regarded by some Tanzanians as a positive example of responsible leadership, led to #WhatWouldMagufuliDo trending on social media across Africa. However, Magufuli's presidency has not matched the initial hype, and he has allowed for some distinctly undemocratic tendencies to emerge such as banning public rallies, arresting opponents, and threatening the mass media who have criticised him.

independent public prosecutor created an enormous backlash, forcing a partial acceptance of wrongdoing by Zuma in 2016. This example illustrates that despite the enormous pressure exerted by the ANC towards the civil service, judiciary, media, and civil society, a dominant party operating within a democratic system cannot always have everything its own way.

Often regarded as a shining light for democratic governance, Botswana is another example of a dominant party state. Since 1966, frequent multiparty elections have been held, but the BDP has always retained power, accentuating its influence in Botswanan society that makes defeat at the polls highly unlikely. However, the BDP's incumbency has been increasingly threatened at the ballot box since the early 1990s, with its number of seats in parliament steadily declining, dropping to their lowest levels in 2014, when it gained 37 of the 57 seats available; perhaps an important indication for the future is that the BDP lost all but one of the wards in the capital Gaborone, which reflects how urbanisation across the continent is increasingly affecting traditional political norms. Despite the length of incumbency and the growing criticism of the BDP's record in office, Botswana consistently ranks highly on governance indices, lying third on the 2017 Mo Ibrahim Index (2017) of good governance.

A second strand within the dominant party state nexus contains ostensibly authoritarian nations such as Angola, Algeria, Cameroon, Equatorial Guinea, and Ethiopia. These countries are closely associated with one-party or military states from the post-colonial era, or a ruling party that came to power through armed liberation struggles. For democracy to be entrenched the formal rules of political behaviour need to be 'institutionalised' to ensure the continued adherence to specific norms (Posner & Young, 2007). Yet across Africa, the democratisation process was not universal and did not fundamentally alter the political system. The result was political and economic power continuing to reside within executives, which consequently allowed political elites, uninterested in respecting the 'rules' of democracy, the opportunities to remain autocratic (Gyimah-Boadi, 2015). In electoral authoritarian regimes, incumbents hold ballots that do not live up to democratic standards of freedom and fairness. Elections are utilised solely as a tool for legitimacy, often directed to appeasing the international community, but little else. The electoral process is therefore fundamentally flawed as opposition groups are harassed; political leaders are arrested; the media is largely state-run and far from impartial; the apparatus of the state is used for the purposes of the party; and if the election results look in doubt, simply rig the outcome – the 2008 Zimbabwean presidential poll was a perfect example of this. These authoritarian nations are dominated by powerful leaders such as Paul Biya (Cameroon) and Paul Kagame (Rwanda), with the continual retention of power the overriding priority. The political system is thus characterised by power centralised around the president, who retains overwhelming dominance over state structures, while the party rubber stamps their demands. Furthermore, the civil service, judiciary, and security services are closely intertwined with the ruling party, acting as an extension of its grip over a nation, and if needs be, suppressing dissent; for example, the Zimbabwe African National Union–Patriotic Front (ZANU–PF) dominates all aspects of Zimbabwe's bureaucracy and police, which have been utilised during every election against the opposition Movement for Democratic Change (MDC). The meshing of the state and the party results in the politicisation of what should be independent entities, and which maintains ongoing neo-patrimonial governance. As a consequence, the vast majority of voters are disenfranchised from the political process.

A significant political change highlighted earlier in the chapter was the adoption of new constitutions across the continent during the 1990s, with most stipulating a two-term limit for presidents. There have been developments which would positively indicate that there is an increased 'institutionalisation' of democratic norms and practices, preventing some elites from extending their rule (Posner & Young, 2007). However, a recent trend is the number of nations experiencing 'constitutional coups', as a host of leaders have sought to rewrite, amend, or simply ignore constitutional stipulations (Reyntjens, 2016). Namibia's Sam Nujoma set a precedent in 1999 by altering the constitution in a move which has subsequently been replicated across the continent since the 2000s. Burundi experienced waves of violence in 2015–2016, after President Pierre Nkurunziza defied the constitution and stood for a third term in office, while Paul Kagame implemented changes to the Rwandan constitution in 2015 which theoretically enable him to govern until 2034. Furthermore, in the Republic of Congo, President Denis Sassou Nguesso passed a constitutional amendment in 2015 which abolished the two-term condition and removed age limits for presidential candidates (it used to be 70 years old as a maximum). Finally, Yoweri Museveni won the 2016 Ugandan election amid accusations of irregularities, after previously changing the constitution in 2005. One of the ironies is that at the turn of the millennium Museveni, alongside Kagame, Meles Zenawi (Ethiopia), and Abdoulaye Wade (Senegal), was regarded as a new breed of leader that would promote democracy, freedom, and constitutionalism. The nations which have experienced constitutional coups are characterised by weak democratic structures; fragile political institutions; a constrained civil society; fractious and disorganised opposition parties; powerful presidential personalities; and highly centralised power which enable neo-patrimonial practices to be sustained (Randall & Svåsand, 2002). As a consequence, elites disinclined towards democracy have very few incentives to respect the constitutional term limits, nor are there institutional barriers preventing them from doing so.

However, not all attempts at constitutional coups have been successful. For example, Blaise Compaoré, who had ruled Burkina Faso for 27 years, sought to amend the constitution in 2014 to maintain his rule. Public protests in the capital Ouagadougou forced Compaoré out of office, and after a period of instability, including an unsuccessful military coup, elections were held in 2015. The election of Roch Marc Kaboré was an important moment in Burkina Faso's history because most of its previous leaders had gained power through coups. In other instances, presidents who do not relinquish power following electoral defeats have led to instability and protest. The most notable case occurred in Côte d'Ivoire where President Laurent Gbagbo refused to concede office in 2010, sparking a civil war that led to UN and French soldiers intervening to stop the violence and install Alassane Ouattara as president.

A major challenge confronting contemporary African politics has been the attempts to broker peaceful post-conflict settlements or to ease electoral violence (Chapter 9). Conflict resolution is an important tool in easing political instability, and seeks to achieve compromises and find solutions to implement and protect the 'institutionalisation' of democratic practices. Unfortunately, elite motivations often outweigh the need for national reconciliation (Chapter 6). Through the manipulation of factors including ethnicity, religion, and resource allocation, elites recognise that continued instability often suits their vested interests; for example, conflict in the DRC (1997–present) aptly demonstrates the intractability of political motivations. One mechanism to try and ease political conflict has been the use of power-sharing agreements and governments of national unity, which are designed to bring rivals together. In 2008, both Zimbabwe and Kenya encouraged the warring parties to join governments of national unity, after the incumbent refused to accept defeat. However, the outcomes were less than satisfactory, because the agreements failed to overcome the core political differences, and ensured continued access to power and patronage for the defeated incumbent. In Zimbabwe, ZANU-PF undermined the power-sharing agreement through blatant violations and coercion, while the legitimacy and influence of the MDC was tarnished because they were unable to enact meaningful political change. Across the continent, nations such as Burundi, Comoros, DRC, and Somalia have all tried power-sharing initiatives, yet they have failed to adequately resolve the conflicts or secure stability. The only tangible 'success' would be the Government of National Unity established in South Africa in 1994, which brought stability and compromise, although it ended after only two years, when the white minority National Party withdrew from the arrangement.

One key political change has been the diminishing influence of the military in contemporary African politics. An unambiguous position has been adopted by the continent's multilateral organisations (Chapter 9) such as the AU, the Economic Community of West African States (ECOWAS), and the Southern African Development Community (SADC), all of which have refused to recognise the legitimacy of military coups. Moreover, where defeated incumbents have refused to step aside after elections, these institutions have even threatened to intervene militarily to instate the rightful victor, most notably in the Gambia, where President Jammeh was unwilling to concede power in January 2017. However, the political role of militaries has not completely abated. Since 2000, there have been 15 successful coups, the most recent of which was in Zimbabwe (2017), albeit the military was fully aware of adverse international opinion, and were therefore at pains to insist that their overthrow of Mugabe was not a coup. Remarkably, two nations which had never experienced a successful coup before the 1990s – the Gambia (1994) and Côte d'Ivoire (1999) – both suffered their first capture of power by the military in the democratisation era. In the case of Algeria (1992), elite self-interest clearly emerged when the military seized power to prevent an Islamist election victory, which was perceived to threaten their privilege. Importantly, where there is a history of coups, the probability of continued military interventions into politics remains high (see Box 4.8). Since 2010, there have been ten unsuccessful coups in countries such as Mali, Lesotho, and Burundi which have been enormously disruptive and undermined efforts at entrenching respect for democratic institutions and practices. Moreover, as the number of coups has decreased, there has been a growing rise

Box 4.8 The 2013 military overthrow of Egyptian democracy

In 2011, Egypt experienced mass protests, centring on Tahir Square in Cairo, which eventually led to the end of Hosni Mubarak's 30 years (1981–2011) of autocratic leadership. The 'Egyptian Revolution' (part of the broader Arab Spring) forced Mubarak to resign, which resulted in a new constitution and democratic elections to be held. In the first election, Mohamed Morsi, a member of the Islamist Muslim Brotherhood, became Egypt's first democratically elected president in June 2012. However, only a year into democratic rule, public protest re-emerged in mid-2013, amid accusations that Morsi had monopolised power in the presidency, subordinated decision making to the Muslim Brotherhood, entrenched the Islamist movement within the state bureaucracy, and clamped down on dissent. With civil unrest growing, the Egyptian military intervened in July, issuing a 48-hour ultimatum, which demanded that Morsi resolve the ongoing civilian political differences with opposition parties. Unsurprisingly, the rapprochement was not forthcoming within the time frame, prompting the Egyptian military general Abdel el-Sisi to remove Morsi, the country's only democratically elected president, after one year in office. Morsi was arrested and the activities of the Muslim Brotherhood highly constrained as a wave of repression was enacted by the military. Although the coup was justified on the failings of Morsi's leadership and the widespread public protests against his rule, it was the growing power of the Islamists, combined with the possibility of new political reforms, that was clearly a challenge to vested military interests. The coup once again reinstated the Egyptian military as an influential powerbroker in the nation's political system, and undermined the authority and legitimacy of civilian institutions.

in army mutinies, which are often motivated by political and economic concerns (Dwyer, 2017); for example, in 2017, there were military revolts in Côte d'Ivoire and Cameroon. Therefore, the military may no longer be such an important political actor, but it would be folly to discount the influence and power they still retain within a number of African nations.

Future prospects

Since 1990, enormous progress towards embedding democratic norms has been achieved. There have been sustained attempts at inculcating democratic practices, including provisions for national elections, adopting new constitutional arrangements, and allowing for the liberalisation of civil society. Africans increasingly demand effective leadership and good governance, and have demonstrated that they are willing to protest against anti-democratic legislation and authoritarian practices when standards of good governance are not fulfilled. The growing commitment to the ideals of democracy and freedom can only be viewed as a positive development. A growing number of elections are regarded internally and internationally as free and fair, providing credence and legitimacy to the broader democratisation process. Moreover, an intriguing recent trend has emerged in which several embattled African leaders have chosen to step down from political office rather than clinging on to power, exemplified by Angola's José Eduardo dos Santos (2017), South Africa's Jacob Zuma (2018), and Ethiopia's Hailemariam Desalegn (2018). Yet, without wanting to be overly pessimistic, things are still not universally positive across Africa. In fact, there is significant evidence that shows that good governance standards are stalling, and in some cases are regressing. For example, Zambian president Edgar Lungu initiated legislation in 2017 that moved the country rapidly towards authoritarian rule, while in the DRC, against a backdrop of mounting public opposition, incumbent president Kabila has since 2016 simply resorted to continual postponements of scheduled elections to an unspecified future date.

There are a series of datasets (the Mo Ibrahim Index; Economist Intelligence Unit; Freedom House) which chart the levels of governance on the continent. According to these assessments, autocratic leadership, political instability, and flawed elections are all gathering apace. For example, the Mo Ibrahim Index (2017) showed that between 2012 and 2016, 20 countries have seen their overall governance score decrease (marked on a scale of 0–100, based on 93 indicators), including four of the top ten ranked countries (see Table 4.5).

Table 4.5 Mo Ibrahim Index on African governance

Top ten performing countries	Bottom ten performing countries
(1) Mauritius	(45) Angola
(2) Seychelles	(46) Equatorial Guinea
(3) Botswana	(47) Chad
(4) Cape Verde	(48) Democratic Republic of Congo
(5) Namibia	(49) Libya
(6) South Africa	(50) Sudan
(7) Tunisia	(51) Central African Republic
(8) Ghana	(52) Eritrea
(9) Rwanda	(53) South Sudan
(10) Senegal	(54) Somalia

Source: Created using data from the Mo Ibrahim Foundation (2017).

What is most instructive about all the different indices on African political development is that smaller nations, particularly the island states, are disproportionately represented as consistently high performers, associated with good governance, the protection of human rights, and freedom. In many respects this is due to fewer ethnic divisions and the geographic conditions for creating a more unified national rather than regionally focused identity, and their ability to hold more manageable elections. The caveat is that small countries such as Equatorial Guinea and Eritrea are among the most repressive and authoritarian because it is easier to exert total control over the population. In comparison, Africa's largest nations are overly represented at the lower reaches of these developmental tables; those with multiparty systems have experienced major electoral challenges exacerbated by political mobilisation around ethnic, religious, or regional concerns. For example, the utilisation of ethnicity in elections has often stoked political violence and instability in Kenyan elections.

Similarly, the Economist Intelligence Unit (2017) has noted some promising democratic gains, including the rise in the amount of peaceful changes of governments and presidents, as well as the decreasing cases of coups since 2006. However, it was highly critical on a range of governance indices, which include the rising number of presidential incumbents; the increasing cases of constitutional alteration or manipulation; and poor levels of general governance as causes for concern. In its rankings, only one nation, Mauritius, is regarded as a full democracy, while 27 North and sub-Saharan African nations are categorised as authoritarian.

What does the future hold? Undoubtedly there are ongoing governance and leadership problems, but the path to democracy is far from simple. Stop and consider just how long it took European nations to adopt democratic norms following centuries of upheaval, instability, and gradual evolution and refinement. Then reflect on how these structures and institutions were imposed swiftly and imperfectly on African nations by departing colonial powers, and then judged immediately against Europe's (albeit flawed) standards of democracy. In the 60 years since independence the continent has come a *very* long way. While the democratisation of the 1990s may not have been completed, the transition is still underway in many African states. Democratic practices are increasingly normalised across the continent, and authoritarianism is declining. The findings of the Afrobarometer (2016) survey showed that 67.8% of Africans polled supported democracy, and a further 82.8% opposed life presidents. African people demand good governance and democracy. Socio-economic developments (especially in education) and the changing demographics of the continent indicate that younger generations, particularly in urban areas, are increasingly intolerant of poor leadership and demand political change when their expectations are not met. Not within the scope of this chapter (see Chapter 10), technological changes such as the growing prevalence of mobile phones and internet access have facilitated the expansion of democracy, providing mechanisms that have transformed access to information and helped to illuminate government misdemeanours, making it more difficult for authoritarian leaders to continually maintain power.

The move towards entrenching democratic norms has also been facilitated by the AU and regional blocs such as ECOWAS, which are now far more willing to take a stand, particularly against military coups (see Chapter 9). Encouragingly, even in some of the continent's electoral authoritarian states such as Zimbabwe, opposition parties are permitted, something which did not occur in the immediate post-colonial era. While full democracy may not have been achieved yet, the hope is that the actions and commitment of political leaders in Mauritius, Nigeria, and Ghana will inculcate best practice and respect for institutionalised norms that will be increasingly replicated across the continent.

 Further reading

For more information on the key political developments and trends across the continent, an excellent continental starting point would be Paul Nugent's (2012) *Africa Since Independence*, followed by Richard Joseph's (1999) *State, Conflict and Democracy in Africa*, Crawford Young's (2012) *The Postcolonial State in Africa*, Robert Jackson and Carl Rosberg's (1982a) *Personal Rule in Black Africa*, and Patrick Chabal and Jean-Pascal Daloz's (2010) *Africa Works: Disorder as Political Instrument*. For discussions on some of the contemporary themes set out in this chapter, consult the edited volume by Nic Cheeseman (2014), *Routledge Handbook of African politics*; and the articles by Daniel Posner and Daniel Young (2007), 'The institutionalization of political power in Africa', and Filip Reyntjen (2016), 'The struggle over term limits in Africa'.

5 THE ECONOMY

The performance of contemporary African nations' economies, which are closely related to issues of governance, poverty, growth, and development, has played a significant role in shaping perceptions of the continent. The narratives of Afro-pessimism and Afro-optimism are closely intertwined with economic indicators. From the 1980s through until the early 2000s, the picture was almost universally bleak, as African nations struggled with escalating debts, growing poverty, external interventions, and a hugely imbalanced trade deficit, resulting in enormous difficulties; the now infamous *Economist* (2000) headline 'The hopeless continent' is testament to how economics and Afro-pessimism went hand in hand. It would be amiss to argue any other way that for over two decades Africa suffered the consequences of poor economic performance, which had grave effects on the political and social development of the continent (see Chapters 2 and 4). Yet, by the mid-2000s, following the restructuring of external debt, rising commodity prices, and the emergence of China as a major player in African affairs, the picture had changed dramatically. African economies almost all markedly improved, with enviable growth rates and increased investment in development and infrastructure projects, prompting the increasing use of the 'Africa Rising' label that depicts a continent uplifting itself from its previous malaise. The pendulum has now swung the other way – one all-encompassing negative perspective of the continent has been replaced with another more positive view.

The purpose of this chapter is to chart the peaks and troughs of Africa's economic situation from independence through to the present day. It will begin by examining the state of the continent in the opening decades of the post-colonial era, demonstrating how mounting domestic and external issues contributed to the economic crisis of the 1980s, followed by an assessment of the external efforts to alleviate the problems, most notably through structural adjustment programmes (SAPs), which had grave consequences for African nations. The latter sections will then turn to assess the recent economic improvements since the millennium, highlighting China's part in facilitating these developments. Africa has been booming economically, and important questions of why this has happened, and whether it is sustainable, will be discussed.

Before commencing with the chapter, three broad points must be raised. The first is that through this assessment of Africa's economic fortunes the book does not wish to make the case for either of the grand narratives set out above. This chapter will seek to explain how the various economic boom and bust cycles arose, and the effects these had across the continent, but it is up to you to decide if the grand narratives fit. Secondly, while there are clearly broad economic patterns that can be witnessed across the continent, each nation's economy is unique. Therefore what applies in one country does not necessarily mean the same circumstances can be found elsewhere. There is no single African economic experience.

The final issue is one of statistics and their reliability. Understandably in a chapter on economics, there will be plenty of figures to highlight growth rates, trade balances, and debt levels from organisations such as the IMF, World Bank, and the African Development Bank. However, we must be extremely cautious about the accuracy of these figures, produced by multilateral organisations often with their own explicit agendas, and also how they are interpreted. Morten Jerven (2013b, 2015) has written at length about the problems of data collection across Africa, the ways in which figures are extrapolated, and the pitfalls that these produce for our understanding of African economics. What we must also be aware of is that African economies can be modern and highly developed, yet simultaneously traditional, informal, and localised all at once. Across the continent there are signs of a rush to 'modernity', with the construction of skyscrapers and the utilisation of information and communication technologies, but these stand side by side with informal traders and those simply struggling to survive. The figures used by economists, politicians, and academics hide the economic reality for many, and exclude a significant proportion of economic activity. Therefore, a healthy level of scepticism should be observed when using any of these figures, recognising that they do not tell the whole story.

1960–1970s: An age of optimism?

Utilising a historically deterministic outlook, it is very easy to write off the entire post-colonial era through a lens of unremitting negativity. Indeed, the usual characterisation is one of a series of failures and missed opportunities, hindered by poor growth (Collier & Gunning, 1999, 4). However, this would be a misrepresentation; the initial stages of post-colonial economic development during the 1960s and early 1970s saw steady progress that helped to transform many African nations. The leaders of newly independent countries understood that a prosperous and economically viable state was fundamental for changing their fortunes and overcoming some of the colonial legacies, while fulfilling the promises of improved welfare provision and employment. Consequently, a focus on rapid economic development became a key priority. In many respects, moderate success was achieved in the 1960s as growth rates proved steady, jobs were created, and investment into infrastructure and social programmes including health and education were implemented.

The job of transforming newly independent nations was certainly made harder against the specific context of their colonial inheritance (see Chapter 3). By and large, African economies had been established to service the needs of Europe with a focus on the export of cheap agricultural produce and unprocessed raw materials for industrial production. At independence, the continent was a crucial global producer of export products such as tea, coffee, groundnuts, and cotton. As a result, the bedrock of most African economies was extremely narrow, based on a select few primary materials. As Table 5.1 shows, there was very little economic

Table 5.1 Select examples of African nations' reliance on primary production and exports

Raw materials	Nations
Oil	Algeria, Angola, Cameroon, DRC, Egypt, Equatorial Guinea, Gabon, Libya, Nigeria, Sudan
Diamonds	Angola, Botswana, CAR, Sierra Leone, South Africa, Zimbabwe
Coffee	Burundi, Côte d'Ivoire, Ethiopia, Kenya, Rwanda, Uganda
Cocoa	Benin, Cameroon, Côte d'Ivoire, Ghana, São Tomé and Príncipe, Sierra Leone, Togo
Copper	DRC, Zambia
Cotton	Benin, Burkina Faso, Chad, Egypt, Mali, Sudan, Togo
Precious metal (gold, silver, platinum)	Ghana, Guinea, Mali, Senegal, South Africa, Tanzania
Uranium	Chad, Niger, Namibia, South Africa
Metal ores (bauxite, iron ore, zinc, etc.)	CAR, DRC, Guinea, Liberia, Madagascar, Mauritania, Morocco, South Africa, Sierra Leone, Togo, Zimbabwe
Groundnuts	Guinea-Bissau, Niger, Senegal, the Gambia

Source: World Bank Group, African Development Indicators, *2000.*

diversification; nations such as Nigeria (oil), Botswana (diamonds), and Zambia (copper) relied almost entirely on the export of a single item for revenue, often to the former colonial power. The legacy of this structural imbalance is still evident today. As will be explained later in the section 'The onset of economic collapse', the overreliance on primary production left the continent at the mercy of international demand and fluctuating harvest yields, with highly volatile prices susceptible to peaks and troughs. Furthermore, the colonial powers had made almost no effort to create an indigenous manufacturing sector, transfer technological processes and knowledge, or develop any form of African self-sufficiency, which in turn necessitated the importation of expensive processed goods from abroad; the consequence was an in-built imbalance of trade terms in favour of developed nations.

Not only were African economies premised on a narrow primary export base, but the situation was exacerbated by the highly skewed internal development of colonial territories. For example, almost all the limited road and rail networks were created specifically by the colonial powers to ensure the exportation of primary products off the continent (Berg, 1981, 12); African economies were geared to be explicitly outward-facing, centred on exportation to Europe, and not on domestic trade or interconnectivity with other African nations. A final legacy was that through the poor provision of educational opportunities the colonial era had left African nations with a scarcity of trained and skilled people, which made the job of modernising and developing fledgling economies even more challenging. The upshot was that it was extremely difficult for independent nations to establish a manufacturing sector, diversify away from the commodity export-led model, or find alternative buyers for their products. The result was that it entrenched Europe's economically advantageous position. For authors such as Amin (1973) and Rodney (1972), or leaders such as Kwame Nkrumah (1965), this was the very essence of neo-colonialism that kept the continent 'underdeveloped' (see Box 5.1).

While it is only right to acknowledge the many fundamental problems left by colonialism, the argument that the continent has been left dependent on external factors systematically ignores the political agency of African leaders. In the 1960s, and beyond, political leaders had choices on how best to transform and manage their nation's economies, with ideological and material assistance available from both sides of the Cold War divide. Yet what is remarkable is the near uniformity of policy direction both socialist (e.g. Ghana, Guinea, Mali, Tanzania) and capitalist (e.g. Côte d'Ivoire, Kenya, Nigeria, Malawi, Morocco, Botswana) leaders took towards economic development, largely based around state-led growth and self-sufficiency, albeit with different levels

Box 5.1 Neo-colonialism

Neo-colonialism is a concept that gained credence in the 1970s which asserted that even after decolonisation, the economic model that underpinned colonialism remained firmly in place. The consequence was that former colonies may have achieved political independence, but continued to be economically dependent on the west. As a result, external forces (i.e. developed nations) had the power to influence and direct economic systems via imbalanced world trade terms, which were stacked heavily in the west's favour. With African economies so heavily premised on extractive industries or cash crop production to function, while having to purchase processed, manufactured products in return, it was argued that there was no way that they could diversify and develop in any meaningful fashion, relegating the continent to a subservient place in the global hierarchy. The outcome: a veneer of freedom, and the perpetuation of poverty and inequality. This is clearly an alluring concept, and is a neat explanation for some of Africa's enduring economic problems. Undoubtedly all the major European powers sought to ensure that they continued to benefit economically without formal political control after independence. Yet the concept of neo-colonialism cannot be applied uniformly across the continent.

In reality, it was only really France that successfully nurtured a genuinely neo-colonial system. In its former west and equatorial colonies (with the exception of Guinea) France convinced the newly independent nations about the benefit of retaining the CFA franc, which surrendered full fiscal autonomy to Paris in return for a fixed exchange rate. Furthermore, the former colonies signed technical agreements, pursued preferential trade deals, and allowed for a continued French military presence across the region. Côte d'Ivoire is the prime example of neo-colonialism in practice, in which President Félix Houphouët-Boigny invited French advisors to assist in many aspects of the country's governance, and allowed for Paris to develop a major stake in the nation's agricultural planning and production. The extensive cultivation of agricultural products, particularly cocoa, enabled the Côte d'Ivoire to rapidly increase its GDP in the 1970s, but this was at the expense of government control and planning. An irony was that after independence more Europeans lived and worked in Côte d'Ivoire than during the French colonial era.

of commitment to these depending on their ideological grounding. Although the rhetoric of economic transformation based on redistribution and egalitarianism was extensively employed by African leaders, the reality was somewhat different. Crawford Young (1982, 183) neatly observed that 'the capitalist pathway in Africa has numerous followers but few partisans'.

The 1960s was a decade of political and economic optimism for Africa. Commodity prices across the world for items such as coffee, tea, copper, and oil remained high, which meant that state revenues were relatively buoyant, enabling investment into industrial development to progress quickly. In the decade 1960–1970, sub-Saharan Africa's gross national product (GNP) increased annually at 4.2% for low income countries and 4.8% for middle income countries (World Bank, 1980, 99). Utilising the steady income available, African leaders implemented policies to modernise and transform economies and societies as quickly as possible. To achieve this transformation, politicians turned to the state as the most effective vehicle for change. While state-led growth is no longer a fashionable development model, it must be remembered that the statist approach was widely used in the 1960s, exemplified by western nations such as France and Britain, and most notably the socialist countries of the Soviet Union and China. Centralised economic planning was regarded as the key path to development and modernity, as it allowed politicians direct control to oversee rapid change. With most African states achieving their independence in the period 1956–1966, when such economic thinking was at its zenith, it should be of little surprise that this model became ubiquitous across the continent. Backed by primary export incomes, infrastructure and industrialisation projects commenced throughout Africa, including the Aswan High Dam in Egypt and the Inga Dam in Zaire (DRC), while major public sector spending was directed to the expansion of welfare provision, most notably for health and education. Indeed, backed by significant financial investment, one of the greatest successes in the opening decades of post-colonial governance was social welfare improvements that benefited the lives of millions of Africans. For example, the increase in health spending helped significantly reduce infant mortality across the continent from 171 per 1,000 in 1955–1960, to 121 per 1,000 by 1975–1980 (UN, 2016).

The primary means of achieving state-led economic development was through the creation of centrally run organisations known as parastatals, along with the nationalisation of strategic industries. An integral part of the managed economy in which African governments sought to establish self-sufficiency was premised on import substitution in order to create a domestic industrial base. These industries were aided by protectionist policies such as high tariff barriers, overvalued currencies, and massive state subsidies. To give a sense of just how prevalent parastatals were across Africa, a World Bank study estimated that, by the 1980s, there were more than 3,000 state-run organisations in sub-Saharan Africa. In the report covering 30 countries, half had more than 100 parastatals – for example, Tanzania operated 400, Senegal 188, and Malawi 101 (Nellis, 1986, 1–5). Throughout the 1960s and early 1970s, with commodity prices remaining high, and an amenable international community assisting fledgling African governments, state-led economies throughout Africa grew at a steady rate; the first decade of independence certainly looked positive (see Box 5.2).

The parastatal which formed the heart of the centralised economic model also served political purposes, providing opportunities for job creation, while fulfilling some of the promises made at independence. However, the parastatal created a Pandora's box of problems that had negative economic consequences. As discussed in Chapter 4, access to the central levers of economic power was fundamental to the patron–client model of political control. This system enabled well-positioned individuals to siphon off wealth, and for political leaders to cement their power through neo-patrimonial practices by placing supporters within parastatals and the civil service. The result was a rapid increase in public sector employment throughout Africa. During the 1960s, civil services grew on average 7% per year annually; the upshot was that by the 1970s, government bureaucracies provided 60% of all wage earners, while costing 50% of state expenditures (Chazan, 1999, 55). In some countries like Ghana, state run-organisations provided 73.9% of all jobs (Berg, 1981, 41). Very rapidly state bureaucracies became overstaffed, inefficient, and enormously costly to government finances. While commodity prices remained high, African states could just about cope with the financial drains, but when prices later collapsed, it caused serious budgetary deficits for many governments such as Ghana (Nellis, 1986).

Furthermore, due to the lack of other opportunities available for wealth creation, the state became the primary vehicle to achieving personal prosperity. The increasing instability of maintaining political control by the late 1960s had meant that when in political power there was a propensity by elites to maximise individual wealth, because once power was lost so too was access to economic opportunity. The result was a short-termist economic outlook, which saw rent-seeking and corrupt practices flourish, and a decline in long-term planning in favour of immediate returns. Not surprisingly, any profit generated was withdrawn, resulting in a lack of investment or diversification of industrial practices; why change a system that benefited the elite? In 1961, the anti-colonial philosopher Frantz Fanon (2001, 122) had predicted this very scenario for independent African states under new, venal nationalist elites.

Box 5.2 The Mauritian success story

Against the backdrop of the continent's economic failures during the first decades of independence, a rather short list of nations stood out as anomalies that successfully bucked the prevailing malaise. One example is the small island nation of Mauritius. However, the initial prognosis was not encouraging; geographically isolated in the Indian Ocean, its colonial inheritance left the economy reliant on sugar exports, while also lacking a natural resource base. The future looked so poor that James Meade (1961), a Nobel Prize-winning economist, predicted that 'the outlook for peaceful development is weak'.

Yet Mauritius successfully overcame these challenges, rapidly transforming itself into a middle income nation, recording annual GDP growth rates of more than 5% during the first three decades of independence. Importantly, the economic gains were transferred to the general populous, with Mauritius having one of the highest per capita incomes in Africa, while the government provides free education and healthcare.

How was this achieved? The story of Mauritius's economic development is one of careful management and a willingness to adapt and evolve to changing conditions. Since independence, the Mauritian government prudently used export-led growth to ensure the creation of a broad and diverse economic system, which enabled rapid economic growth that brought material benefits for the population. A key underlying element was the political system in Mauritius (see Chapter 4) that was democratic, transparent, financially prudent, and committed to maintaining independent functioning institutions. The stability of the political system, particularly in comparison to much of the continent, proved a major draw to international investors and subsequently brought large foreign direct investment (FDI) inflows. The first step towards economic prosperity was that the government encouraged, rather than penalised, the sugar industry, which was aided by preferential export trade deals with the European Economic Community in the 1970s. The revenue generated by sugar was used as the basis to diversify the economy into light manufacturing and textiles through the creation of Export Processing Zones supported by highly protectionist government policies and incentives for export-focused companies. By the 1990s, Mauritius once again evolved its economic base on the back of exports with the creation of a thriving service sector, centred on ICT, financial institutions, and a vibrant tourism industry.

Theoretically, the move towards import substitution was a sensible model for creating a self-sufficient industrial base and for unshackling African states' dependency on external forces; the 'Asian Tigers' offer an obvious example of this successfully working. Yet the drive for self-sufficiency ran aground due to a multitude of interconnected problems. A major issue was one of cost. Not only did investing in the creation of an industrial base cost a phenomenal amount of money, but the returns did not offset the outlay. Most of the components and machinery for the industrial processes had to be imported from abroad, and because there was a very small domestic market for the products being produced, there were no economies of scale. The finished products were thus expensive, and often of inferior quality compared to competitor nations, which meant that there was a limited export market. Lacking from investment, and requiring external borrowing to sustain the projects, the parastatals became increasingly costly to maintain.

Perhaps the most important political decision, which had the greatest impact on precipitating economic decline, was the widespread neglect of agriculture. The rapid shift to economic modernity was overwhelmingly urban-focused, and funded largely on the back of agricultural production. At independence, 81% of sub-Saharan Africans were employed in agriculture, forming 48% of GDP, and thus generated a significant proportion of state revenues (Berg, 1981, 145, 178). Yet for many leaders the neglect of agriculture was a conscious political decision. Farming was widely regarded as backwards and unsuitable for the basis of a modern economy. Rather than ensuring the returns from agricultural production remained healthy, many African leaders chose to actively exploit rural producers in order to fund industrialisation projects, boost state revenues, and maintain the support of urban constituents (Bates, 1981).

Utilising the colonial-era marketing boards, these state-run monopolies purchased agricultural products at set prices, selling them on at a profit. In order to generate ever greater profit margins, marketing boards increasingly set prices well below the actual cost of production. For example, in 1965, Nkrumah's government paid Ghanaian cocoa farmers only 37% of the actual price their crops were sold for (Fieldhouse, 1986, 34). Through punitive taxation and reduced revenues for their products, there was a disincentive for farmers to engage in mass agricultural production. Fully appreciating they were being exploited, farmers chose to decouple from state control, shifting instead to subsistence farming, smuggling, or to the informal economy by selling directly to consumers; a study of Senegalese farmers described the 'illegal' exportation of groundnuts as the 'peasant malaise' (Schumacher, 1975, 183–185). On the whole, the continent-wide exploitation of farmers resulted in a catastrophic decline of agricultural yields, at a time when demand from growing populations increased. As a consequence, governments were forced to start costly food imports, which ironically reduced the pursuit of self-sufficiency and drained state finances. The continent, which had been a net exporter of food, became a net importer. For example, Nigeria, by the 1970s, was dependent on food imports amounting to $2 billion (Meredith, 2006, 281).

An anomaly to this continental trend was Tanzania, whose leader Julius Nyerere regarded agriculture as the bedrock for an effective socialist economy. Through the policy of Ujamaa (see Chapter 4) he sought to encourage greater production through collectivisation of farms to improve productivity. Although the policy would ultimately fail as rural communities resisted state intervention, Nyerere chose a different path to pursue economic development. Moreover, by the late 1970s, as socialist-inspired governments took control in countries such as Mozambique and Ethiopia, they also experimented with agricultural collectivisation, albeit with limited success, hampered by inefficiency and overburdened central planning.

The onset of economic collapse

By the mid-1970s, after moderate, but unspectacular economic growth compared to the rest of the world, the continental picture began to decline as a series of calamities undermined progress and sent African governments into financial meltdown. The warning signs were already visible. Cumulatively, the denigration of agriculture and the cost of maintaining large state bureaucracies had put a growing strain on state finances leading to a loss of tax revenue, a lack of capital to support and invest in fledgling industrialisation projects, and ever greater urban migration that put further pressure on already overburdened services. These revenue shortfalls were exacerbated by a series of external shocks that sent commodity prices tumbling and created straightened global economic conditions that worsened Africa's already disadvantaged position in the global system.

The first external issue was a severe drought which affected much of the Sahel region from 1968 to 1974. The sustained drought led to further declines in agricultural production, and thus export revenues, leading to increased food imports and price inflation. For example, from the early 1960s, year-on-year net food imports of cereals increased by 9%, which were augmented by an increasing reliance on international food aid to mitigate production shortfalls (Berg, 1981, 45–49). The shortage of food hurt the poorest the most, forcing some governments such as that in Zambia to provide subsidies to reduce the impact of prices rises.

The most serious turn of events was the oil shocks of the 1970s that prompted what has been described as the 'lost decades', resulting in economic decline, stagnation, and unsustainable debts. In 1973 and then again in 1979, the decision of the Organization of the Petroleum Exporting Countries (OPEC) to sharply increase oil prices, which most African states imported, triggered a global recession. International demand declined significantly, which in turn reduced commodity prices – a disaster for Africa's export-led economies. The 80% increase in real oil prices between 1978 and 1980 meant that oil imports cost the continent 23% of all export earnings, and 6% of GDP. African states' terms of trade (export revenues compared to import prices) decreased rapidly in the 1970s, with mineral-exporting countries experiencing a –7.1% annual decline throughout the decade (Berg, 1981, 18–19). Owing to Africa's position at the bottom of the global supply chain, the collapse in commodity prices was ruinous, leaving almost no alternative options to generate extra finance to support their economies. For the vast majority of the continent it was a disaster, pushing overstretched nations to the precipice of economic ruin. Governments across the continent were essentially bankrupt.

For a few African oil exporters such as Algeria, Republic of Congo, Egypt, Gabon, and Nigeria, the increased oil prices proved enormously beneficial. In Nigeria, the economy expanded rapidly with GDP growing at 7.5% annually throughout the 1970s, and by 1980, oil exports generated $25 billion (Berg, 1981, 144). However, the oil revenue bonanza sparked irresponsible spending and complacency, which saw Nigerian politicians squander huge sums of money, while neglecting domestic agriculture and industrial manufacturing further. For example, groundnut cultivation all but ceased. However, oil prices did not stay high for long, so when revenues started to decrease, oil-rich economies were sent into freefall, mirroring many of the problems experienced elsewhere in Africa.

The only solution left available was to seek loans from international financial organisations, which were flush with new capital invested by recently minted OPEC nations. However, what had seemed like a short-term solution to plug a temporary revenue shortfall soon escalated into an unsustainable debt crisis. Throughout the 1970s, Africa's economic picture did not substantially improve, as commodity prices remained low and importation costs continued to rise. The outcome was the need for further loans, on top of earlier borrowing, simply to sustain state finances. Owing to the very nature of African economies premised on primary resources and a fragile manufacturing base, the collapse in commodity prices made it increasingly unlikely that the debts could be repaid (see Table 5.2). African states were caught in a debt cycle of needing to take out new loans just to service existing liabilities.

Table 5.2 Select examples of African indebtedness

	External public debt ($ millions)		Debt service as percentage of exports and services	
	1970	1982	1970	1982
Côte d'Ivoire	256	4,861	6.8	36.9
Ethiopia	169	875	11.4	9.5
Ghana	489	1,116	5.0	6.8
Guinea	314	1,230	–	–
Malawi	122	692	7.1	22.8
Mauritania	27	1,001	3.1	11.8
Morocco	711	9,030	7.7	36.8
Nigeria	480	6,085	4.2	9.5
Rwanda	2	189	1.3	3.2
Sudan	319	5,093	10.7	7.5
Tanzania	248	1,659	4.9	5.1
Tunisia	541	3,472	17.5	15.1
Zaire	311	4,087	4.4	–
Zambia	623	2,381	5.9	17.4

Source: Created using data from World Bank (1984), World Development Report (Oxford University Press), 1984.

Blame for this worsening situation must be apportioned to both African leaders and the irresponsible lending of international institutions. African leaders were unwilling to implement austerity measures to stem the mounting crisis because of the political imperative to retain economic control and maintain spending for patronage purposes. Many leaders such as President Mobutu took out loans with little intention of repaying them, or mortgaged future raw material yields as collateral, exemplified by the Nigerian military juntas in the 1970s. Simultaneously, the major international lenders that continued to accept new liabilities from an already vastly overburdened continent cannot be absolved of responsibility either, having assumed that nations could not fail and would honour their financial commitments; the number of loans and the interest repayments went on with little thought for the future.

Structural adjustment

By the 1980s, almost all African nations were experiencing serious economic difficulties, confronted with stagnant or declining growth, enormous external debts, escalating interest repayments, a negative trade imbalance, and diminishing state revenues. According to the World Bank (1989, 222) GDP for sub-Saharan Africa was extremely poor, with only a handful registering any form of positive growth: Botswana, Lesotho, Mauritius, and Cameroon achieved above 5% per annum, while Mozambique, Tanzania, São Tomé and Príncipe, Togo, and Nigeria were among nine that registered negative growth rates. These poor growth rates were exacerbated as other regions such as South America continued to grow at a much faster rate, further widening the inequality gap (see Table 5.3). The continent was in a serious bind.

The only viable solution came from international financial institutions in the form of the IMF and World Bank. Unfortunately for African states, these western institutions had entered a new era of neo-liberalism influenced by ideologically conservative leaders such as Ronald Reagan and Margaret Thatcher. The new economic orthodoxy created a very specific western perspective on the cause and solution to Africa's economic demise. The western financial consensus had moved away from the 1960s state-centred development models and instead preached the power of free market economics. The so-called 'Washington Consensus' regarded the state as being inefficient, hampering growth, and proving unsuitable for economic decision making. To generate growth, the prescribed solution was that the state should be dramatically reduced in size,

Table 5.3 World regions' GDP growth

Regions (low and middle income countries)	GDP: Annual growth rate %	
	1965–1980	1980–1988
Sub-Saharan Africa	4.8	0.8
East Asia	7.2	8.5
South Asia	3.7	5.1
Europe, Middle East, and North Africa	6.1	–
Latin America and Caribbean	6.0	1.5
Average	**6.0**	**1.5**

Source: World Bank. 1990. World development report 1990: Poverty. New York: Oxford University Press. © World Bank. https://openknowledge.worldbank.org/handle/10986/5973 License: CC BY 3.0 IGO.

services including social welfare provision cut back, parastatals privatised, and economies opened up to market forces (see Box 5.3).

The package of financial assistance introduced were SAPs. Importantly, SAPs were not 'free' international aid to African governments, but rather a series of loans with stringent economic stipulations attached. The conditions covered an array of demands such as market liberalisation, the removal of tariff and trade barriers, fiscal austerity, and privatisation. If African governments did not agree to the prescribed conditions, their access to funds could be denied. The tough conditions imposed generated a lot of controversy as they went well beyond simply offering economic solutions, straying into political and social affairs. As a consequence, the west was now dictating terms, forcing a wholescale reorientation of African economic policy. African governments lost much of their fiscal autonomy to external interference, combined with a growing narrative of paternalism and condescension from the west; neo-colonialism was alive and well.

Although there was deep unease among African leaders about SAP conditionality, the financial situation left them with no choice. Across the continent, socialist, capitalist, and oil-exporting nations were all in turn forced to turn to the west for help, albeit with varying degrees of commitment to the imposed conditions. The first country to take on structural adjustment was Senegal in 1979, and by the 1990s, 36 African nations would take out 241 SAP loans in order to support their ailing economies

Box 5.3 The Berg Report: The blueprint for structural adjustment in Africa

The key document which set out the neo-liberal case for Africa's economic reform was enshrined by *Accelerated Development in Sub-Saharan Africa*, commonly referred to as the Berg Report (Berg, 1981). Imbued with new western thinking, this World Bank report placed the blame for the crisis squarely with African governments for poor growth rates and indebtedness; there was some acknowledgement of structural factors such as colonial legacies, and environmental factors, but the importance of these were diminished in favour of 'domestic inadequacies' (Berg, 1981, 4). In order to rectify the problems three core themes were identified to generate export-led growth: (1) suitable trade and exchange-rate policies, (2) increased public sector efficiency, and (3) improved agricultural policies (Berg, 1981, 5). The key message was to utilise resources more effectively away from consumption by the state towards a greater focus on production. These were radical, far-reaching reforms. In order to achieve the necessary growth African governments would be expected to incentivise farmers to boost production; devalue inflated currencies; remove state subsidies; reduce tariff barriers to open markets to international competition; enact cuts to the public sector and privatise state monopolies; and to engage in better economic management. The underlying aim was to reduce the government monopoly over the economy in favour of a market-driven approach. However, the Berg Report was not all about reductions. One section (Berg, 1981, 81–90) did stress the need for a greater focus on human development in education, health, and training to go hand in hand with any reforms, but as sweeping cuts to services were implemented these recommendations fell by the wayside, having an enormous impact on social indicators across the continent.

(van de Walle, 2001, 1, 7). Some nations such as Senegal, Ghana, Kenya, and Madagascar were all forced to take on multiple loans. In 1989, even greater western interference was justified after a re-evaluation of SAP outcomes saw the World Bank acknowledge that the expected growth rates had not been achieved. However, any failures of the programme were identified as being the lack of commitment to implementing reforms in nations such as Sierra Leone and Zambia (see World Bank, 1989, 1994). Yet given the centrality of the economy to maintaining political control through neo-patrimonialism, it is of little surprise that leaders would not fully enact fundamental changes that would jeopardise their already flimsy position. Conceding that economic change would also require political will, Africa's autocratic leaders increasingly came under the spotlight. The proposed solution in 1989 was an explicit demand for 'good governance', which coincided with the wave of democratisation in the early 1990s (see Chapter 4).

Did SAPs solve the continent's economic problems? It is difficult to make a conclusive economic judgement, but the consensus is that the effects of structural adjustment had an enormous and long-lasting impact on the political and social climate of Africa.

The World Bank's (1994) own self-congratulatory assessment of SAPs argued that the programme had been successful in not only restoring growth to Africa, but also tackling poverty. In a survey of 29 African nations, they posited that six countries (Ghana, Tanzania, the Gambia, Burkina Faso, Nigeria, and Zimbabwe) had made significant gains and 'enjoyed the strongest resurgence in economic performance' by recording GDP growth of 2% or more, through an extensive adherence to the reform programme (World Bank, 1994, 1, 57–58). Yet delving behind the headline 'improvements', by their own assessment, nine countries had made small improvements and eleven had actually regressed (World Bank, 1994, 58). However, these far from conclusive outcomes were reimagined as a success. The blame for the economic and social problems associated with SAPs was once again deflected onto African governments, such as Rwanda, Mozambique, and Cameroon, for failing to fully implement liberalisation programmes. The report declared that:

> Adjustment has contributed to faster GDP per capita growth in half the countries examined in this report, and there is every reason to think that it has helped the poor, based on the strong linkage between growth and poverty reduction elsewhere in the world. But in many adjusting African countries, policy implementation has been very partial, and growth has not shown much, if any, recovery. Often the poor would have benefited from *more* adjustment. (World Bank, 1994, 163; emphasis in original)

An alternative perspective on the SAP was provided by the UN Economic Commission on Africa (UNECA), which in a scathing report (1989, iii–iv) argued that there was no direct evidence that SAPs could be associated with GDP growth, and accused the World Bank of creating a 'mythical optimistic picture'. Furthermore, it went on to state that: 'any attempt to portray the economic situation currently prevailing in Africa in [a] rosy picture …, and to depict the effects of structural adjustment programmes as having always been positive does not only detract from the reality of the situation but is also cynical in the extreme.'

In terms of growth, the economic outcomes of structural adjustment remain unclear. There is no overarching narrative that can decisively state whether SAPs worked or not: a few countries grew, but others stagnated, or declined significantly. Whether this situation was the fault of the World Bank or the African leaders that refused to implement the full reform package, it is impossible to tell. However, in 2000, a World Bank (2000, 17) assessment of the previous 20 years recorded an overall downward economic trajectory for the continent: in 1975–1984, GDP per annum was 3.3%, in 1985–1989 it was 2.5%, and from 1990 to 1998 it was 2.3%. Admittedly several countries such as Ethiopia, Equatorial Guinea, and Uganda registered substantial improvements, but for most the situation actually worsened. The lack of sustained, positive growth meant Africa lagged far behind other continents, and was not progressing as quickly as it needed to in order to catch up. A crucial inhibitor to African growth under the SAPs regime was that the proposed solution focused on the increased production and export of primary commodities, particularly in the agricultural sector. Yet once a large number of countries started expanding their exports the result was overproduction, creating gluts on the world market and therefore a reduction in prices. The consequence was that the unequal world system was further cemented, as primary products became cheaper for industrialised nations and African producers got less revenue in return.

One conclusive outcome was that as a strategy to solve Africa's debt crisis SAPs proved wholly inappropriate and actually made the continent more indebted. According to van de Walle (2001, 6), in 1980, Africa's external debts stood at $84 billion, but by 1996 these had increased to $227 billion; even Ghana, often heralded as a success, had debts that had risen from $1.4 billion to $4.2 billion. The upshot was that by the millennium African nations continued to be highly indebted and were spending a significant proportion of their GDP servicing these debts (World Bank, 2000, 180–182). In 1996, the Heavily Indebted Poor Countries Initiative (HIPC) was set up by the IMF and World Bank to begin the process of assisting nations with unsustainable debt burdens through consolidation and debt relief, while simultaneously implementing policies to combat poverty.

Although there are questions regarding the 'success' of SAPs, the social impact they had is one of the most contentious issues regarding contemporary Africa. Not only is there little evidence to suggest improved economic growth was achieved, but the far-reaching societal consequences were catastrophic (see Image 5.1). Economic dogma and the fetish of continual growth rates driven by the market ignored the material impact the policies had on Africans, particularly the poorest. UNECA (1989, ii) argued that SAPs' 'human and social costs have often been seen as out of proportion with their real or intended benefits'. The drastic rollback of the state demanded by SAPs not only saw an increase in unemployment levels as civil services were reduced and domestic jobs were lost to international competition, but it also prompted a sharp decline in the investment and subsidies for social welfare; the expectation was that users would now pay for access to health, education, and other state services. Already impoverished African citizens could now no longer afford many basic services, which led to a decline in many of the indicators of social well-being such as literacy, life expectancy, and infant mortality. For example, in the period 1984–1997, 20 countries had 30% or more of the population living in poverty, while Chad, the Gambia, Sierra Leone, and Zambia had rates higher than 60% (World Bank, 2000, 318). Moreover, the rollback of health services coincided with a dramatic increase in HIV/AIDs across the continent, with large parts of eastern and southern Africa affected. These cuts to services fell disproportionately on those who could least afford it, especially women and children. This was a dramatic reversal of a key success in the post-colonial era. Furthermore, by reducing employment levels and service provision, people had less money available, resulting in decreased local demand for products, precipitating the rise in the informal economy (a major, yet often unaccounted, component of African economies), and extensive economic inequality.

As the state was forced to withdraw from many core functions, a new phenomenon emerged: the reliance on foreign aid and the rise of the powerful western NGO. Faced with reduced revenues many African governments were forced to rely heavily on official development assistance (ODA). Almost every African nation received official aid (the exceptions were Libya and Liberia), although the scale varied depending on need (see Table 5.4). In 1995, 25 states received aid which amounted to 14% or more of GDP, and in some cases, for example, Cape Verde, Eritrea, and Guinea-Bissau, it exceeded 25% (World Bank, 2000, 301). The consequence was that external assistance meant governments were increasingly dependent and beholden to the demands of donor institutions and nations.

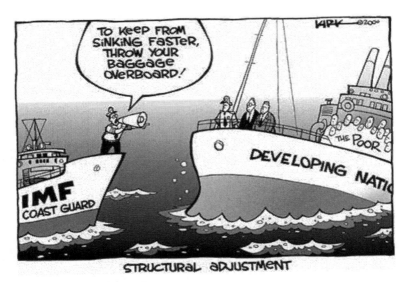

Image 5.1 Structural adjustment

Source: Kirk Anderson, www.kirk.co (2018).

Furthermore, African nations found that not only were their economic policies being dictated to from abroad, but the issues of poverty, health, and education that had been exacerbated by the reform process were now the focus of western intervention and moralising. While the rapid expansion of NGO activity (see Chapter 7) clearly cushioned some of the worst societal problems, it did little to solve the structural causes affecting poverty across the continent. Perhaps more damaging for Africa's reputation was that the competing NGOs needed to raise funds through marketing activities which perpetuated a resoundingly bleak picture of the continent, casting Africa as requiring external assistance; the continent once again needed saving.

By the end of the 1990s, it was increasingly clear that structural adjustment had not had the desired economic effect for generating sustainable long-term growth, and solving the ever worsening debt crisis. Furthermore, there was a belated realisation that the impact of conditionalities on social development indicators had set the continent back decades, harming the poorest most. The turn of the millennium thus saw a greater emphasis on campaigns for debt relief, and policies that would establish economic prosperity for Africa.

Table 5.4 Net official development assistance from donors as a share (%) of recipient GDP (select countries)

	1980	1990	1992	1994	1997
Burkina Faso	12.4	12.1	22	23.5	15.6
Burundi	12.8	23.4	28.7	33.9	12.5
Djibouti	–	45.8	24.1	26.5	17.3
Egypt	6.1	12.6	8.6	5.2	2.6
Equatorial Guinea	–	46.8	40.3	24.1	4.9
Mozambique	4.8	40.1	75.1	54.3	28
São Tomé and Príncipe	9.1	109.8	125.2	101.1	76.3
Tanzania	–	27.8	27.4	23	13.6
Zambia	8.2	14.6	32.5	21.5	15.7

Source: World Bank, African Development Indicators, 2000.

The road to recovery?

The reversal of Africa's economic fortunes since the millennium has been nothing short of dramatic, prompting a U-turn in opinion, in which the continent has now turned a corner on the path towards prosperity. Throughout the 2000s, the continent sustained impressive year-on-year increases, amounting to an average 5.5% annual GDP growth for the decade (AfDB, 2011, 253). Across Africa, nations with very different resource inheritance or economic structures have flourished; for example, Ethiopia, Mozambique, and Rwanda all made enormous gains (see Table 5.5). Indeed from 2003 to 2011 no less than 17 African nations had annual GDP growth rates of more than 6% (AfDB, 2012, 240–241). This is nothing short of remarkable when put in the context of the situation found in the 1980s and 1990s. The narrative has now begun to shift to one of Afro-positivism, in which the continent is now progressing rapidly: Africa is deemed to be 'rising' following more than a decade and a half of sustained upwards growth (Robertson & Okonjo-Iweala, 2012; Rotberg, 2013; IMF, 2014). Even the 2008 global recession did little to drastically alter Africa's rise, which offered indications that the economic revival was not simply a flash in the pan, but one that could be sustained.

How can these changes be explained? Without doubt, much of the growth had been based on high commodity prices, especially for oil

Table 5.5 Select annual GDP growth rates (%), 2002–2010

	2002	2003	2004	2005	2006	2007	2008	2009	2010
Angola	14.5	3.3	11.2	20.6	18.6	22.6	13.8	2.4	3.4
Côte d'Ivoire	-1.6	-1.7	1.6	1.8	0.7	1.6	2.3	3.8	2.4
DRC	3.5	5.8	6.6	7.8	5.6	6.3	6.2	2.8	7.2
Egypt	3.2	3.2	4.1	4.5	6.8	7.1	7.2	4.7	5.1
Equatorial Guinea	20.4	14.4	32.7	8.8	1.3	21.4	10.7	5.7	-0.8
Ethiopia	1.6	-2.2	13.6	11.8	10.8	11.5	10.8	8.8	11.4
Ghana	4.5	5.2	5.6	5.9	6.4	6.5	8.4	4.0	7.7
Kenya	0.5	2.9	5.1	5.9	6.3	7.0	1.5	2.6	5.6
Nigeria	21.3	10.2	10.5	6.5	6.0	6.4	6.0	7.0	7.8
Rwanda	9.4	2.2	7.4	9.4	9.2	7.6	11.5	6.0	7.2
Sierra Leone	27.4	9.5	7.4	7.3	7.4	6.4	5.5	3.2	5.0
Tanzania	7.2	6.9	7.8	7.4	6.7	7.1	7.4	6.0	7.0
Zimbabwe	-5.9	-17.2	-6.9	-2.2	-3.5	-3.7	-17.7	6.0	9.0
Africa	5.7	5.3	6.1	5.9	6.2	6.5	5.5	3.1	5.0

Source: Created using data from AfDB (2011), 254–255, and AfDB (2012), 242–243.

and metals, fuelled by China's insatiable demand for raw materials during the first decade of the twenty-first century; this has clearly brought about positive change, but implicitly holds many risks for Africa. But, raw materials do not constitute the whole story, as a plethora of local and international factors have provided the platform to enable transformations, which point, albeit cautiously, to a more sustainable economic future for the continent (see Box 5.4).

While in no way trying to defend structural adjustment policies, particularly given the damage they inflicted across the continent, aspects of the liberalisation agenda did result in the implementation of structural reforms that have since allowed African nations to benefit from the current global economic status quo. Africa's previously closed economies, protected by overvalued currencies, were replaced by more 'open' markets and new trade practices that have created opportunities for better international connectivity, which has benefited the continent greatly. By and large, the increasing move away from state-led development (nations such as South Africa that still retain several parastatals are anomalies), combined with the implementation of fiscally responsible policies, the reduction of debts to manageable levels, stringent efforts to curb inflation, and the build-up of foreign reserves, has created a more conducive business environment. For example, between 2005 and 2013, 20 countries in Africa were ranked among the top 50 most-improved world economies in business regulatory efficiency, with Rwanda improving the most (AfDB, 2014, 22).

These measures have enabled the private sector to flourish, where previously it was constrained by political interference. This development has begun to shift employment and wealth creation opportunities away from the public sector and into a newly expanded private sector, which generated 90% of African jobs and two-thirds of the continent's investment (AfDB, 2014, 21). In turn, these new and increased employment opportunities have begun to gradually reduce poverty levels (although still stubbornly high), enabling the growth of a visible middle class, which stands at around 350 million people across Africa. Consequently, the middle class has helped drive domestic production via the consumption of goods and services; this is particularly important, as it highlights that not all of Africa's GDP comes from commodity or services exports, but is also internally driven. However, it is important to note that the wealth of the middle classes is still underpinned primarily by commodity exports, which means that growing prosperity stills remains fragile. The urgent diversification of African economies is badly required.

There has also been a realisation by African leaders that the continent has to work together if there is going to be sustained economic uplift. As mentioned earlier in the chapter, African economies are traditionally outward-facing, with consequently very little intercontinental trade; it stood at only 14% in 2013, compared to Europe's 70% (UNCTAD, 2015, 3). In 2012, the AU adopted a decision to establish a Continental Free Trade Area (CFTA) by 2017, with the goal of uniting African countries within a single continental market for goods and services; although not implemented yet, the CFTA would perhaps realise the Pan-African dream of the 1960s. One step towards the creation of the CFTA was initiated in 2015, with the announcement of the Tripartite Free Trade Area (TFTA), which brought together three of Africa's major regional economic communities: SADC, the East African Community (EAC), and the Common Market for Eastern and Southern Africa (COMESA). If successful, these continental trading agreements could prove a crucial catalyst to sustained economic growth and dynamism (see Chapter 9).

The broader economic policy changes can be linked to the waves of democratisation, both in the early 1990s and again in the 2000s, which saw improved government policies, overseen by increasingly democratic rulers (however, this is under threat; see Chapter 4). Governments across the continent are implementing ambitious strategies to create thriving economies and move their nations towards middle-income status, such as Kenya's Vision 2030 project. The bedrock of good governance prompted a wider continental adherence to democratic norms, aided by more accountable political leadership, which has encouraged international trade to flourish. Furthermore, the broader political stability has, albeit with some major exceptions in Libya and the Horn of Africa, led to a decline in conflict and instability. A more peaceful continent has removed business uncertainty and created conditions for increased international FDI and ODA. The total external financial flows (including FDI, ODA, and remittances) to Africa were $208.3 billion in 2015, and rising to more than $220 billion in 2016 (AfDB, 2016, 52–53). The continent is gradually being regarded as a good destination for businesses and governments to invest.

It must be acknowledged that the destination of FDI is highly uneven, and a small number of nations such as Egypt, South Africa, DRC, Morocco, and Ethiopia receive the vast majority of overseas investment. Although China continues to be a crucial partner for Africa, along with other emerging economies such as Brazil and India, it must not be forgotten that traditional external partners such as the EU and the USA remain vitally important to economic development through trade and investment. Furthermore, the impact that other African nations have on facilitating investment should also be recognised, especially the South African government and businesses, which since 1994 have acted as a major investor across the continent in a range of sectors (Louw-Vaudran, 2016).

An often neglected aspect of financial inflows that has helped African nations' economies progress is remittances sent home from migrants. There are an estimated 32.6 million African migrants in either developed nations or elsewhere in Africa, and their remittances amount to $64.6 billion. Although western nations such as the USA, France, and UK account for around half of remittances, importantly African countries such as South Africa also contribute extensively to the total. For several nations, remittances are a crucial component of their economies; in Liberia, the Gambia, Comoros, and Lesotho, remittances consist of 20% of their GDPs. However, remittance flows are unstable, predicated on the prosperity of economies in the West and Middle East, and the destination of money is uneven with a significant proportion of inflows heading to North and West Africa (AfDB, 2015, 2016).

Box 5.4 Assessing Ethiopia's rapid economic growth

Since the early 2000s, Ethiopia has experienced dramatic economic transformation, assisted by average GDP growth rates of over 10% during the last decade, making it one of the fastest growing countries worldwide. For many analysts, Ethiopia's success embodies the 'Africa Rising' narrative. In fact, what makes Ethiopia's growth even more remarkable is that it has not been achieved on the back of primary commodity exports such as oil and minerals. In the 1990s, former President Meles Zenawi pronounced Ethiopia a democratic development state (although the democratic component was quietly forgotten about), which entailed significant economic reform under the direction of a strong centralised state. The ambitious economic objectives set out by the EPRDF were designed to ensure Ethiopia is a middle income country by 2020.

Without oil or metals to export, the 'miracle' relies almost entirely on government-led investment, with five-year economic models such as the Growth and Transformation Plan (2010–2015) the key engine for growth. The EPRDF-led government has since directed over 60% of total expenditure towards poverty-alleviating initiatives, including infrastructural spending on transport such as the Addis Ababa light railway, and energy projects such as the Grand Ethiopian Renaissance Dam. This state-led spending has been augmented by the growth of a diversified manufacturing base, an increase in service sector employment (worth 46.6% of GDP), and explicit efforts to support intensive commercial agriculture (38.8% of GDP) (AfDB, 2016, 287). These efforts have been assisted by growing FDI inflows, particularly from China, and external development aid, targeted increasingly at the manufacturing and retail sectors.

There are, however, some major problems with Ethiopia's 'miracle' economic growth. Much of the success has been secured under an authoritarian leadership, which crushed political opposition and dissent; the lack of democracy was justified by the ERPDF as a necessary step for achieving long-term prosperity. Furthermore, Ethiopia remains highly dependent on foreign aid to maintain its government-spending commitments, while droughts have meant that around 10 million people rely on food aid simply to survive. This brings into question whether GDP growth has actually trickled down to the poorest in society, while domestic inequality has increased (see the end of this chapter).

A major structural change, which undoubtedly accelerated African economic transformation, was widespread debt relief from western nations and institutions. In the early to mid-2000s, a series of measures were enacted which allowed for Africa's poorest nations to be unshackled from their unsustainable debts, helping to alleviate poverty. The HIPC initiative that was already in place to oversee debt reduction was augmented in 2000, by the UN Millennium Development Goals (MDGs) which were established to achieve eight ambitious targets by 2015, including the eradication of poverty, reduction in deadly diseases, and the promotion of sustainable development (UNDP, 2015). However, the progress of these initiatives was irregular (not all the targets were met by the 2015 deadline) and stymied by the obvious debt crisis afflicting the world's poorest nations.

In 2005, a groundswell of civil society action led by the Global Call for Action against Poverty, and assisted by organisations such as Make Poverty History, organised the Live8 concerts, which were designed to lobby G8 leaders into taking decisive actions. At the 2005 G8 meeting at Gleneagles, Scotland, it was acknowledged that many of the poorest nations could never pay off their debts, and simply servicing them was an inhibitor to sustained economic growth. Therefore to assist the HIPC initiative and MDGs, the G8 leaders, encouraged by then British Prime Minister Tony Blair, established the Multilateral Debt Relief Initiative (MDRI), which allowed nations that fully completed HIPC to access 100% debt relief from the IMF, World Bank, and African Development Fund (see Table 5.6). By 2018, 30 African nations had gone through the process, which amounted to $116.4 billion of debt cancelation (IMF, 2018). For some countries such as Ghana, Tanzania, and Zambia, it meant a 75% reduction in their overall debt burden (Oxfam, 2013). Understandably, African nations that achieved debt relief were subsequently able to commit to a range of developmental and economic spending policies, which had previously been unavailable due to debt servicing.

Table 5.6 African nations and multilateral debt relief efforts

Countries successfully completed HIPC/MDRI	Eligible, but non-compliant states
Benin, Burkina Faso, Burundi, Cameroon, CAR, Chad, Comoros, Côte d'Ivoire, DRC, Ethiopia, the Gambia, Ghana, Guinea, Guinea-Bissau, Liberia, Madagascar, Malawi, Mali, Mauritania, Mozambique, Niger, Republic of Congo, Rwanda, São Tomé and Príncipe, Senegal, Sierra Leone, Tanzania, Togo, Uganda, Zambia	Eritrea, Somalia, Sudan

Source: Created using data from IMF (2017), HIPC Statistics, 5–7.

Enter the dragon: China's role in Africa since the millennium

The changes outlined above have been clearly important structural steps towards improving Africa's economic fortunes, but two intertwined factors have proved fundamental to the rapid growth since 2000: rising commodity prices and the increasingly active role of China across the continent. China's rapid expansion into Africa is closely aligned with its own dramatic rise to superpower status since the turn of the millennium. The Chinese state's engagement with Africa is not new, having established links with liberation movements such as Zimbabwe's Zimbabwe African National Union (ZANU) during the Cold War, as well as funding infrastructure projects such as the construction of the TAZARA railway in the 1970s, linking Zambian copper mines with Dar es Salaam in Tanzania. However, the renewed interest with Africa was rekindled in the 1990s, when China implemented the 'Go out strategy' in 1999, which was designed to gain access to raw materials and open up opportunities for its businesses on the international market. The consequence has been a staggering increase in political and economic ties across the continent from Algeria to South Africa. China is now a visible and active actor across Africa, with virtually every nation, not just commodity exporters, benefiting from Chinese investments (Image 5.1). Total trade with the continent (see Chart 5.1) has grown exponentially from $6.4 billion in 1999 to over $221.6 billion by 2014; its key African trading partners are Angola, South Africa, Sudan, Nigeria, and Egypt. In the same period, China's share of African trade grew rapidly from 4.4% to 21%. China has been crucial for Africa's economic upturn. It is easy to get carried away by China's expanded role and presence, but it is important to recognise that there is not a single overarching 'Africa plan' by Beijing, with many transactions and investments specific to an individual locale run by Chinese companies and entrepreneurs, and not just the state.

A main priority for China had been to secure access to energy supplies and raw materials to fuel its domestic growth. Offering unparalleled trade opportunities, concessional loans, and cheap infrastructural development, China secured cooperation agreements and preferential access to key African commodity exporters. For Africa's export-led nations such as Angola (oil), Equatorial Guinea (oil), Cameroon (commercial logging), and Zambia (copper), the commodity boom of the 2000s was extremely beneficial, as demand and thus prices rose rapidly, which in turn improved domestic budgets, providing much needed revenue. Furthermore, in its attempt to secure future energy reserves, China provided the impetus and expertise to expand oil exploration in countries such as Sudan, Mozambique, Tanzania, and Uganda, as well as funding new mining concessions for iron ore and metals in the DRC.

A myth commonly promoted in western circles is that China's unrelenting focus on raw materials entails a 'new scramble for Africa' because Beijing has gained exclusive access to commodities to meet its current and future economic needs. However, the data shows that Chinese interests and investments are prevalent across the continent (Brautigam, 2015); while resource exporters such as Gabon and South Africa remain central to Chinese interests, those non-commodity exporters including Kenya and Malawi have also benefited greatly. Not only is China buying African raw materials, but in return it is exporting significant quantities of consumer goods to the continent; products made in China are now ubiquitous in shops and markets across the continent, with companies such as electronics firm Huawei establishing a strong foothold.

A central component of China's economic interactions with the continent has been massive investment into infrastructural projects. Many African states have long suffered from poor infrastructure capabilities lacking reliable energy supplies or adequate transport networks,

Image 5.2 Ethiopian man standing in front of a Chinese billboard in Addis Ababa

Source: Eric Lafforgue/Art in All of Us/Corbis via Getty Images.

which has harmed economic development; a World Bank report (Foster & Briceño-Garmendia, 2009) argued that the continent's poor infrastructure cut economic growth by 2% per year and reduced productivity by 40%. Even leading African economies such as Nigeria and South Africa suffer from power shortages, with so-called 'load shedding' causing huge problems for the industrial sector. While institutions such as the World Bank have long acknowledged the infrastructural deficit of the continent, it is China that has taken the lead in rectifying the situation. Backed by state-led initiatives, China is the largest global source of finance for infrastructure projects in Africa, amounting to $13.4 billion (Baker & McKenzie, 2015, 15). Across the continent, projects are being established to fund the construction of roads, railways, energy projects, and communication networks in countries including Sudan, Nigeria, DRC, and Ethiopia. For example, the enormous investment into communications has allowed several nations such as Kenya and Rwanda to make vast technological leaps, especially in regards to internet and mobile networks that hold the potential to kick-start tech-industries and reach out to previously economically disenfranchised citizens (see Chapter 10 for more details); Kenya's M-Pesa and Mozambique's M-Kesh are two such instances of mobile technologies enabling people, even in remote communities, to transfer money simply and quickly via their phones, without the need for traditional banking services.

The investment in African infrastructure looks likely to continue for some time, and will be crucial to future economic development. In December 2015, President Xi Jinping announced at the China–Africa Summit in Johannesburg $10 billion for the China–Africa Development Fund, as well as launching the China–Africa Industrial Cooperation Fund, committing a further $10 billion of investment; the increased focus on industrialisation as part of these plans will go some way to facilitate the continent's much needed economic diversification.

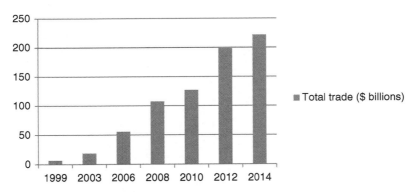

Chart 5.1 China's total trade with Africa

Source: Created using data from the China Statistical Yearbook, 2000–2015, available at: www.stats.gov.cn/english/statisticaldata/AnnualData/

China's interests are not limited solely to accessing resources and establishing economic infrastructure, but have also funded a range of other projects, including the construction of the new AU buildings in Ethiopia, as well as a host of football stadiums across the continent including in Benin, Gabon, and Mozambique. The focus on infrastructure and building projects makes not only economic sense, but also buys political capital. It must be stressed that Chinese investment and trade with Africa is by no means benevolent, and is serving Beijing's needs rather than those of the continent (see Box 5.5); the terms of trade are heavily stacked in China's favour, with its 'investment in and trade with Africa represent[ing] 3 percent and 5 percent of its global investment and trade, respectively' (Sun, 2014, 2). Consequently, Africa needs China for its economic well-being far more than Beijing does.

Another important dimension of Chinese investment and trade is an explicit policy of non-interference, which has made it an attractive partner for many of the continent's less democratically aligned governments. When we consider western insistence on conditions and good governance attached to aid and loans, China has provided a powerful and appealing alternative. For autocratic leaders such as Chadian President Déby and Sudan's al-Bashir Chinese interests have been extremely useful in propping up not only their political power base, but also their ailing economies. For example, Chinese loans proved very useful for former Zimbabwean President Robert Mugabe to circumvent western economic sanctions of Zimbabwe.

Box 5.5 China's challenges

It is sometimes difficult to distinguish between fact and fiction when considering China's impact on Africa. While China's interactions with African nations have clearly been enormously beneficial, there is some concern and criticism of the uneven relationship that has developed; in reality, the continent is very much the junior partner. A series of examples highlight the mounting grievances, which range from ignoring environmental concerns, poor health and safety standards, the lack of local jobs being created, and the destruction of local industries. In Niger, the government protested against the poor deal they received from China, arguing that they had practically given away their oil resources, while Chinese refinery workers and engineers were brought in, thus providing almost no benefit for the state or ordinary citizens. It is estimated that around 1 million Chinese workers now live across the continent. In Chad, it was discovered that China National Petroleum was dumping crude oil in ditches south of the capital, N'Djamena, and then making Chadian workers remove it with no protection, prompting the government to close China's interests in the country (*New York Times*, 2013). At the Collum Coal Mine in Zambia during a strike over pay and working conditions in 2012, mine workers killed a Chinese foreman and injured several others in protest. The imbalanced power relationship has also seen imported Chinese products flood African markets, sweeping away domestic industries, and consequently causing job losses; by the late 2000s, the South African textiles industry was severely damaged. Moreover, in January 2018 the asymmetrical power dynamic was dramatically highlighted when China was alleged to have electronically 'bugged' the Chinese-built AU headquarters to access its confidential materials. These were hardly the actions of an ally with the best interests of the continent in mind.

A sustainable recovery?

There is little doubt that the African continent has taken enormous steps in the right direction, but the economic 'miracle' that has been so widely lauded must come with some serious health warnings. The first observation is that growth across the continent is highly uneven. The continental picture shows East Africa continuing to thrive, yet northern and southern Africa struggling to make significant headway; even within these regions, some nations such as Ethiopia far outstrip those of their immediate neighbours. What is apparent is that there is not an overarching economic story for Africa. Even though the continent still continues to record positive GDP growth, unlike the 1980s, the average rates have begun to stall, which has set alarm bells ringing about the depth and sustainability of Africa's transformation (Table 5.7).

Since 2012, Africa has increasingly experienced declining growth rates triggered by international and local factors. As previously indicated, China proved to be a major catalyst for the continent's economic revival, yet its own supercharged domestic growth has slowed considerably. Moreover, China's slowdown coincided with a stagnant international economy that resulted in sluggish growth and declining demand for raw materials. A sharp fall in commodity prices followed including oil, iron

Table 5.7 Select annual GDP growth rates (%), 2011–2017

	2011	2012	2013	2014	2015	2016	2017
Angola	3.9	5.2	6.8	4.8	3.8	3.3	3.5
Côte d'Ivoire	−4.7	10.7	8.7	7.9	8.8	8.6	8.3
DRC	6.9	7.2	8.5	9.2	7.7	7.0	8.0
Egypt	1.8	2.2	2.1	2.2	4.2	4.3	4.5
Equatorial Guinea	7.7	9.5	−12.1	2.3	−10.2	−8.0	−3.4
Ethiopia	11.2	8.6	10.6	10.3	10.2	8.1	7.7
Kenya	6.1	4.6	5.7	5.3	5.5	6.0	6.4
Libya	−61.4	92.1	−12.3	−23.5	−6.0	−0.8	3.9
Nigeria	4.9	4.3	5.4	6.2	3.0	3.8	5.0
Sierra Leone	6.0	15.2	20.1	4.6	−21.5	0.2	3.7
South Africa	3.2	2.2	2.2	1.5	1.3	0.7	1.8
Tanzania	7.9	5.1	7.3	7.0	7.0	7.2	7.2
Zimbabwe	11.9	10.6	4.5	3.8	1.5	1.6	3.1
Africa	2.9	6.4	3.9	3.7	3.6	3.7	4.5

Source: Created using data from AFDB (2016), 338–339.

ore, platinum, and agricultural products, affecting export-dependent nations such as Mauritania and Zambia the most. In particular, the rapid drop in global oil prices by around 70% from 2014 to 2016 was especially harmful for oil-rich nations such as Nigeria, Equatorial Guinea, and Gabon. In two countries, Angola and South Sudan, where oil revenues constituted over 90% of government budgets, the global price collapse negatively impacted on state finances, prompted an increase in inflation, led to a drop in foreign currency reserves, and impinged on other economic activities.

The often overlooked structural flaw in the 'miracle growth' narrative was the unreformed nature of most African economies, which remain overwhelmingly reliant on exporting raw materials. Perhaps more surprising is that African economies have become more reliant on primary resources than ever before. The continent experienced growth on the back of primary export activity from 2000, yet most governments failed to implement policy initiatives aimed at diversifying economic activity. What should have happened is a greater shift towards industrialisation, which has been implemented relatively successfully in Ethiopia and

Kenya. However, for the majority of the continent this has not been the case. If diversification has materialised it has often been in the service sector, which does not generate production or significant GDP growth. Remarkably, Africa has experienced de-industrialisation, when in fact industrialisation is fundamental for providing the basic platform for sustainable growth and creating employment. Figures indicate that manufacturing as a percentage of GDP dropped to 10.1% of all economic activity on the continent in 2013, down from 13.2% in 2000 (UNCTAD, 2016, 356). An urgent task of African leaders is to implement viable industrialisation policies in order to give their economies greater opportunities in the future (UNECA, 2016).

A worrying development reminiscent of the 1970s is that revenue shortfalls from declining commodity exports have been mitigated by increased government spending and external borrowing to maintain budgets in nations including Cameroon, Republic of Congo, and Tanzania (IMF, 2016, 4–7). Once again, the result has been a rapid rise in several nations' external debt, exacerbated by higher borrowing costs since 2015. As a consequence, several nations are once again in serious financial difficulties. In terms of their debt as a percentage of GDP, the following countries have been identified as at significant risk: Cape Verde (91%), São Tomé and Príncipe (91%), Mozambique (69.9%), Republic of Congo (52.6%), and Angola (46.8%) (IMF, 2016, 107). In 2015, Ghana was forced to turn to the IMF for a $918 million bailout after debts rose unsustainably and growth nosedived (IMF, 2015).

A further set of destabilising factors since 2010 include pandemics, environmental change, and political conflict, which continue to have a major impact on economic growth and development. In West Africa, the 2013–2016 Ebola epidemic that broke out in Guinea, Liberia, and Sierra Leone halted almost all economic activity in these countries. These three countries rely on exporting commodities such as iron ore and aluminium, so were also hit hard by the drop in global prices. The outbreak of Ebola has since been curbed (see Chapter 7), but it will take some time for a full economic recovery. Environmental factors which are hard to prevent have also been instrumental in impacting on regional economies. In 2015–2017, southern Africa experienced a severe drought affecting Malawi, Namibia, South Africa, and Zimbabwe with serious consequences for agricultural production, forcing governments to increase expensive food imports. Finally, ongoing political instability and violence in countries such as Burundi, Libya, Somalia, and South Sudan have prevented economic development and investment from growing.

A potentially looming crisis for many African governments will be how best to deal with the continent's growing population in the coming decades. For authors such as Rotberg (2013), the demographic changes are a dividend which will allow the potential of a youthful population to be harnessed to boost productivity and growth across the continent. However, for this to occur there will have to be faster and more sustained growth, and a greater focus on job creation. The above points indicate that leaders across the continent will have to move swiftly and decisively in order to create meaningful employment opportunities for Africa's burgeoning youth population. However, an alternative, bottom-up initiative for job creation has emerged across the continent through microlending schemes at a community level, especially led by women. Women own about 48% of all enterprises in Africa, but have long suffered from the inability to access traditional finance. This situation prompted collective action to enable change in countries such as South Africa and Kenya where groups of women have come together to gain funds through microfinancing, which is designed to limit lender risk and enable small businesses to grow (UN, 2009). The result has been the rise of grass-root strategies to overcome economic marginalisation.

An important question that is often ignored concerns whether growth rates, FDI, and trade actually have an effect on ordinary citizens? The statistics indicating the emergence of a vibrant middle class across Africa are celebrated as demonstrating that tangible material benefits are emerging. Or are they? The African Development Bank (AfDB, 2014) definition of middle class is someone who earns more than $2 per day, which is somewhat pushing the boundaries of credibility. It would appear that if you earn more than the global poverty line ($1.25/day) you are now ranked as middle class. More crucially, earning $2 per day is hardly likely to ensure enough purchasing power to consume the goods one might expect of a middle-class lifestyle, or to generate economic growth. As a consequence, the African Development Bank definition has been criticised for overestimating the size of the middle classes, and for ignoring factors such as expenditure, professional attitudes, and lifestyle. However, the growth of sizeable middle classes across Africa will be vital for generating future economic prosperity, yet in their current form, there is little chance that they will prove to be the vehicle for sustained growth that analysts and politicians are hoping for.

Likewise we must be cautious about obsessively focusing on GDP growth rates. Can we link GDP growth with societal uplift? Unfortunately, the statistics do not bear out this assertion. The GDP figures recorded by nations such as Ethiopia and Tanzania are extremely impressive, and are the envy of many. However, the GDP statistics bear little correlation with poverty alleviation; even the IMF (Martinez & Mlachila, 2013, 22) conceded this point. For instance, sub-Saharan

Africa's gross national income (GNI) per person is $3,339, which places the continent at the bottom compared to other developing regions. Perhaps what is most surprising is that nations with the highest GDP rates since 2000 have among the lowest GNIs on the continent. For example, Côte d'Ivoire, Ethiopia, Kenya, Mozambique, Rwanda, and Tanzania all have achieved improved GDPs, but have among the lowest GNIs at less than $3,000 per person. In comparison, those with slow or declining GDP growth such as Algeria, Egypt, Seychelles, and South Africa all have GNIs above $12,000 (UNHDR, 2015, 246–249). Furthermore, as Table 5.8 demonstrates, a significant proportion of Africans still live below the international poverty line. The question then to consider is whether the impressive economic growth is actually trickling down to the majority in the form of employment and improved wages. The statistics would indicate that this is simply not the case. For example, in 2018 Nigeria had the largest number of people living in extreme poverty globally, with an estimated 86.9 million of the population falling into this category. The reality is that the rich have got richer, and the poorer have got poorer. Inequality across Africa has actually increased, demonstrated by the Gini co-efficient: six of the top ten most unequal societies are African. Therefore, once we delve behind the overarching figures, we soon discover a very different picture, one of persistent inequality and poverty.

Table 5.8 Select nations, percentage of population living on less than $1.25/day

Nation	Percentage of population living below international poverty line of $1.25 a day
Benin	51.6
Burundi	81.3
CAR	62.8
DRC	87.7
Ethiopia	36.8
Liberia	83.8
Mozambique	60.7
Nigeria	62.0
Tanzania	43.5
Zambia	74.3

Source: Created using data from the UN Development Report (2015) http://report.hdr.undp. org/, 228–229.

Is it legitimate to claim whether Africa is 'rising' economically? The continent has undoubtedly experienced a dramatic revival in its fortunes since 2000, and many nations have begun the process of transforming their economies for the better. The outcome has been sustained growth rates, which in turn has contributed to a far more positive outlook for Africa. This is something that should be rightly praised. But to assert that the whole continent is rising offers only a partial truth, masking a range of factors that once examined more closely are far from rosy. The structure of African economies still remains dangerously imbalanced, and the overreliance on commodities continues to leave the continent at the mercy of international trends. African leaders must take urgent steps towards diversifying their economies in the future, or current issues will persist. Connected to the need for economic restructuring, there has to be conscious efforts to ensure the fruits of GDP growth actually reach ordinary people and lift them out of poverty. There is much to be optimistic about, but there is plenty of work still to be done.

 Further reading

A good starting point on Africa's post-colonial economic inheritance would be Samir Amin's (1973) *Neo-colonialism in West Africa*, as well as Kwame Nkrumah's (1965) perspective in *Neo-colonialism: The Last Stage of Imperialism*. For more information on the economic crises, important analyses are Nicolas van de Walle's (2001) *African Economies and the Politics of Permanent Crisis, 1979–1999*, Giles Mohan's (2000) *Structural Adjustment: Theory, Practice and Impacts*, Thandika Mkandawire and Charles Soludo's (1999) *Our Continent, Our Future: African Perspectives on Structural Adjustment*, and Gavin Williams's (1994) 'Why structural adjustment is necessary and why it doesn't work'. For the economist's perspective, see Paul Collier's (2008) *The Bottom Billion: Why the Poorest Countries Are Failing and What Can be Done About It*, as well as the various World Bank reports, including the Berg Report, *Accelerated Development in Southern Africa: An Agenda for Africa* (Berg, 1981). A crucial book to consult when considering the problem of data collection and its interpretation is Morten Jerven's (2015) *Africa: Why Economists Get It Wrong*. Finally, to get a sense of the changing economic narratives, see Robert Rotberg's (2013) *Africa Emerges*, Meine Pieter van Dijk's (2009) *The New Presence of China in Africa*, and Deborah Brautigam's (2009) *The Dragon's Gift: The Real Story of China in Africa*.

6 POLITICAL VIOLENCE

One of the most powerful external images regarding Africa is of a continent beset by violence, political conflict, and instability. Such a pessimistic narrative of violent unrest was reinforced in the 1990s, a decade which witnessed a dramatic upsurge not only in the number of conflicts in the post-Cold War era, but also in the brutality of them. The most notable examples occurred in Rwanda and Sierra Leone where the violence was largely directed towards civilian populations. The continent has experienced a number of debilitating conflicts in the post-independence era, which have been enormously destructive, killing millions of people, displacing millions more, while disrupting economic activities, destroying infrastructure, straining societal bonds, and damaging political institutions. The prevalence of conflict, in its various forms, has been a major impediment to development and stability for many post-colonial African states. For example, since 1956, a third of the world's civil wars have occurred in Africa. The consequences have been predictably catastrophic, and certainly perpetuated many of the negative external perspectives of Africa.

However, developing a true understanding of why Africa has experienced so many conflicts is certainly lacking from most depictions of the continent. The common explanations verge towards the simplistic and mono-causal, reducing specific and often localised occurrences to a narrow set of tags that encompass factors including the legacies of colonialism, greed, grievance, resources, religion, and ethnicity. Underpinning some of these reductive assessments is an implicit level of racism, particularly in relation to ethnicity. A widely held misconception is the notion that the 'tribal' or ethnic composition of African society is a key precursor to primordial outbreaks of inter-ethnic conflict; the early reporting of the Rwandan genocide is testament to such sentiments (Thompson, 2007, 252–53). Furthermore, blaming the ills of colonialism as a core factor for conflict is a highly problematic approach. While the pervasive and long-lasting effects of colonialism cannot be discounted entirely, particularly in reference to the wars of liberation, for example in Algeria and Mozambique, they still do not offer a full explanation for conflict. The colonial interpretation for violence becomes increasingly problematic when you consider the variance in the types of European rule, the different post-independence trajectories (i.e. that many nations have in fact remained peaceful), and that such an argument removes African agency from the picture (see Chapters 3 and 4). Undoubtedly, all of the various factors mentioned have, in different nations and specific circumstances, played a part in contributing to violence, but importantly, they rarely act as the primary cause. As always, the reality is far less clear-cut.

Instead, when looking for explanations for many of the outbreaks of conflict, the underlying cause is frequently the retention or pursuit of power, in which the utilisation of violence serves elite ambitions, cloaked by pretexts such as ethnic mobilisation or ideological affinity. In part, the system of neo-patrimonial governance discussed in Chapter 4 contains inherent characteristics which can create the parameters for violence through declining legitimacy, political instability and weakness, factionalism, and exclusionary social dynamics. For example, exclusion from the political system has been a key component of neo-patrimonialism. This exclusion can in certain circumstances provide the conditions and motivations for revolt from marginalised groups; yet importantly, the primary impetus for rebellion remains inherently political. Although neo-patrimonialism does not intrinsically establish the framework for violence, instability during times of political crisis increases the likelihood of conflict dramatically as patronage networks crumble, exemplified by the upsurge of unrest during the democratisation process of the early 1990s (Reno, 2007). The consequence is that weak political entities are more likely to utilise violence in an effort to retain power given the winner-takes-all nature of African politics, while simultaneously, the very same weakness of centralised authority creates the opportunities for non-state interests to act.

There are many forms of political conflict and violence across Africa, encompassing a range of different situations including intra-state conflicts, such as the Uganda–Tanzania War in 1978–1979; state-based conflicts where governments engage in the use of armed force targeting at least one opposing group challenging its authority, for instance the Angolan Civil War (1975–2002); non-state armed conflict, comprising rebel groups, militias, and Islamist jihadists, functioning on the periphery of weak states, which fight not only the government, but other similar groups as well (Cilliers & Schünemann, 2013), including, but not limited to, the Lord's Resistance Army (LRA) in central-eastern Africa, and al-Shabaab in Somalia; and by no means finally, riots and protests, often connected to contested elections, or service delivery, which have occurred in multiple nations since the turn of the millennium, such as Egypt, Kenya, and South Africa. The Armed Conflict Location and Event Data Project (ACLED, 2017, 2), which has been recording and mapping all these reported instances of political violence and conflict across the continent since 1997, found that while violence and conflict remain high, the nature of unrest is changing as 'battles and large scale wars are on the decline, as they have been for quite some time. In their place are multiple, co-existing agents who engage in a variety of strategies to make their place within the political landscape.' What transpires is that violence remains a key mechanism for elites to stake their position within the political system.

While the chapter stresses the need for readers to appreciate the wide variance in the nature, form, and causality of violence across the continent since decolonisation, it will only serve as a window to examine a representative few themes and examples due to the sheer scale and range of case studies that could be consulted. Moreover, efforts at peacekeeping and conflict resolution will be examined in Chapter 9.

Political structures

As will be argued throughout this chapter, the crucial underlying factor behind armed conflict in Africa is political. The general overview of autocratic or neo-patrimonial forms of governance across Africa, as well as a long-running democratic deficit evident in many states, has established the conditions for conflict. The prominent characteristics of neo-patrimonial rule (Chapter 4) promote a fragmentary and factionalised system of governance premised on exclusionary practices in the political and economic spheres. Although this system of governance does not intrinsically lead to armed violence, the degree to which 'political inequalities' are entrenched through government policies has a major influence on the likelihood that disenfranchised groups will turn to conflict (Raleigh, 2014, 93).

African governments have long grappled with issues of extending their legitimacy and political authority over their citizens, and distributing a nation's resources. Under neo-patrimonialism, when any one of these factors begins to weaken, the fragile social contract can start to crumble. By creating schisms within society, and with limited opportunities for democratic alternatives, neo-patrimonialism can establish the incentives for groups to resort to violence as a mechanism for enacting change against autocratic leaders. This was highlighted by the Africa Centre for Security Studies (2016), which found there was a strong correlation between autocratic rule and political violence across the continent (see Map 6.1). According to ACLED (2017, 2–3), 'across Africa, governments and citizens have lived in states of disorder that reflect the political dynamics of

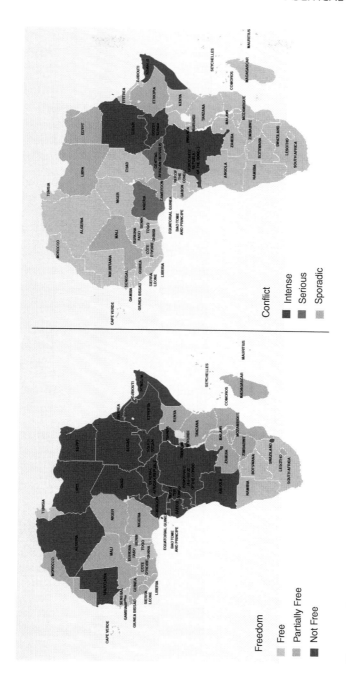

Map 6.1 Africa Centre for Security Studies 2016 map of autocracy and conflict

Source: http://africacenter.org/spotlight/overlapping-effects-autocracy-conflict-africa/

the moment', and while there are clearly many different ways to 'oppose, challenge and enforce governments and government policy', the increasing number of incidents in countries such as Burundi, Ethiopia, and Mozambique demonstrates that violence is frequently used as a political instrument. While political conflict is most commonly found in those areas experiencing civil wars or rebel insurgencies such as Libya, South Sudan, and Somalia, it is important to note that many nations that are not in an overt state of crisis remain susceptible to violence. For example, in Gabon, Morocco, and South Africa violent protests have occurred as dissent against the electoral process or the access to services escalated. In turn these protests have been met by increasingly forceful government responses to subdue the opposition. As a consequence, both state and non-state political elites across Africa realise that they can 'use violence to influence political dynamics or consolidate their position vis à vis other competitors' (ACLED, 2017, 4). With the lack of alternative options for change, it means that violence remains a potent weapon in the political process across the continent.

In the post-colonial era, which witnessed the widespread implementation of one-party states or exclusionary policy decisions, the only way to achieve political change was through rebellion or a military coup (Chapter 4). In several instances, including the Igbo secessionist attempt in Biafra (the eastern region of Nigeria) in 1967–1970, a flawed electoral process, the inability of the central authority to create an inclusive governing dispensation, and perceived ethnic exclusion, all created the conditions for violent conflict. Likewise, the civil war in Chad was prompted by President Ngarta Tombalbaye's imposition of a one-party state in 1963, and the diversion of the exclusive spoils of power to the Sara ethnic group which sparked a localised rebellion against his rule in 1965. The rebellion, however, descended into over two decades of conflict as state functions and authority all but collapsed, with large swathes of Chad subject to armed rebel groups, violent reprisals, and foreign intervention (particularly from Libya after 1973) operating in the areas outside of the limited influence or control of the central government.

By the 1990s, a large number of conflicts had emerged across the continent as the fragile economic and political balance began to crumble, exacerbated by a series of interconnected crises that revealed the inherent weaknesses of many African states. Neo-patrimonial rule was under threat like never before as the end of the Cold War brought with it diminishing external military and economic support, combined with local and international demands for democratisation. Elite legitimacy was further eroded by a range of grievances including the shrinking resource base needed to sustain neo-patrimonial cronyism; the inability of state institutions to function adequately; widespread public dissatisfaction; and exclusion from the political process (Chabal & Daloz, 1999, 37). Moreover, two academic studies on guerrilla insurgencies in Africa (Clapham, 1998; Bøås & Dunn, 2007) both identified frustrations over the lack of political opportunities which contributed to armed activities by opposition groups, where they raged 'against the machine' of the failing state.

Without the economic resources to maintain power (see Chapter 5), violence increasingly became the only tool of ensuring elite survival. Yet the very nature of the neo-patrimonial state meant it was extremely difficult for centralised authorities to exert influence over an entire country, which increased the potential for rebellions to emerge on the periphery. Indeed, as leaders such as Samuel Doe (Liberia, 1980–1990) found, the fragmented and uneven nature of political legitimacy, a declining economic base, and a demoralised and purposefully weakened military (to avoid coups) meant that relatively small groups such as Charles Taylor's National Patriotic Front of Liberia (NPFL) could easily challenge state structures. Furthermore, within the wider context of the Cold War collapse, there was a surfeit of weapons available from the former Soviet bloc, which arms dealers were more than happy to sell to emerging rebel groups across the continent. Rebel groups across Africa were thus in a position to escalate their armed challenges at a point when many states were least able to respond effectively. Throughout the 1990s, the twin pressures of economic collapse and political crisis (especially the move towards democratisation) had established the platform for a range of conflicts to emerge against ailing leaders, for example in Liberia, Sierra Leone, Somalia, Rwanda, and Zaire (DRC).

Although there has been a shift towards greater democratisation since the millennium, the nature of the political system across Africa has not altered drastically; a lack of legitimacy, insufficient resources, corruption, and political exclusion still prevail. The slow pace of change has consequently meant that political violence continues to trouble several nations. While the number of interstate conflicts and civil wars has notably declined, it is evident that violence continues to manifest itself across Africa, as governments and non-state actors resort to coercion for political purposes. For example, since the overthrow of Colonel Gaddafi in 2011, the breakdown of central authority in Libya has meant that internecine violence is widespread with rebel groups using armed force within the broader political vacuum to seek ultimate power. In 2018, the country was divided between the internationally recognised Tobruk government, and a host of rival groups including the National Salvation government, all of which lacked sufficient legitimacy, authority, or power to unite Libya. The fragmentation of Libya socially and politically only aggravated the ongoing violence. Furthermore, Somalia has been beset by violence and conflict since the late 1980s, and despite carefully managed presidential elections in February 2017, the country remains affected by instability. The UN-aided government in Mogadishu is ineffective and lacks authority, hampered by the country's clan divisions and the presence of al-Shabaab in large parts of Somalia, which continues to disrupt any efforts to implement a functioning government. The result has been instability and political violence against state institutions and civilians.

However, the recent trend in conflict across Africa has not been the emergence of insurgent rebel groups which so characterised the violence of the 1990s, but rather the increasing utilisation of militias for political purposes. Raleigh (2016, 284) has argued that political elites within and outside of state structures have enlisted the use of militias to in order to 'compete over access to power, settle territorial and resource disputes, strengthen local power disparities, and continue historical disagreements'. These militias are most commonly found in situations where weak governments are struggling to maintain power (CAR) or during elections (Côte d'Ivoire, 2010–2011 and DRC 2016), where politicians battle it out over the spoils of office. The growing use of political militias is directly linked to competing elite interests, who are attempting to gain access to power. Therefore the violence that these militias cause is not linked to traditional interpretations such as ethnicity or resource allocation per se, but are instead facilitated and utilised by different elite actors who rely on these organisations to influence the prevailing political system. Examples of these militia movements include the War Veterans in Zimbabwe, who had played a role in preserving Robert Mugabe and ZANU-PF's power, while the Imbonerakure in Burundi were extremely violent during the 2016 electoral unrest within the country.

Another key development has been the growing willingness of governments across the continent to resort to repressive violence against civilians to counteract unrest, witnessed in Cameroon, Egypt, Ethiopia, and Sudan. For example, in September 2016, Ali Bongo extended his grasp on power by using Gabon's security forces to crush public protests following a disputed and closely run election, which saw street protests turn violent. However, the most serious government repression has been in Ethiopia, which experienced regular bouts of unrest between late 2015 and early 2018 in the Oromia region of the country, with protesters predominantly targeting disputed state development projects. Facing sustained unrest, the EPRDF government implemented a state of emergency that was renewed yet again in February 2018, cracked down on internet access, and resorted to increasing levels of violence to crush the opposition that has left an estimated 1,000 people killed, and 29,000 more arrested.

When considering political violence in Africa we must therefore look to systems of governance to understand some of the root causes. At its heart, elite competition, driven by factionalism, weak government institutions, and the desire to gain access to political power and resources, has been instrumental in creating the conditions in which violence can flourish. In some settings, violence has become a key mechanism within the political process as entrenched governments or non-state actors seeking positions of power utilise force for their own ends. Those political leaders who are willing or able to exert the most force are then best placed to impose their will or influence on the political process.

The impact of the Cold War

In the common narratives of the Cold War, Africa is regularly ignored or relegated to a mere footnote in the public discourse of the global super-power rivalry. However, such a perspective is a disservice, and wilfully neglects the sheer impact that the Cold War had across the continent; as Ryszard Kapuscinski (2003) argued, 'the Cold War in Africa is one of the darkest, most disgraceful pages in contemporary history'. The implications and influence of the Cold War were far-reaching and profound, and in terms of violence, played a decisive part in escalating conflicts in Angola, Ethiopia, and Somalia. The Cold War in Africa was very much 'hot', and an estimated 2.5 million people died in the combined conflicts in Angola and Ethiopia.

The decolonisation process that swept across Africa (see Chapters 3 and 4) from the mid-1950s onwards coincided with the mounting geopolitical tensions between the USA and the Soviet Union, which had wide-ranging impacts for many nations. With political and military deadlock in the northern hemisphere, the independence of Africa provided the superpowers the prospect of exporting their ideologies, securing new allies, and safeguarding areas of strategic interest. The resulting rivalry placed new leaders in an insidious position in this global game of chess, as the two major powers competed for influence and allegiance on a rapidly changing continent. The Cold War in Africa started slowly, with gradual and pragmatic, rhetorical, and financial interventions predominantly in northern and central Africa, such as the Soviet Union's support for Egypt in the finalisation of the Aswan High Dam. For the Socialist bloc, particularly the Soviet Union and Cuba (although China, the GDR, and Yugoslavia were also active at various points), interest in Africa was in part motivated by aiding oppressed peoples (the Southern African liberation movements), preventing the west from gaining strategic advantages (Somalia), promoting international socialism (Ethiopia and Mozambique), and pragmatic support for those requesting help (Guinea and Egypt). The west was similarly driven by strategic concerns (Morocco and South Africa), ideological containment of communism by aiding 'friendly tyrants', and supporting 'moderate' political groups (Congo/Zaire), as well as economic and political considerations (Kenya).

While it could be perceived that the Cold War prompted a series of unwarranted external interventions, many African leaders actively courted foreign support; the superpowers could not have acted as they did without domestic collaboration by elites who chose to engage with them. In several cases, the division between the capitalist and socialist worlds created myriad opportunities for development and security. For some African leaders, the Cold War was enormously beneficial for their rule, as powerful external patrons provided international legitimacy, support, and economic assistance. For example, President Mobutu was extremely adept at exploiting these global tensions to his own advantage, receiving huge amounts of military and economic aid from the USA. However, nations such as Ethiopia and Somalia were far less fortunate as the superpowers became increasingly belligerent and interventionist – their actions turning what were localised battles for political power into much more internationalised conflicts, bringing with them untold violence and destruction. Moreover, for those not embroiled in overt conflict, the Cold War led to the militarisation of the continent, which resulted in the western and eastern powers supplying huge quantities of military hardware.

By the 1960s, African decolonisation was incomplete; with the white minority regimes particularly in Southern Africa steadfastly refusing to grant majority rule, armed liberation movements emerged across the region. Southern Africa is not usually regarded as a key Cold War battleground, but it had an enormous regional impact as the Soviet bloc, Cuba, China, and the west all became entangled in various ways. Movements such as the ANC, the Mozambique Liberation Front (FRELIMO), and ZANU all adopted some form of socialist ideology and organisational tropes; in turn, this attracted the attention of both the Soviet Union and the USA. For many of the liberation movements, the support of the Soviet bloc maintained their struggles through the provision of weapons, training, and financial aid (Shubin, 2008; Graham, 2015). For example, in Mozambique, Guinea-Bissau, and Rhodesia, guerrilla fighters trained and armed by the Soviet bloc were able to carve out liberated zones in which they could launch attacks, predominantly against the security forces of the white minority state, which deeply concerned the USA (Westad, 2007, 213). The insurgencies and counter-insurgency strategies destabilised Southern Africa, creating a cycle of violence and instability as Marxist-backed liberation movements battled western-funded white minority regimes. When Mozambique gained its independence in 1975, guerrilla movements such as ZANU and the ANC were able to use the country as a base from which to target Rhodesia and South Africa, fuelling a wider escalation of violence in both countries.

The emergence of independent, Marxist-inspired regimes in Angola and Mozambique provided support to other socialist-backed liberation movements in Southern Africa. This in turn was utilised by the South African government as a propaganda tool to gain crucial western support for the morally bankrupt apartheid system. South Africa positioned itself as a Cold War warrior and a strategically important anti-communist state. By the 1980s, the 'threat of communism' saw South Africa regularly impinge state sovereignty across the region to target the military bases of the ANC and the South West African People's Organisation (SWAPO), carry out extra-judicial killings and bombing raids, as well as destroy the infrastructure of neighbouring nations, with socialist-governed Mozambique suffering the most (Hanlon, 1986). Without the shield of the Cold War, Pretoria would have been unable to carry out such actions, or for so long, without the tacit diplomatic approval of western powers in the name of confronting communism.

Box 6.1 The Congo Crisis

An important example of how the Cold War exacerbated and perpetuated domestic instability and political rivalries into a much broader and deadly conflict was in 1960, during the Congo Crisis. During Belgium's rapid and disorganised withdrawal from the Congo, Patrice Lumumba came to prominence as a charismatic politician, later becoming prime minister of an uneasy governing coalition, in partnership with his rival Joseph Kasavubu, who became president. However, the weak central authority of the Congolese government provided the opportunities for ambitious politicians in the resource-rich regions of Katanga and South Kasai to secede within weeks of Congo's independence, which plunged the Lumumba government into disarray. Lumumba, frustrated by the lack of western and UN support to help end the two secessions, turned to the Soviet Union for assistance. This decision by Lumumba to 'look' East convinced the USA that he was a communist, and fearing they would lose influence over the centre of the continent and its vast resource base to the Soviet Union they chose to intervene. They urged first Kasavubu and then the Army Chief of Staff Mobutu to take action against him. After the Americans backed Kasavubu's seizure of power, Lumumba was soon arrested and later executed by Katanga rebels with the help of the USA and Belgium (De Witte, 2002).

The execution of Lumumba did little to stem the crisis. Bickering, power-hungry politicians and divisive forms of regional and ethnic nationalism saw the Congo descend into further chaos, with the country effectively split in four, with each region supported by various external patrons. By 1964, rebellions in the east of the country inspired by the Chinese Communist revolution, and employing Maoist tactics, emerged to challenge the central government, who soon captured large parts of the country. The USA once again intervened, helping to support the pro-western Congolese through extensive funding and military logistics, in what became a costly and deadly conflict. This particular Cold War confrontation also caught the attention of Cuba, who sent Che Guevara at the head of a small force in 1965 to assist the growing Simba rebellion. However, the rebels were disorganised, lacked a coherent strategy, and were clearly not remotely revolutionary inclined, which persuaded a disillusioned Guevara and the Cuban force to withdraw. In the Congo, the USA had cynically intervened in the affairs of a sovereign state, helped assassinate its prime minister, and assisted in the rise of Mobutu to power, who became a useful anti-communist ally for Washington.

The key battle grounds of the 'hot' Cold War emerged in the 1970s in Angola, Ethiopia, and Somalia, where the superpowers relied on client groups to confront one another. Perhaps one of the most intriguing examples occurred in 1977 when Soviet-backed Somalia invaded Ethiopia, which had only recently installed a Marxist-Leninist government that was also seeking assistance from the Soviet Union. The conflict was a diplomatic dilemma for Moscow, who naturally had wanted to nurture as many Cold War allies as possible, especially in the strategically important Horn of Africa. However, the intractable differences between the two nations resulted in Somalia being jettisoned in favour of Ethiopia, whose adherence to Marxism was regarded as more genuine. Backed by Soviet weaponry and Cuban soldiers, the Ethiopians easily defeated Somalia, whose leader Siad Barre had made a dramatic ideological U-turn by seeking western assistance instead. What this demonstrated was the fluidity of Cold War alliances, the cynicism of the superpowers, and the fragility of the ideological commitment by 'client' states.

Box 6.2 The Angolan Civil War and Cold War confrontation

One of the most destructive Cold War conflicts was in Angola, where the decolonisation process degenerated into a violent civil war between three rival movements: the Popular Movement for the Liberation of Angola (MPLA), the National Front for the Liberation of

Angola (FNLA) and the National Union for the Total Independence of Angola (UNITA). These organisations were divided on ideological and ethnic lines, and fought one another for power in the build-up to independence in 1975. The movements appealed to various external supporters for military and financial assistance, exemplified by Holden Roberto, leader of the FNLA, declaring that his movement would 'accept help from anyone, regardless of its origins' (Jackson, 1995, 392). Roberto's sentiment was shared by the other liberation movements who, despite their radically different ideological positions, sought assistance from any willing backer (Westad, 2007, 210–211). Each movement attracted assistance from across the Cold War divide receiving military, economic, and political aid. The USA supported the FNLA in the early stages of the Civil War, and later backed UNITA, who were also allied with apartheid South Africa, while the MPLA were sustained by the Soviet Union and Cuba. These external interventions in Angola resulted in what was essentially a local battle for political power escalating into a clash between the forces of communism and western democracy.

As the civil war intensified, the MPLA gained the upper hand through regular supplies of sophisticated weapons from the Soviets. In turn, the USA covertly increased its involvement in Angola, despite repeated warnings by American foreign policy experts not to become too deeply embroiled (Davis, 1978; Stockwell, 1979). By October 1975, the apartheid regime was increasingly concerned by the emerging communist threat on its borders. In an effort to decisively turn the tide of the war in support of its ally UNITA, South Africa invaded Angola with the tacit backing of the USA (Graham, 2011). However, the MPLA, facing imminent defeat by its rivals and their external backers, gained salvation when Cuba decisively intervened by sending thousands of troops and millions of dollars' worth of military equipment to the country. The course of the war had swung in the MPLA's favour, with Cuban and Soviet assistance helping to temporarily defeat the combined challenges of the FNLA and UNITA (Gleijeses, 2002).

Once the MPLA had secured power, it relied heavily on the material assistance of the Soviet Union, and the active presence of thousands of Cuban troops to maintain its position. By 1981, the election of Ronald Reagan as US president, combined with South Africa's aggressive anti-communist 'Total Strategy' policy which explicitly sought to destabilise Southern Africa's Marxist nations, saw both nations support UNITA, enabling it to challenge the MPLA once again. With this extensive external support UNITA conquered large parts of Angola by the mid-1980s, with the adversaries fighting pitched battles across the country resulting in widespread destruction and destitution for millions. The most infamous battle was Cuito Cuanavale in 1987–1988, which resulted in a huge number of casualties; there was no decisive winner, but the stalemate was the first step towards international negotiations, and ultimately a peace settlement in 1991.

Ethnicity

Ethnic rivalry is often cited as an important reason for conflict across the continent, and is a factor publicly associated with violence in Africa. The argument frequently heard is that 'tribalism' is to blame, as if it is a characteristic intrinsic only to African conflicts. To some extent, violence can be partially attributed to ethnicity when different groups are driven by self-interest, hatred, or fear of the 'other' (Braathen, 2000). However, to view African conflicts in such a light is simplistic in the extreme, and intrinsically racist. If ethnicity was a key cause of conflict, then ethnic groups across the world would be constantly at war, which is simply not the case. The question that must be asked is why ethnicity is so frequently referred to as an explanation for African conflicts, and what other factors might be at play.

Ethnicity can be viewed as a form of human identity in which shared identifiers such as ancestry, history, language, culture, religion, and locale are used to bind peoples together. Therefore ethnicity is an inherited, not a biological state, and through establishing a specific identity, particular norms prescribe and regulate behaviours, explicitly in relation to 'others'. However, ethnicity is not a static concept, as people can shift between ethnic groups through the assimilation or rejection of particular traits; as such, ethnicity should not be viewed as being an homogeneous label, as there is scope for the fluidity of people and ideas. Furthermore, the notion of African 'tribes' is a relatively new phenomenon, shaped largely by European colonialism. Believing that Africans were intrinsically tribal, groups were sought out by the colonisers as a means of bureaucratic administration to establish hierarchies, as well as making governance easier through divide and rule tactics (see Chapter 3). Where tribal groups were not evident, they were simply invented. For some African peoples, such as the Igbo in Nigeria or the Tutsi in Rwanda, the designation by the colonisers as a 'favoured' ethnic group provided opportunities for material benefit.

For others it brought greater subjugation and exclusion. Therefore ethnicity was socially constructed and in many places institutionalised and internalised through colonialism. In the post-colonial era, newly endowed elites often reverted to utilising ethnicity as a form of political mobilisation in order to achieve power and distribute patronage. These political decisions had the potential to exacerbate exclusionary practices and establish grievances associated with neo-patrimonial rule. However, ethnicity does not have to be a divisive force in African politics, with leaders such as Jomo Kenyatta in Kenya demonstrating particular skill in binding disparate groups together. But it must be recognised that in contemporary African life ethnicity remains an important part of the social and political milieu. Therefore, many African conflicts certainly have an ethnic dimension associated to them. For example, even in ostensibly Cold War conflicts, rival liberation movements in Angola and Zimbabwe were divided along ethnic lines as much as they were ideologically.

It is crucial to recognise that ethnicity does not cause violence or start wars. However, if it is constructed, shaped, and mobilised by elites pursuing a potent political agenda then it can potentially be an extremely destructive force. A persuasive argument is that ethnic identity creates the necessary conditions for violence only when it is combined with additional societal and political pressures, such as the exclusion from state power, and then manipulated and utilised by political leaders who can effectively coalesce these grievances (Cederman, 2010).

A good example of this scenario would be the Darfur war in Sudan that broke out in 2003. At first glance this appeared to be another chapter in the long-running internal war between the north and south Sudanese, in what could crudely be regarded as an ethnic conflict between the 'Arab' and 'African' populations. There were long-standing grievances in the south that Sudan's 'Arab' population, through exclusionary government policies, had discriminated, marginalised, and neglected the nations 'black' Africans. In 2003, the Sudan Liberation Army and the Justice and Equality Movement began a successful rebellion against the government in Khartoum, fighting for greater autonomy and powers for the south. To combat the growing threat, the al-Bashir government recruited and funded the 'Arab' militias known as the Janjaweed to put down the black African rebels in South Sudan by carrying out massacres and using scorched earth tactics to target the local populace (de Waal, 2004). As the conflict unfolded, these tactics soon saw the Sudanese government accused of ethnic cleansing and genocide in Darfur, leading to the International Criminal Court (ICC) laying charges against al-Bashir for crimes against humanity.

However, to see this in solely ethnic terms would misread a complex political situation. There were a multitude of factors at play, of which ethnicity was just one of them (Flint & de Waal, 2005). In Sudan, a series of political grievances were refracted through appeals to ethnic identity by elites, in order to gain domestic and international support. Since independence in 1956, Sudanese authority and power had been centred in the northern capital, Khartoum, with elites paying little heed to the peripheral regions. Much of the historic unrest and rebellions since independence had been from marginalised groups such as the Sudan People's Liberation Army (SPLA) who wanted increased powers from a poorly governed and brutal central authority. Furthermore, the unstable neo-patrimonial governance structure of Sudan also pitted elites against one another which created room for conflict and alternative power bases (Prunier, 2005b). Throw into this mix a religious dimension that saw not only the imposition of Islamic tradition and practice on the largely Christian south which angered the local population, but also a theological split within the elite governing structures of the government about which Islamic doctrine to follow (El Din, 2007). Moreover, in the Darfur region there was a national and local struggle developing over the access and control of resources. At the local level, there were grievances and clashes over the access to water and agricultural land, exacerbated by recurring droughts and climate change, to which the Janjaweed were promised control of in return for their cooperation against the rebels (Faris, 2007). Nationally, the al-Bashir government was eager to secure control over the oil resources in the region, as the export revenue made up a significant proportion of the national budget. As can be seen in Sudan, the war was simplified into ethnic binaries, but in reality it was a combination of factors that plunged the country into conflict.

Box 6.3 The Rwandan genocide, 1994

On 6 April 1994, President Habyarimana's plane was shot down, a spark that led to 100 days of genocidal slaughter (see Image 6.1), which saw Rwanda's Hutu population predominantly target the minority Tutsis; the result was between 500,000 and 1 million deaths (Mamdani, 2001; Prunier; 2005a). The genocide was depicted, particularly in the international media, and aided by Hutu state propaganda, as a spontaneous movement of the population to 'kill the enemy Tutsi' (Prunier, 2005a, 247) or as 'pure tribal enmity' (*Time Magazine*, 1994), in which the events were the result solely of historical ethnic tensions. The general perception that the genocide was driven by ethnicity remains a prevalent interpretation, despite the academic consensus refuting this argument.

Image 6.1 Mass burial site in Kigali

Source: PASCAL GUYOT/AFP/Getty Images.

However, the Rwandan genocide was political in origin and should be viewed as state-orchestrated ethnic cleansing that had little to do with the purported historical rivalry between the two main groups. Viewing the violence through an ethnic lens fails to acknowledge the fundamental importance of political ambition and wider societal issues as the principal causes of the Rwandan genocide (Hintjens, 1999). In fact, the Hutu state had cultivated and propagated a narrative of historical ethnic hatred and tensions over a significant period of time, which engrained racist prejudice among a significant proportion of Rwanda's population, but also excluded Tutsis from positions of power (Uvin, 1997).

Hutu and Tutsi were originally social labels, which were attributed ethnic importance initially to facilitate the aims of the colonial state. In fact, the Hutu and Tutsi shared a number of commonalities, with few distinguishable distinctions, many of which were based on superficial identifiers such as height and wealth (Des Forges, 1999, 32–35). The perceived ethnic divisions were developed in the colonial period, which cast the minority Tutsi into a position of power. When Belgium granted independence to Rwanda in 1962, they switched allegiances, transferring state authority to the Hutus, who favoured ethnic exclusivity over inclusiveness (Thompson, 2007, 21).

By retaining and extending colonial governance structures, this political decision by the Hutu elite to preserve their dominance over power structures served only to deepen the institutionalised ethnic divisions in the post-colonial era.

By the late 1980s, as the Hutu elite encountered a number of multifaceted crises including famine, unemployment, and poverty, ethnic hatred became the cloak with which an autocratic regime tried desperately to cling to power. For example, the years prior to the genocide were characterised by growing overpopulation and a sharp socio-economic decline that aroused widespread discontent. The situation offered the perfect opportunity for Hutu hardliners to fight back against these developments, recasting the crisis as one of ethnicity in order to rally the Hutu population behind a common enemy: the Tutsis.

The narrative of a people divided along ethnic lines provided a justification for the actions of the Hutu regime, which allowed the Rwandan government to meticulously plan and enable the acts of genocide. What might at first glance appear to be a 'tribal' conflict was in fact a highly orchestrated and careful manufactured series of political manoeuvres designed to protect an ailing regime. The discourse of ethnic hatred and fear, propagated via the Rwandan media, was effectively utilised as a tool for societal mobilisation against the 'other'. Despite the popular representations of the genocide, it must be recognised that the slaughter was not solely targeted at the Tutsis, as moderate Hutus were among the first to be murdered, while a significant proportion of the Hutu population *did not* participate in the violence (Mueller, 2000; Straus, 2004). To fully understand the Rwandan genocide, we must look first to the wider political and societal factors, and the role of unscrupulous and desperate elites who, through constructed ethnic antagonism, were able to encourage widespread violence.

Religious belief

Religious beliefs and identities are extremely powerful in contemporary Africa and permeate all levels of society (Ellis & ter Haar, 1998). Similar to ethnicity, religion has an important role in social interaction and identity, binding peoples together (see Chapter 7). Religious beliefs in another spiritual dimension can establish unique individual and group identities, provide the mechanism for societal interactions, and enshrine and influence forms of ethical behaviour and practice. There are many forms of religious behaviour and practice across Africa, encompassing traditional belief in the power of spirits and ancestors, which is attuned to the natural environment of the continent, to the more formalised worship of Islam and Christianity. As outlined in Chapter 3, from 641, the spread of Islam in particular had a major influence across much of north, western, and later eastern regions of the continent, while Christian missionaries, from the nineteenth century, introduced variants of Catholicism and Protestantism in the south. On a very basic level, the general geography of religious beliefs across Africa is of an Islamic north and a Christian south, which at first glance looks like a potential point of division. Even within countries such as Nigeria and Sudan, the division between Christian south and Islamic north is often characterised as being a key source of dispute. Furthermore, the recent rise of al-Shabaab or Boko Haram has created an impression in the west of an impending violent Islamic jihadist conquest of the Sahel region.

A crucial aspect of religious scripture is that there is often no single 'truth' or path, which means texts such as the Bible and Qur'an can be interpreted very differently. For example, the Qur'an and Shari'a law provide guidance on a range of issues addressing, among other things, how Muslims should act, live their lives, and pray. Importantly, there are a multitude of religious interpretations and indeed forms of worship (such as the Sunni/Shia division within Islam) that can vary enormously between nations. The space that alternative interpretations establish can create schisms, as group identities and practices can be shaped, influenced, or utilised by leaders, especially in relation to others. For example, the re-emergence of conflict in 1990s Sudan was due in part to the al-Bashir regime introducing a new governing interpretation of Shari'a, which was designed to exclude the rival SPLA, creating a scenario in which a challenge to state authority was now categorised as one of religious rebellion (de waal & Abdel Salam, 2004, 73). Therefore, in particular circumstances, religious practice can play an important part in stoking tension, militancy, and ultimately violence.

Yet, mirroring ethnicity, we must not jump to simple conclusions about religion and its correlation to violence. Once again, we can identify an array of factors and motivations, of which religious belief is one of several. The significance of religion has long been recognised by elites across Africa. In divided localities, religious practice offers a useful political mobilising tool, which can be utilised to gather popular support around specific issues, or to engender action against state institutions and rival groups (Ellis & ter Haar, 1998, 178, 188). Therefore, it is crucial to recognise a holistic mix of issues at play, and note that religious differences do not in the majority of cases result in violence.

However, we cannot simply write off religious beliefs as a motivating factor, because devotion can be crucial in spurring individual action or militancy. For example, an Islamist conquest of much of Mali in 2012 threatened to topple the government, which lacked legitimacy or authority. The Malian government was ultimately saved by French military intervention, which had been prompted in part by western concerns of growing militant Islamic influences in the region. However, Dowd and Raleigh (2013, 505) argued that while the coalition of Malian groups placed themselves strategically within a global narrative of violent Islamic jihadism, 'understanding them in these globalized terms divorces them from the context in which they emerge and operate'. In reality, competing political elites, marginalisation, and societal dissatisfaction were all crucial local drivers of the violence spearhead by the Islamist coalition.

There have been a number of conflict settings in which religious violence has been regarded as being a major contributing factor. For example, northern Nigeria has experienced frequent bouts of extreme violence which has seen both Muslim and Christians killed in large numbers. During the outbreaks of violence, religious association clearly played an important role in the atrocities. Although religion was used to justify certain group actions, the underlying causality included access to jobs, exclusion from the political process, and local elites manipulating religious convictions. In Algeria, the autocratic ruling FLN were seriously challenged by the rise of Front Islamique du Salut (FIS), which had made enormous gains in the first round of the 1991 elections. The FIS were demanding the creation of an Islamic state based on Shari'a law, and had called for a jihad against the FLN government. In January 1992, fearing near certain Islamist rule, the Algerian military cancelled the elections, banned FIS, and arrested thousands of its supporters. The result was the onset of a civil war in which Islamist-inspired fighters engaged in guerrilla tactics against the government. This was a destructive and costly civil war, in which the massacre of civilians became an increasingly horrific tactic utilised by the rebels; when the conflict officially ended in 1999, an estimated 100,000 people had been killed. While the initial stages of the protest certainly had a religious dimension, Algeria had suffered from an ongoing socio-economic crisis since the 1980s, and was confounded by the breakdown in the FLN government's legitimacy. As the conflict unfolded, support for the violence of the FIS dissipated, with the struggle increasingly centred over the spoils of political and economic power. Despite the ceasefire, some guerrilla soldiers refused to surrender the Islamist fight, and went on to play an important role in the emergence of Al-Qaeda in the Islamic Mahgreb, a terrorist organisation which spans Algeria, Mali, and Mauritania.

Box 6.4 Al-Shabaab and Somalia

Successfully emerging out of two decades of anarchy and chaos in Somalia, the Islamic Courts Union (ICU), a coalition of Islamic Shari'a courts, gained political control of much of the country, including the capital Mogadishu. However, fearing a powerful militant Islamist government in the Horn of Africa, Ethiopia was encouraged by the USA in 2006 to invade Somalia in order to overthrow the ICU and install the Transitional Federal Government (TFG) in power. By late 2006, the ICU had lost much of its territory and authority as it rapidly disintegrated in the face of the Ethiopian invasion. ICU's loss of power and authority saw the radical al-Shabaab emerge as a splinter group, committed to Islamic jihad against the TFG. Al-Shabaab began a guerrilla war across swathes of Somalia, explicitly targeting the institutions of state power, which enabled it to successfully capture much of the south. Somalia's violence is connected to a wider pattern of global Islamic terrorism, as the organisation pledged its allegiance to al-Qaeda in 2009, and has since 2007 exported terror attacks across East Africa including Kenya and Uganda. The most infamous attack was at Nairobi's exclusive Westgate shopping mall in 2013, where 67 people were killed. The spiral of conflict and violence has wider regional implications with Uganda's and Kenya's military actively involved in Somalia to try and stem the power and influence of al-Shabaab's jihadist goals. Yet regional military intervention has fanned the flames of conflict, provoking a series of serious attacks predominantly targeting Kenya; the most notable acts were at Mpeketoni in June 2014, where 50 non-Muslims were murdered (Anderson & McKnight, 2015, 24), and in January 2017, when 57 Kenyan soldiers were killed at their military base in Kulbiyow, Somalia (Burke, 2017). Al-Shabaab are able to utilise the unifying tool of religion to recruit followers in Kenya and Somalia disillusioned by political marginalisation, a lack of a legitimate outlets through which to express discontentment, widespread poverty, and an absence of economic development.

A more recent case of the military intervening to prevent Islamist gains was in Egypt. The Muslim Brotherhood rose to a position of influence during the 2011 Egyptian Revolution in which President Hosni Mubarak was overthrown. By 2012, the Muslim Brotherhood had achieved political power following the elections, in which Mohamed Morsi became president. However, his presidency was marred by allegations of unconstitutional acts and the promotion of overtly Islamist policies, which prompted mass public demonstrations. Fearing the entrenchment of Islamic policies within Egyptian politics, the military stepped in to remove the Muslim Brotherhood from office in July 2013.

On the whole, religious differences only become an important dimension in Africa's conflict and violence when political, social, and economic issues are combined alongside spiritual justifications. In most cases, religion helps to unify groups behind a common ideology, and is an important factor in contemporary African politics. However, when religious belief is mobilised against specific grievances, such as the exclusion from political power, it can create the necessary conditions for violence. In settings such as Somalia and Sudan, alternative visions of Islam are crucial to our understanding of the violence, yet in Mali, despite the outward appearance of a religious conflict, the rebellion of disparate groups, despite being united by faith, were in fact concerned primarily with political and economic issues.

Resources

Perhaps one of the most iconic explanations for conflict in Africa is the competition for the control of resources. Films like *Blood Diamond* depict a scenario where warring militias pillage valuable natural resources such as diamonds to enrich themselves, with seemingly little or no interest in political power. In the post-Cold War setting, a number of conflicts established the alluring concept of 'resource' wars. For example, in Angola both the MPLA and the UNITA fought for control of the oil fields and diamond mines; in Sierra Leone the Revolutionary United Front (RUF) also exploited diamond deposits; while in the eastern Congo militias such as M23, and neighbouring states including Uganda and Rwanda, fought over access to minerals including gold, tin, tantalum, and tungsten. Thus the argument is that rebellion offers an ideal opportunity for profit, and as such 'the insurgents are indistinguishable from bandits or pirates' (Grossman, 1999, 269). This perspective is enshrined in the 'greed and grievance' explanation outlined more fully by Collier and Hoeffler (2004) which seemed to fit the bill for much of Africa's contemporary violence. On the international stage, the importance of resource competition as an explanation for African conflicts was identified in multilateral deals such as the Kimberley Process, signed in 2003 to stop the trade in 'conflict diamonds', while in 2010, the US government signed the Dodd–Frank Wall Street Reform, which included a subsection forcing companies to disclose their use of conflict materials from the DRC. The sentiment enshrines the view that resources motivate, facilitate, and sustain rebel groups

(Keen, 1998). While resource abundance is the most common explanation, it must be noted that the scarcity of access to resources such as food, water, and land have all been cited as offering incentives for conflict (see Chapter 2). For example, in Darfur the availability of grazing land has been a source of competition, while access to water around the rapidly shrinking Lake Chad has also sparked violent clashes.

However, using resources as an explanatory framework once again narrows the multidimensional nature of war, and posits that resources, or lack of, can be directly attributed to conflict. In doing so, this establishes an economically deterministic argument. Indeed, by engaging with such a perspective this once again removes political agency from the equation, as well as a series of other interconnected motivations. Resources alone do not cause violence. Nations such as Botswana, which has extensive diamond deposits, have not been 'cursed' by their resources base, nor afflicted by violence. If the 'resource curse' was such a key component in conflict, then far more states with primary commodities would be susceptible to armed rebellion. Furthermore, in contemporary Africa there has been a sharp distinction in how resources have been conceptualised and potentially fought over. During the Cold War era, none of the conflicts could be labelled as 'resource' wars. It was only after 1990, when external backers ceased assisting client governments or rebel groups, did resources begin to take on greater importance in conflict situations. But crucially these conflicts were still not primarily about resources. High-value minerals and oil reserves do not act as the underlying motivation for groups to engage in rebellion. It is only after conflicts have started do they take on significance, as the control, management, and profiteering from them provide the means to sustain a rebellion against the political system.

An excellent example of this situation is Angola. The 1975–1991 period of the civil war was a fractious political contest for power between the MPLA and UNITA that was intensified by the geopolitical concerns of the Cold War. However, resources only featured prominently in the conflict after the war resumed following the 1992 election. For the MPLA government, its war effort was financed by controlling the offshore oil reserves, while UNITA could only maintain its rebellion by securing Angola's diamond deposits. After the 1992 elections, UNITA gained control of 60–70% of Angola's diamond production, which Global Witness (1998, 3) argued had generated US$ 3.7 billion in illicit sales on the global market, providing the movement with funds to capture two-thirds of the country. These diamond sales were fundamental to UNITA's ability to continue the war effort until Savimbi's death in 2002. Importantly, this was not a 'resource war'; Jonas Savimbi's primary aim was to secure political power in Angola, not personal enrichment.

163

Likewise, the conflicts in Liberia (1989–2003) and Sierra Leone (1991–2002), which were closely intertwined, became synonymous with outright brutality and resource piracy. The rebellions led by Charles Taylor's NPFL and Foday Sankoh's RUF emerged in direct response to declining government legitimacy, widespread corruption, the erosion of central authority, and increasing socio-economic problems in both countries (Ellis, 1999; Hirsch 2001). Once the NPFL and RUF were prevented from taking total political power, these conflicts morphed into ideologically devoid struggles, characterised by extreme violence, the widespread use of child soldiers, and importantly the control of resources. The ultimate seizure of power always remained the primary goal, but once checked, the utilisation of resources became a decisive factor in the unfolding wars. For example, Taylor's NPFL was able to secure Liberia's diamond and gold mines, and in collaboration with multinational firms sell them on the international market (Reno, 1998, 94), which helped fund the purchase of military supplies. Meanwhile, in Sierra Leone, the besieged government, bereft of revenue from the RUF-controlled diamond mines, was forced to rely on the private military company Executive Outcomes to secure its position, whose assistance was 'bought' in return for a stake in the diamond mining revenues (Howe, 1998).

Box 6.5 The DRC, Africa's 'world war', and conflict resources

The conflict that broke out in eastern Zaire (DRC), which lasted from 1996 to 2003, was one of Africa's most costly and destructive. The war, borne out of complex political and social factors, has left an enduring scar on the political, economic, and social fabric of the region to this day, in which an estimated 6 million people died.

By the mid-1990s, President Mobutu's regime was in disarray, having lost almost all semblance of authority after the Cold War. Within the context of Mobutu's diminishing central authority, the Hutu perpetrators of the Rwandan genocide fled to the north-east of the country (Cyrus Reed, 1998). In 1996, Rwanda and Uganda invaded Zaire to remove the increasingly powerful Hutu opposition, assisted by a coalition of rebel groups – the Alliance of Democratic Forces for the Liberation of Congo-Zaire (AFDL) led by Laurent Kabila. With the military aid of Rwanda, the AFDL swept through Zaire as Mobutu's poorly funded and demoralised army capitulated. By 1997, they had successfully overthrown Mobutu, who was replaced in power by Kabila; yet Kabila soon removed all opposition to his rule and ejected the Rwandans who had been fundamental in his rise to power. The alienation of erstwhile supporters resulted in renewed political grievances and the formation of a new rebel group, the Rally for Congolese Democracy (RCD), now backed by Rwanda and Uganda. In August 1998, the Rwanda military, using the pretext of protecting ethnic Tutsis in the Congo, waged war on Kabila. His government would have been defeated had it not been for the intervention of Angola, Chad, Namibia, and Zimbabwe, which internationalised the conflict in what has been labelled 'Africa's World War' (Turner, 2007; Prunier, 2009; Reyntjens, 2009). In the ensuing chaos and political breakdown, a fractured RCD was able to secure parts of the eastern Congo, while a range of other rebel groups including the Hutu-dominated Democratic Forces for the Liberation of Rwanda (FDLR), staked their territorial claims.

As the anarchy spread and a political solution receded, the various belligerent forces turned to plundering the natural resource base of the DRC. The rebel militias and military personnel of the foreign armies reappropriated millions of dollars of resources from their controlled areas, which were used to finance continued conflict and amass personal wealth. In 2002, the UN identified an elite network of military and political figures that used the cover of the DRC's insecurity to secure resources and illegally trade them abroad. Using their monopoly on violence and serving elite interests, these various armed groups exploited the DRC's resources, with the full complicity of global multinational companies and international criminal gangs. In the report, high-ranking figures from Rwanda, Uganda, and Zimbabwe were implicated in the profiteering, declaring that they had 'built up a self-financing war economy centred on mineral exploitation', and that the Zimbabwean elite 'network ha[d] transferred ownership of at least US$5 billion of assets from the State mining sector' (UN, 2002, 7). Although a peace deal was finally signed in 2006, which saw the main actors cease the hostilities, instability continues to ravage the region. Warring militias such as FDLR and M23 are still engaged in a destructive conflict in the Kivu region, despite the presence of a UN peacekeeping force.

It is clear that the resources in the Congo did not establish the conditions for war, yet as the violence spread, they provided the opportunities for profiteering. Elite motivations for power and influence across the region were the driving forces behind the conflict, but the DRC's resources have enabled the violence to be perpetuated, while enriching a small minority.

It is therefore important to appreciate that resources themselves do not cause conflict; rather, it is the political and social dimensions which turn these resources into a vital component that facilitate further violence and act as a limiter to peace. Englebert and Ron (2004, 76) sum this sentiment up nicely: 'No matter how tempting natural resources might be and how they may exacerbate ongoing instability and armed conflict, they are unlikely to stimulate civil war on their own unless the political context is already unstable.'

 Further reading

An important book that has informed this chapter and is one of the most comprehensive assessments on political violence in Africa is Paul Williams's (2016) *War and Conflict in Africa*, which should then be followed by William Reno's (1998) *Warlord Politics and African States*, and Morten Bøås and Kevin Dunn's (2007) *African Guerrillas Raging Against the Machine*. For specific case studies see some of the various contributions from Mahmood Mamdani (2001) *When Victims Become Killers: Colonialism, Nativism, and the Genocide in Rwanda*; Alison des Forges (1999) *'Leave None to Tell the Tale': Genocide in Rwanda*; Gerard Prunier (2005a) *The Rwanda Crisis: History of a Genocide*; Stephen Ellis (1999) *The Mask of Anarchy: The Destruction of Liberia and the Religious Dimensions of an African War*; Gerard Prunier (2009) *Africa's World War: Congo, the Rwandan Genocide, and the Making of a Continental Catastrophe*; Filip Reyntjens (2009) *The Great African War: Congo and Regional Geopolitics, 1996–2006*; and Odd Arne Westad (2007) *The Global Cold War: Third World Interventions and the Making of Our Times*.

7 SOCIAL MOVEMENTS AND CIVIL SOCIETY

In general assessments of contemporary Africa, social movements and civil society organisations continue to receive very little attention, despite the presence of an array of diverse popular movements that seek to achieve political, economic, and social change. One problem for understanding these collective movements is that there is no consensus on what social movements in Africa constitute (see Ellis & van Kessel, 2009; Larmer, 2010). In short they can be seen as non-state, collective movements of people uniting to combat, challenge, and protest issues of exclusion and inequality. These movements are often informal, and seek to empower people taking 'action from below' against the state to achieve change. They also operate within the public space which is often termed 'civil society', where non-state actors provide vehicles for collective action to achieve specific aims. Civil society organisations on the other hand also operate within this same public space, but with objectives that include providing services and lobbying governments. Therefore civil society organisations can include charities, NGOs, trade unions, and think tanks, which are usually independent of government interference, although some generate their funding through state grants.

As noted in previous chapters, post-colonial states experienced a series of contradictions and problems, which saw large numbers of African citizens suffer from an inability to directly influence their material conditions, including but not limited to themes of political participation, economic exclusion, environmental issues, or access to social welfare and services. The shadow of unequal power relations loom large across Africa, in which one-party states and corporations dominate the landscape, establishing the need for social movements and civil society organisations to offer opportunities to articulate alternative visions and represent their constituent demands. Since independence, a diversity of movements have therefore emerged across the continent, both formally and informally, in a bid to enact transformations: nationalist movements, NGOs, churches, trade unions, civil society, and single-issue protest groups have, in local, national, and transnational settings, sought to contest and materially alter their immediate conditions (Larmer, 2010, 252). This in part is why it is so hard to precisely define social movements in Africa, due to the variety of causes and demands, as well as the diverse mechanisms through which they are expressed.

A key tension is whether African movements can be viewed in universal terms, based on the experiences and influences of those in Europe and Latin America, or whether there is something unique about those that emerge on the continent. International factors have clearly had an important role, through interacting and influencing African organisations, for example aiding the spread of global ideas such as human rights, organisational and campaigning strategies, and, perhaps crucially, funding. It has led some scholars such as Williams and Young (2012) and Gould (2005) to argue that African movements have to some extent been co-opted and utilised by external forces, which makes them beholden to international actors. Yet such a perspective neglects local agency, as well as the inherent hybridity of African social movements, whose characteristics are blurred by interspersed social, political, and religious features (Ellis & van Kessel, 2009, 15), which in turn are shaped and constrained by the specific context and environment that they operate within (de Waal & Ibreck, 2013, 304). Furthermore, it must be recognised that depending on the cause in question, social movements can vary enormously in socio-economic composition (i.e. wealth or levels of education among activists); the association or 'dependency' on state or international funding; the level of autonomy in neo-patrimonial settings; the 'reach' of the message (e.g. the Kimberley Process against blood diamonds in Angola and Sierra Leone became a global issue); and the legitimacy among the constituents they pertain to speak for. Therefore, when looking at any African movement these factors must be acknowledged.

Clearly social movements and civil society organisations across Africa have a long and diverse history. However, when thinking about their emergence and evolution, a useful way to understand them is to divide their trajectory into four broad overarching periods that map onto wider continental political, economic, and social developments (Larmer, 2010; Zeilig et al., 2012). The first is the rise of anti-colonial nationalism in the post-World War II era (see Chapter 3), where often disjointed coalitions were united by the ultimate goal of independence. Educated nationalist elites, such as Senegal's Léopold Senghor, utilised a plethora of organisations such as trade unions and churches to create a popular groundswell of opposition in support of decolonisation. Yet once independence was achieved, a second stage unfolded, which saw the majority of nationalist leaders implement one-party states in the 1960s and 1970s; the very same social movements that had brought about change were instead reimagined as a threat to state power, with new leaders co-opting or alternatively repressing them. However, the economic decline of the 1970s and 1980s (see Chapter 5), and the subsequent implementation of SAPs which demanded the rollback of the state, especially from the provision of social services, consequently had a negative impact on the lives of millions of Africans. In response, new forms of social movements and civil society organisations emerged, including the rise of international NGOs, which stepped in to try to alleviate the economic and social crises across the continent. Many such movements still continue to operate throughout Africa to provide wide-ranging forms of assistance in a number of fields including education and medical care.

The final broad stage in our periodisation was the revival of pro-democracy movements in the 1990s (see Chapter 4), which challenged autocratic leaders, seeking to enact wider political, economic, and societal changes. In the post-Cold War setting, international ideals of human rights and democratisation became closely connected with such movements, offering a point of reference in which demands could be articulated. Yet the incomplete nature of the 'third wave' of democratisation, and the recent retrenchment in democratic governance in Africa, has demonstrated the continued importance of individuals and groups in challenging state power to achieve change. A good example was the emergence in 2010–2014 of a complex and multicausal network of social movements across North Africa, commonly referred to as the Arab Spring, that led to the overthrow of leaders in Tunisia, Egypt, and Libya (Lafi, 2017).

This chapter could not possibly cover all of Africa's social movement and civil society developments, rather it will sketch out in broad brush-strokes some of the most prevalent forms in order to provide a continental overview. To give a sense of the multitude of social formations across Africa, and some of the historical and contemporary activities that civil society organisations have undertaken, the chapter is divided into various subsections which highlight African nationalism, trade unions, NGOs, specific issue movements, traditional authority, and religious institutions.

African nationalism

In the struggle against colonial rule, mass movements emerged across Africa during the 1950s to demand freedom from external powers (see Chapter 3). At the forefront of these efforts to achieve decolonisation were nationalist movements that articulated a vision of independence and self-determination. However, the term African nationalism, applied via a European prism, is actually misleading. The modern African state was created by Europeans and not Africans, which meant the 'nation' was an artificial construction in which a multitude of peoples, often with very little in common, were housed; colonial rule actively encouraged ethnic, linguistic, and religious differences and rivalries as a means of political control, which in turn saw Africans adopt and utilise these sub-national categorisations for their own benefit (Ranger, 1983). Therefore, before independence was achieved, almost no African would have identified as being say Malawian or Senegalese, drawing on their ethnic or linguistic ties as a form of collective identity, rather than the nation-state they resided within. Consequently, these divisions were a major problem for nationalist movements across the continent.

In the post-World War II period, when the fight against colonialism developed more forcefully, the anti-colonial struggle was framed by leaders such as Nkrumah and Senghor under the banner of freedom (a multifaceted yet undefined notion) and collective unity against imperial control. However, the ultimate goal was not nationalist in the traditional sense, because once European control had been removed there was no intention of redrawing the map to establish 'new' ethnically or culturally representative nations. Instead once political independence had been won, the modern nation would be forged within the confines of the colonial borders, irrespective of diversity and differences. Therefore, the appeal for unity transcended the historical reality – Africans were asked to subsume their sub-national identities in favour of the common cause of the nation, when division and competition were more likely. In fact, many nationalist leaders recognised the political danger of these inherent divisions, while also viewing them as a distinctly 'un-modern' phenomenon. For example, Mozambique's first president Samora Machel argued that 'for the nation to live, the tribe must die'. The appeal for African unity was promoted under the guise of a common yet unspecified heritage, so as to overcome domestic and international pressures following independence. In order to establish a sense of unity, early nationalist leaders deployed a range of ideological mechanisms to achieve this aim. For example, the Ghanaian president Nkrumah promoted the concept of Pan-Africanism, which went beyond the realm of the nation-state towards a shared continental identity; Tanzania's Nyerere focused instead on primarily achieving domestic unity through Ujamaa (see Chapter 4); while Kaunda promoted humanism in Zambia.

In terms of social movement formation, nationalist leaders worked hard to establish popular organisations that could be utilised to support the broader anti-colonial struggle. There was a realisation that the strength of mass mobilisation, both urban and rural, would not only help to exert pressure on colonial authorities to cede power, but allow any aspiring leader to secure power once independence was achieved. The apparent unity, both rhetorically and organisationally, provided a useful tool to agitate for change, but was essentially a myth. Given the internal contradictions already identified, the reality was that nationalist movements were coalitions of the disaffected, briefly united by the concepts of freedom and independence. In fact, the rhetoric of African nationalism was a façade that masked uneasy, divided, and loosely connected groups, which encompassed a diverse set of political, ethnic, cultural, and economic interests. For many of the social movements and civil society organisations under the nationalist umbrella, it was therefore not necessarily the concept of a Eurocentric notion of 'nationhood' that was being sought, but often specific, non-national interests (Hodgkin, 1956).

Once independence had been achieved, the mirage of national unity rapidly eroded, revealing the deep fissures within African nationalism. For the small number of African elites that had utilised but never fully harnessed the support of social movements and civil society organisations, such as trade unions and women's groups, the unifying thread of anti-colonialism gave way to conflicts and social divisions over the fruits of freedom. As the nationalist project disintegrated, groups including student associations, trade unions, and regional organisations found that their constituent demands were not being met, which led to unrest and protest. The internal contradictions fragmented these nationalist projects, and were replaced instead by the utilisation or reformulation of ethnic loyalty or regional affiliations by African elites; this is why so many post-colonial leaders established one-party states and relied so heavily on such narrow support bases to maintain their political control (see Chapter 4). Civil society as an agent of popular change had obviously been discouraged by colonial rulers, which meant that there was no historical link to the state, and 'what there was of civil society was part of the nationalist elite or was viewed by it with suspicion or as something to be used to achieve independence and then controlled' (Young, 1988, 45). Instead of embracing civil society as a means to build nationhood, these movements and organisations were viewed by post-colonial elites as agents of division. The implementation of centralised one-party states under the auspices of 'national unity' in countries as varied as Guinea and Uganda meant that social movements that campaigned for social justice, human rights, women's emancipation, or education were either co-opted by the state or simply banned. The consequence was that the public space for non-state actors to operate was curtailed and underdeveloped, and the interests of African people were vastly diminished as authoritarian and unrepresentative political structures were created.

Contemporary movements in Africa

Trade unions

Trade unions are organised groups of workers designed to protect and enhance the interests of their members, especially in relation to powerful political and economic forces. Throughout Africa, trade unions have not only sought to serve the economic and social well-being of workers, but also played an important role in the political process, first during decolonisation and later in the struggles for democratisation since the 1990s. These organisations have experienced fluctuations in the extent of their influence and impact, but must be considered a crucial component in our understanding of African social movements. Under colonialism, industrial action became more apparent in the 1940s as a form of collective protest, which saw a series of disputes break out, such as the 1947 railway strike in Senegal, which ground the country to a halt (Cooper, 1996b). Across the continent, unions mobilised their members in strikes and non-cooperation activities, which made them a powerful counterpoint to the colonial state, and consequently aligned them with the evolving nationalist struggles. For example, Ghana, Kenya, and Nigeria all experienced worker agitation over material and social issues, which were utilised as part of the anti-colonial fight. Most unions did not operate with an explicit political platform, yet it was perhaps unavoidable that huge displays of popular support were regarded as being intertwined with demands for self-determination. In some cases, such as with Guinea's Sékou Touré, leaders used their role within the union movement to enhance their leadership credentials for the post-colonial dispensation. While there was clearly a crossover between the aims of unions and those of nationalists, which led to the creation of tentative alliances across the continent, there was some unease by union leaders about the power and motivations of elites using worker mobilisation as a mechanism to gain independence.

The suspicions of trade unions became a reality after independence, as their room for manoeuvre was severely curtailed by successive post-colonial states. Having seen how influential unions were in the anti-colonial struggle, one-party states either co-opted workers' leaders into government ministerial positions, created 'official' unions which were under centralised control, or simply banned any independent-minded organisations. There were a few countries such as Nigeria where powerful workers' organisations were able to resist total co-option by the state, but these were exceptions rather than the norm. However, the onset of economic decline and the IMF's implementation of structural adjustment policies by the 1980s (see Chapter 5) created an environment in which inequality and mass job losses became more pronounced. These clearly demonstrated the inability of 'official' unions to represent their natural constituents. The suppression and co-option of trade unions ensured there was little opportunity to express frustrations and discontent, nor the ability to achieve tangible material change in the face of deepening austerity; in 1983, the Tunisian government removed food subsidies, which caused mass rioting, yet the state-sanctioned trade union did not support the public protests (Zghal, 1995). The consequence was that for much of the immediate post-colonial period the ability of unions to offer effective representation, or influence policy decisions, was diminished considerably.

Box 7.1 Congress of South African Trade Unions (COSATU)

During the anti-apartheid struggle, trade unions became a powerful symbol of popular, mass resistance to white minority rule. The recommendation to legalise black unions in South Africa was first tabled in 1979 by the Wiehahn Commission, which led to the flourishing of black workers' movements seeking to represent political and economic concerns within the confines of an oppressive system. In 1985, the multiracial COSATU was established as a formidable federation representing over 33 union organisations to act as a focal point for community action and labour concerns. The creation of COSATU 'marked a major new force both in industrial relations and in politics' (Gerhart, 2010, 87). Throughout the late 1980s, COSATU worked closely with other civil society groups such as the United Democratic Front to sustain protests, boycotts, and strikes (such as the 1986 May Day stay-away of 1.5 million people), which in tandem with international sanctions helped cripple South Africa's economy. Many of COSATU's actions were centred on workers' rights, such as the 1987 Living Wage Campaign, but these were still inherently highly political issues because the apartheid system restricted black opportunities.

During the transition process (1990–1994), COSATU was represented as part of the ANC's negotiating team to form a new democratic dispensation, which was reflected by a number of union leaders such as Jay Naidoo and Cyril Ramaphosa (South Africa's current president) serving in the first post-apartheid government, as well as the initial adoption of the 'leftist' socio-economic policy, the Reconstruction and Development Programme. Since 1994, COSATU has been officially part of the 'tripartite alliance' that governs South Africa along with the ANC and South African Communist Party (SACP), although it has found its influence over economic policy has been severely constrained, most notably by the introduction of the neo-liberal policy Growth, Employment and Redistribution, the huge private sector job losses experienced under Thabo Mbeki, and the co-option of its leadership into government structures. However, COSATU's relationship with the ANC has become increasingly uneasy as the economy declines and workers continue to endure persistent inequality, which were exacerbated by former president Jacob Zuma's autocratic rule. In May 2017, COSATU openly diverged from the ANC by publicly stating that it would campaign against Zuma's presidency and seek a greater focus on workers' rights by the ANC.

Importantly, the economic decline of the 1980s had weakened the legitimacy and strength of authoritarian governments, kindling growing societal unrest. For instance, in Mali and Congo-Brazzaville trade unions seized this opportunity to stake their independence away from state control, which enabled them to act as conduits to channel widespread social discontent. By the early 1990s, unions emerged at the forefront of the democratisation process, and their actions and initiatives forced the political agenda through strikes and mass action, especially throughout West Africa. One of the most notable examples was in Zambia, where the formation of the Movement for Multiparty Democracy – developed out of the Zambia Congress of Trade Union's militancy – by leader Frederick Chiluba proved instrumental in forcing the incumbent Kenneth Kaunda into constitutional changes and then elections in 1991. Another instance of unions campaigning to effect change was in Zimbabwe, where workers' movements were fundamental in the protests against Robert Mugabe's autocratic rule and economic mismanagement; these efforts resulted in the formation of the MDC in 1999, which under the leadership of former trade union secretary-general Morgan Tsvangirai came close to unseating Mugabe in 2002. Subsequently, the MDC entered into a power-sharing agreement in 2008, but its power and influence waned as Mugabe continued to retain overall control.

Therefore trade unions were and continue to be a vital social movement formation that enabled some degree of freedom and democracy to be realised after decades of authoritarianism. However, the democratisation process is far from complete, and the global economic inequalities that continue to afflict the continent have maintained structural poverty for many. African trade unions have found the recent political and economic environment dominated by the wealthy nations and the ideologies of neo-liberalism particularly challenging to navigate. Social movements now have far more freedom and space to work within than ever before (with exceptions such as Swaziland), but the inability of governments to fundamentally alter neo-liberal economic policies to serve the majority has meant that achieving effective and material change is now extremely difficult for trade unions (Zeilig, 2010, 20–21). Globalisation has certainly impacted on the influence and power of unions, because weak economies, unstable working conditions, and a growing informal sector have made employment both scarce and insecure (in South Africa, youth unemployment was 63.5% in 2018). The consequence is that unions now have fewer members than previously, and are generally less militant (OECD, 2016). Nevertheless, African trade unions remain a crucial social movement, providing alternative voices in political and economic debates, offering ongoing efforts to protect workers' material interests, while remaining an important source of power.

NGOs

Since the 1980s, the presence of international and local NGOs has expanded rapidly across Africa. NGOs act as powerful and influential civil society organisations which are able to intervene in, and work on, issues related to political and economic development, inequality, human rights, and the environment. There are a multiplicity of NGOs throughout Africa, and they vary enormously in terms of their size and scale, ranging from the truly international such as Oxfam and Médecins Sans Frontières (MSF) to small local initiatives; the source of their funding, be it through government and development agencies or via charitable donations; their overarching purpose(s) such as providing humanitarian relief or campaigning on issues such as HIV/AIDs awareness; and whether they are concerned with local capacity building or committed to delivering externally planned projects (Jennings, 2013, 323). In order to fully appreciate the complexity of NGO activity in Africa it is fundamental to recognise these complex layers with regards to their structure, operation, and focus – many organisations will exhibit various characteristics of each. Furthermore, all too often NGOs are regarded through a western lens, which conceptualises external agencies implementing top-down initiatives and policies, with little input from the communities they are operating in. Yet taking such a perspective obscures the significant role and influence that African organisations have had in establishing spaces within civil society which ensure 'action from below' and citizens' participation to assist in altering local conditions. Clearly, then, the label NGO conceals a diverse set of distinctive activities and organisations, but in simple terms NGOs are non-state, non-profit actors that are concerned with resolving specific development issues.

The common perception is that NGO activity in Africa is a recent phenomenon, but non-state institutions – for instance church groups – were extremely active in providing education and health provisions during the colonial period. Britain in particular was unwilling to fund welfare provision to Africans, for example choosing instead 'to "outsource" most of the education to private voluntary agencies' (Frankema, 2012, 337). Kenya, for example, saw an 'expansive network of faith-based NGOs … [which] busied themselves with extensive social welfare work' (Hershey, 2013, 672). Despite being independent from the colonial authorities, these NGOs were still closely tied to the imperial project and treated African people based on ideas of the 'civilising mission' and paternalism, rather than any true sense of social justice; some of these tendencies are still evident today.

The rapid proliferation and growing influence of international NGOs really began in the 1980s, as the aforementioned economic and political decline meant heavily indebted African governments were forced to adopt SAPs that facilitated the wholesale withdrawal of the state from many key welfare functions. The growing influence of NGOs in Africa mirrored the ongoing western ideological shift in economic thinking, which advocated less government provision for services in favour of leaving many of these functions to non-state organisations. The consequential rollback of the state hit the poorest hard, and many countries were forced to rely on international NGOs to provide services that had once been the domain of governments (Shivji, 2007). As these NGOs gained a more prominent position in African affairs, international funding agencies began to seek them out as preferred partners for development and poverty reduction programmes, rather than working directly with governments. Both local African and international NGOs were now able to tap into external sources of funding for their work, which saw the prestige, influence, and number of organisations rise. This also raised significant questions about the depth of dependency and accountability of non-state actors within African nation-states to external funding agencies.

Box 7.2 Médecins Sans Frontières (MSF) and the 2013–2016 Ebola crisis

The outbreak of the deadly Ebola epidemic in West Africa first appeared in late 2013 and affected Liberia, Sierra Leone, and Guinea; led to the infection of 28,000 people; and killed 11,310 (WHO, 2016b). Early warning signs about the emergence of Ebola were ignored by local and international agencies, and the virus spread rapidly across the region, aided by poverty, mistrust of politicians, weak governments, and poorly funded and overwhelmed health services. The regional crisis was described by the World Health Organization (WHO 2014b) as an emergency of international concern, which prompted a response from over 30 NGO groups, which came to assist these states in trying to contain the virus and cure those infected.

MSF, which had been set up after the Biafra War and works extensively on medical care throughout Africa, was a key NGO that offered humanitarian assistance during the Ebola crisis. In the multinational struggle to contain the epidemic, MSF was the largest medical presence in the region providing isolation units, emergence care, health education, and advice on strategies to prevent the spread (Image 7.1). To achieve these goals, in 2014 alone MSF had 4,000 local and 1,300 international staff members in the region (14 of whom died); had shipped in mobile incinerators to cremate bodies; distributed 70,000 Ebola prevention kits; and had also begun clinical trials to test vaccines, which would later prove to be effective against one strand of the disease (MSF, 2014). These various measures, along with those of other organisations and governments, helped to contain the epidemic, which was declared over in January 2016. Despite the work done by MSF, the organisation was highly critical of the global response to the virus and spoke out on the need for more efficient international strategies to cope with health emergencies.

Image 7.1 MSF Ebola treatment centre in Liberia

Source: © Louise Gubb/CORBIS SABA/Corbis via Getty Images.

Another boost to NGO presence across Africa was closely linked to the wave of democratisation that spread during the 1990s (see Chapter 4), and which opened up greater opportunities for civil society work. The new agenda of 'good governance' was closely linked to the neo-liberal project, with western governments and financial institutions such as the IMF explicitly regarding NGOs as useful mechanisms to promote a 'liberal' agenda (Larmer, 2010, 256). NGOs were conceptualised not only as service providers, but also as the defenders of transparency, human rights, and social justice. With a growing focus on advocacy work, lawyers in nations such as Nigeria had an important role in overseeing specific standards were upheld. Increasingly NGOs have a major presence in most African nations; while exact figures are hard to come by, one estimate was that there were 100,000 operating in South Africa alone (Stuart, 2013).

Without wanting to undermine the work of NGOs, which has had a vital role in assisting millions of people and promoting greater civil society freedoms, there have been several criticisms voiced about their role and influence. A key theme is that the rise of international NGOs is linked to neo-liberalism, which has perpetuated inequality and poverty through the enforced retreat of the state. The consequence was that 'outsourced' service provision, for instance healthcare, undermined state sovereignty and entrenched structural problems rather than providing more permanent solutions. The fundamental critique has been that the provision of international aid will not really transform either the economy or society in any meaningful way. Hence NGOs are a sticking plaster for much more deep-rooted issues and mask the need for fundamental changes. Furthermore, those NGOs relying heavily on external funding have consequently been far more responsive to donor concerns than to local needs. In turn, this can create a situation where projects are devised in overseas countries and then implemented with little consideration for the locality in which they are to be carried out. For example, Playpump was an international initiative to install water pumps connected to merry-go-rounds, which as children played on them would draw water to the surface. The scheme sounded like a marketing dream and was endorsed by celebrities such as Jay-Z. However, while Playpump attracted huge sums of overseas finance, the device was far too expensive (four times more than a normal pump), too complex for local maintenance, reliant on the efforts of children, and simply couldn't draw enough water for local demands.

Perhaps more dangerous and harmful are the overwhelmingly negative perceptions that some NGOs perpetuate. There is a common idea that Africa needs 'saving' which creates a cycle of dependency on western 'aid', while reinforcing a narrative of the continent as a 'basket case'. Given the sheer number of NGOs operating throughout Africa, in order to gain public recognition and therefore donations the media message is unremittingly bleak. It projects visual and textual representations of starving children or war-torn communities; while these exist in present-day Africa, they are far from representative. For example, look at the message that the UK charity Comic Relief conveys to get a sense of the ways in which stereotypes are reinforced about Africa. Closely linked to these themes is also the 'white saviour' narrative which sees westerners visit 'Africa' to work on school building projects or environmental sanctuaries. Another example is actress Louise Linton, who published a book in 2016 called *In Congo's Shadow* which caused outrage as it was full of inaccuracies, racist assumptions, and lazy stereotypes. While NGO activity is well meaning, many do little to overcome foreign perceptions of the continent or to establish meaningful change.

An interesting recent development has been the increased scrutiny of NGO activity via satire that has sought to offer alternative perspectives and ways of thinking about poverty. Several examples include the website *Radi-aid* which highlights the best and worst of NGO campaigning and has also released a series of satirical videos such as 'Africa for Norway' and 'who wants to be a volunteer?'; the Instagram and Twitter account *barbiesavior* where a white doll is pictured travelling the continent in designer wear 'volunteering'; and the 2016 film set in Uganda, *N.G.O (Nothing Going On)*, whose tagline is 'in Africa, if you want to be rich, create a rebel group, a church, or an N.G.O'.

Single-issue movements

As seen with the other forms of social movements and civil society organisations above, the key period that allowed them to flourish and have a more decisive influence can be directly attributed to the economic and political developments of the late 1980s and early 1990s. The creation of relatively free public spaces ensured that citizens could begin to organise for collective action, often on very local issues. Governments were obviously wary of such groups and their demands, but the decline in legitimacy and authority meant that it was difficult to monitor or crush dissent. Yet increasingly, governments throughout Africa continue to display a level of distrust about civil society, with some such as Algeria, Egypt, and Tanzania all seeking to restrict and obstruct many organisations and movements that are regarded as a threat to their rule. Therefore recently, single-issue movements have become much more important in offering a voice to the voiceless, and holding governments to account in the pursuit of genuine change.

Across the continent, movements representing a diverse set of local and international causes have successfully emerged to intervene in a variety of economic and social issues since the 1990s. These range from campaigns on HIV/AIDs to wildlife conservation and anti-poaching efforts to the implementation of the Kimberley Process to curb 'blood diamonds'. African civil society activities demonstrate the ability of diverse and often fragmented groups to unify people behind a common cause in order to make a difference. Movements of this nature function and campaign in very different ways, depending on whether they can tap into national or international discourses, which can in turn have an effect on sources of funding; the target of advocacy efforts; who joins the campaign; the 'reach' of the message; and ultimately the impact. It should be pointed out that movements of this type can also rise and fall relatively rapidly depending on the success or failure of their message to capture the public imagination. This section will give an indication of some of these single-issue movements of which there are thousands, but some examples of those not included here are the global anti-apartheid movement; the struggles for LGBT rights to be enshrined and respected; the Treatment Action Campaign (TAC) for access to antiretroviral drugs for HIV/AIDs; campaigns against slavery in Mauritania; and mass rioting over food prices in countries such as Mali in 2008.

An excellent example of a social movement associated not only with peace but also social inclusivity is Liberia's women's organisations (see Chapter 4), which not only helped to end the country's civil war in 2003, but also facilitated the election of Africa's first female president Ellen Johnson Sirleaf in 2005. The women's movement in Liberia was a campaign from below, which consciously mobilised across socio-economic and ethnic lines to be as representative as possible. The aim was to use their shared collective wartime experiences (that often involved horrific rates of sexual violence) to challenge notions of male superiority and violence, especially at local levels. Using various tactics such as non-violent campaigning, a 'sex strike', and wearing symbolic white T-shirts, women were able to force the warring factions to negotiate a peace deal and to firmly entrench gender concerns in post-conflict Liberian society. These local efforts were supported by international agencies which created spaces for dialogue and organisational structures to develop between activists, as well as providing funding and support. Ultimately successful in its aims, this women's movement was united behind the goal of peace and the promotion of gender equality; however, the women's movement has since begun to crumble, given that it served as an umbrella organisation for a range of competing ideas and interests (Fuest, 2009). The activities demonstrated the power that collective action can have, but also the potential time limit of a single-issue movement.

One of the most famous demonstrations of the power of civil society and NGO activism was the campaign around 'blood diamonds' which led to the creation of the Kimberley Process. Blood diamonds, the alluvial minerals utilised by rebel groups across Africa, particularly in Angola and Sierra Leone, in order to fund on-going warfare, caught the public imagination in the late 1990s. In Sierra Leone, the Network Movement for Justice and Development (NMJD), a local NGO, collaborated with the internationally based Partnership Africa Canada (PAC) to delve into the supposedly ideologically devoid war being waged by the RUF (see Chapter 6). In 2000, their joint report highlighted the corruption and complicity of politicians, multinational companies, and warlords in the unregulated mining and sale of diamonds. On a global level, the publicity of these findings helped to galvanise action, while simultaneously within Sierra Leone NMJD worked hard to establish civil society coalitions in order to influence and change the government's policy on dia-mond mining. Moreover, this coalition of African and international NGOs successfully got the issue on the global agenda – in May 2000, a series of meetings involving NGOs, diamond mining companies, and governments first began at Kimberley in South Africa, to discuss a multi-lateral solution. However, frustrated by the lack of progress and perceived government inaction, NGOs, with the assistance of the media, ran a series of damning reports and stories that shamed international actors into action around this moral issue; the result was the signing of the Kimberley Process in 2003 endorsed by the UN and 70 nations that established the introduction of certificates of origin for all rough diamonds. Within three years, a small, barely recognised issue in Sierra Leone became an inter-national cause célèbre through a partnership of NGOs who were able to force the global agenda (see Gberie, 2009).

Box 7.3 Youth movements in the DRC

The DRC has experienced its fair share of political turmoil, which was exacerbated by the decision of incumbent president Joseph Kabila not to relinquish power in December 2016. Against the backdrop of Kabila's decision, ongoing state failure, and the cyclical violence in the east of the country perpetuated by the M23 rebellion (see Chapter 6), the youth movement 'Lucha' (struggle for change) was formed by disaffected university students in 2012. From humble beginnings Lucha has become a significant and influential youth-orientated social movement, which demands wide-ranging reforms and social justice in the DRC. It is not a political party (nor does it seek to be), but rather a collective organisation, which has a significant proportion of women participation, and works predominantly at a very local level campaigning over issues such as service delivery and empowerment through education. Furthermore, despite ongoing government repression and violence against the movement, Lucha is explicitly non-violent in its mobilisation and campaign activities, utilising various methods including marches and sit-ins, while social media, which has altered the way people can mobilise across the continent, has proved important in attracting support. Although much of the activism has a bottom-up approach, focused on improving local conditions such as access to water and electricity, Lucha's national objectives include political transparency and governmental reform, which in turn will allow for greater social and material transformation in the DRC.

These examples demonstrate the powerful impact that single-issue movements have. By coalescing people and organisational energies behind a single demand or idea, they can ensure lasting changes can be achieved. Although some campaigns will obviously not succeed, single-issue movements throughout Africa have been fruitful in educating citizens, enshrining rights, entrenching democratic norms through local activism, and struggling against activities that harm the environment. Clearly single-issue movements are and remain a crucial dimension of the fabric of African civil society.

Traditional authority

An often overlooked yet important part of contemporary African societies is traditional leadership, which at a local level continues to have a role in ordering and influencing people's lives. Although not necessarily fitting the normal definition of a social movement or civil society, traditional authorities have retained the ability to coalesce large numbers of people on a national and local level, dispense services and patronage, preside over laws and disputes within their domain, and protect cultural identities such as Zulu. During the decolonisation process, most traditional leaders lost their overriding power to nationalist elites, yet in Swaziland King Sobhuza II was able to retain the absolute power of the monarchy; in 1986, his son King Mswati III was crowned king and still continues to wield monarchical power. There is no single pattern of traditional power across Africa, because some current leaders hold their status due to pre-colonial ancestral lineage, while more problematically others do so through the invention of colonial administrators, who created chiefs and tribes where none existed beforehand as a means of indirect rule (see Chapter 3). Therefore the term traditional leadership encompasses a spectrum of different characteristics, with much of the legitimacy stemming from the past. Nonetheless, these leaders have also been able to evolve within the modern state to carve out continued political and economic opportunities for themselves and their constituents.

Box 7.4 Burkina Faso's Mogho Naba

In October 2014, Burkina Faso's traditional king of the Mossi people Baongo II, known as the Mogho Naba, shot to prominence as a conflict mediator – first when President Blaise Compaoré tried to amend the constitution to retain power and then afterwards, in 2015, in preventing an attempted military coup. The Mogho Naba remains an influential and respected powerbroker within Burkinabe society, with politicians required to seek endorsement from him to govern, and in times of difficulty the monarchy acts as a neutral mechanism for dialogue and compromise. During the 2014 political crisis, leaders from the various warring factions met with Baongo II for talks, with the king maintaining channels of communication to ensure the military did not retain political power.

In the post-colonial era, most nationalist leaders regarded traditional authority as distinctly unmodern. As a result, some independent states such as Tanzania and Mozambique moved rapidly to deny the power of chiefs, others including Togo under President Eyadéma sought to co-opt traditional leaders by inserting their own supporters into positions of authority, while many simply did nothing to alter their structures. It is evident that traditional leaders continued to hold significant local power and influence, regularly acting as mediators between people and governments in divided states. Despite the various efforts to curb traditional authority during the 1990s, there was a resurgence across the continent in the recognition and role of these leaders in countries such as Uganda, Ghana, and South Africa; for example, the South African constitution enshrined the role of traditional leaders, such as the Zulu king Goodwill Zwelithini. Traditional leaders retain a strong albeit problematic social status especially in relation to issues concerning 'modernity' versus 'tradition'. For some, chiefs are best able to represent their people, their communities, and cultural identities by providing a crucial democratic link with an otherwise unresponsive state. Yet simultaneously, they can be viewed as a legacy of a bygone era unbefitting of a modern governance system, who entrench patriarchal and undemocratic norms. Whatever your perspective, traditional authority is firmly part of the political and social landscape and remains popular; in 2016, the Afrobarometer found that across 36 countries, Africans expressed more trust in informal institutions such as traditional leadership (61%) than in the state (54%).

Religious movements

Africa is a deeply religious continent, with spiritual beliefs and practices informing social interactions, ethnic identity, and political power. Religious behaviour is shaped both by formal denominations such as Islam and Christianity and by a diversity of traditional belief systems that are closely linked to spirits, magic, and respected ancestors. The spread of Islam can be mapped onto the various historical waves of Arabic expansion in the northern, eastern, and Sahel regions, while European missionaries brought various forms of Christianity, namely Catholicism and Protestantism, to central and southern Africa (see Chapter 3). However, an important difference is in north-east Africa, where the spread of Christianity was not through European missionaries. In Egypt, Ethiopia, and Eritrea, the traditions of Orthodox Christianity still remain, which first emerged in the region through the mission of St Mark the Evangelist in the first century AD. It should be recognised, though, that traditional and formalised religion in Africa are not mutually exclusive belief systems, instead demonstrating remarkable evolution, overlap, and hybridity depending on the geographic setting (Moyo, 2001). For instance, despite the conversion to Christianity, the influence and theology of European churches have been superseded by independent African denominations which have incorporated traditional elements such as spiritualism, faith healing, and music into their worship; the rise of Pentecostal churches in Nigeria is testament to this development, which is more attuned to the demands of their congregations. Likewise, Islam has undergone various revisions, regularly adapting to the specific social and political environment in each nation by infusing traditional customs into worship. Recently, there has been a denunciation of these traditional practices that have been adopted by some Muslims in West Africa, particularly in Senegal, which has seen the emergence of a growing socially conservative Salafist movement, demanding a purer, orthodox form of Islam.

Moreover, it must be acknowledged that the broad three categories Christian, Muslim, and traditional beliefs do not adequately capture the diversity of religious practice in Africa, with numerous competing strands and theological positions. For example, within Islam there is the rivalry between Sunni and Shia Muslims, and under the umbrella of Protestantism there are numerous different branches including

Anglican, Baptist, and Presbyterian. Furthermore, religious affiliation has ensured that these social networks are integrated into wider global discourses, allowing for the international spread of ideas and people (Ellis & ter Haar, 2004). The consequence of this 'internationalisation' is that religion has provided a vital mechanism for social movements to flourish from a politicised form of Islamism, in the shape of al-Qaeda in the Islamic Maghreb, to evangelical Christian missionaries from Nigeria who travel both near and far to preach. Therefore religious practice and beliefs can vary enormously, and be influenced by very local or international factors.

Box 7.5 Pentecostalism in Africa

The rapid rise and spread in the membership of Pentecostal churches across the continent, especially in Nigeria and the DRC, have been a key feature of contemporary Christianity in Africa, and is a major social force. Although the Pentecostal Church has its roots in the USA, it breaks from the traditional pious doctrines of European Christianity in favour of a faith system based on charismatic worship, an emphasis on personal self-renewal, and an acceptance of spirits and faith healing that closely resemble traditional African religions. Furthermore, a key tenet of Pentecostalism is one of self-enrichment, which is particularly attractive to the continent's urban poor, with the church seen as offering a spiritual path away from poverty to a new life of prosperity. The Pentecostal movement is an appealing form of Christianity in Africa, creating a dynamic and energetic community of followers, while also establishing a space free from patriarchal norms that has allowed women to have a prominent position in the church as spiritual leaders and healers. Building on these foundations, Pentecostal churches, many of which resemble business empires, attract followers through a variety of means including mass participation in megachurches; musical, interactive services; public faith healings; the publication of books, DVDs, and CDs; advertising via print and electronic media; and energetic missionary work. A good example of the reach and power of an African Pentecostal Church is the Living Faith Church Worldwide, sometimes referred to as the 'Winners Chapel', formed by Bishop David Oyedepo in 1983. The denomination is now a global phenomenon, with its main Lagos church able to hold over 50,000 people.

In terms of civil society, religion is clearly a powerful and influential force across the continent, providing a moral underpinning for mobilisation and community action. Importantly, and often forgotten, is that religious organisations had a role in the anti-colonial resistance, exemplified by the Maji Maji rebellion in 1906 against German rule, or the regular jihads against the British in Somalia. In the post-colonial era, although many nations adopted a position of secularism (notable exceptions were the Islamic states of Libya, Mauritania, and Sudan), religious institutions often had an ambiguous relationship with the state: some utilised their position for dissent, while others were co-opted into the political process. For example, the Dutch Reformed Church was an ardent supporter of apartheid in South Africa until a moral U-turn in 1986, while the Catholic Church in Rwanda was complicit in the 1994 genocide by the Hutu extremists. However, in many cases, the closing of civil society spaces by nationalist elites meant that religious organisations provided a rare outlet for dissent, with few governments willing to attempt outright suppression. In several instances, as the crisis of political legitimacy increased in the 1980s, it was the clergy and the imams who utilised their relative freedoms to articulate alternative visions for the future; the best examples of religious leaders taking a stand against autocratic leaders were against Hastings Banda (Malawi) and Daniel arap Moi (Kenya).

As the continent has experienced greater democratic norms take root, religious movements have increasingly played a prominent role in public life, acting as protest movements, a forum for policy debates, a vehicle to lobby governments, and a key societal influencer. Perhaps surprisingly in the democratic era, religious organisations, both Muslim and Christian, have not explicitly sought state power, with the notable exceptions being a highly politicised form of Islam evident in North African nations such as Algeria, Egypt, and Sudan. Although African society is extremely devout, the vast majority of states remain secular, which has led to most religious organisations choosing to eschew total state dominance in preference of securing greater and more assertive representation within the public sphere. For example, in francophone West Africa, the majority of Muslims have shown a strong support for democracy, because the religious concerns advocated by Islamic social movements are adequately fulfilled by democratic state structures (Villalon, 2013, 141). Although most groups remain content with active civil society participation within secular states, there has been a recent emergence of vocal fringe organisations wishing to achieve more exclusivist objectives under the guise of religious motivations. In Nigeria, a country divided between Christians and Muslims, the onset of democratic elections in 1999 created conditions that enabled 12 northern states to implement Shari'a law by 2002, which was in response to popular local demands, and to appease the concerns about the rapid spread of Pentecostalism (Soares, 2009). The widespread use of Shari'a in northern Nigeria created a public space in which more fundamentalist Islamist views could flourish, resulting in the formation of Boko Haram, which demanded a stricter implementation of Shari'a, along with a rejection of western and secular education. As the Nigerian state continued to ignore the religious and social demands of Boko Haram, it became increasingly radicalised, resulting in it morphing from protest movement into an extremist jihadi group by 2009, which has since wreaked havoc across the region. Incidentally, the abduction of 276 schoolgirls by Boko Haram in 2014 sparked a grassroots protest movement in Nigeria over government inaction that rapidly became a global social campaign under the banner #BringBackOurGirls, attracting support from millions of people, including the Obamas.

As this chapter has set out, social movements and civil society organisations play an important role in contemporary Africa, providing a space that ensures the concerns and needs of ordinary citizens can be addressed. Although there is now more freedom than ever before for non-state actors in Africa to represent their constituents or to intervene in a particular issue, there remains a tenuous relationship between many governments and civil society. The growing clamp down on civil society spaces from Tunisia to Malawi has begun to reduce the opportunities available for movements to operate, which is connected to the democratic backsliding that is occurring in several countries (see Chapter 5). Yet the increasing penetration and use of the internet across the continent (Chapter 10), especially through social media platforms such as Facebook, WhatsApp, and Telegram, has enabled groups to mobilise more effectively, and unite people behind a particular cause. These tools offer greater opportunities to reach more people, and to act as another strategy to challenge state institutions. Social movements and civil society organisations remain a significant force in many states, allowing for citizens to campaign and protest against unresponsive governments, offering opportunities to create and reinforce democratic cultures, while meeting the needs of the population, often at a very local level, through the provision of basic services.

 ## Further reading

The best sources to start with to gain a broad sense of the diversity of social movements across the continent are Stephen Ellis and Ineke van Kessel's (2009) *Movers and Shakers: Social Movements in Africa*; Peter Dwyer and Leo Zeilig's (2012) *African Struggles Today*; and the relevant chapters – N. Lafi, 'The "Arab Spring" in global perspective: Social movements, changing contexts and political transitions in the

Arab world (2010–2014)' and A. Eckert, 'Social movements in Africa' – of Stefan Berger and Holger Nehring's (2017) *The History of Social Movements in Global Perspectives*. For a greater insight into religious movements in Africa, turn to Ruth Marshall (2009) *Political Spiritualties: The Pentecostal Revolution in Nigeria*; and Louis Brenner (1993) *Muslim Identity and Social Change in Sub-Saharan Africa*. There are also several useful studies into the role and activities of NGOs, including Ondine Barrow and Michael Jenning's (2001) *The Charitable Impulse: NGOs & Development in East and North-East Africa*; and Stephen Ndegwa's (1996) *The Two Faces of Civil Society: NGOs and Politics in Africa*; as well as the powerful critique of western development projects in James Ferguson's (1994) *Anti-Politics Machine*.

8 POPULAR CULTURE

Given the sheer diversity of the continent and its peoples, 'culture' can become an unwieldly and unhelpful term. Culture is extremely difficult to pin down, and the term hides a multitude of meanings, value judgements, political connotations, and social norms, which can be drastically different from community to community. Furthermore, there is a distinction between 'high' and 'popular' culture, in which the former often includes 'sophisticated' or elite-dominated frames of reference such as art and philosophy which set them apart from the rest of society, while the latter includes activities or attitudes enjoyed by the majority of the populace.

To ensure a clear sense of purpose, and to provide a manageable assessment of forms of African culture, this chapter will focus only on literature, film, music, and sport. In and of itself this selection of specific cultures excludes other important material aspects such as visual art, theatre, television, and fashion, all of which have an influential role in African societies and the diaspora. The reason for the narrow selection is to capture an overview of cultural forms, while offering a lens into a range of mass societal activities and experiences across the continent.

Crucially, this chapter emphasises that the four areas of African culture selected here are inherently political, and are sites of struggle, resistance, and reappropriation by various communities. In addition, other themes that can be regarded as cultural such as behavioural norms and group identities which include religious organisations (Chapter 7) or ethnic identity (Chapters 3 and 4) are addressed elsewhere in the book.

Literature

For those unfamiliar with African literature, then browsing a bookshop or online catalogue is probably the worst way to try and get your bearings, because all too regularly publishers fall into the trope of portraying 'the single story' (Adiche, 2009). On book covers, the continent is depicted all too often by acacia trees, big skies, and silhouettes no matter the subject, nor which country it is set in. Such lazy stereotypes do little to change the image of the continent in the west, but more importantly diminish a rich history of African literature. In fact, there is a diverse and lively field of African literature, encompassing an array of topics from critiques of colonialism to science fiction, which have an important role in popular culture, both domestically and abroad. While there are a number of critically acclaimed authors from across the continent, recognition for the works of African writers has so far been slow to materialise. To underline this lack of global acknowledgement, the Nobel Prize in Literature has, since its foundation in 1901, been awarded to African writers a mere five times: Albert Camus (Algeria, 1957), Wole Soyinka (Nigeria, 1986), Naguib Mahfouz (Egypt, 1988), Nadine Gordimer (South Africa, 1991), and J.M. Coetzee (South Africa, 2003).

Although most people would regard the term 'literature' solely through the traditional Eurocentric perspective that holds the written word supreme, it should be recognised that 'oral arts' through the spoken word or song are an important literary form. While there is clearly no single form of 'African literature', oral traditions are one of the few cultural similarities found across the continent, with recognisable folk tales concerning ancestors and spirits in languages such as Yoruba, Swahili, and Zulu. Throughout Africa, this long history of oral tradition has had a key place in the social and cultural fabric of many communities, in which elders or specifically designated wordsmiths would be relied on to retell histories, myths, and ancestral lineage. This is far from a static art form, because the basis or moral of the tale is continuously updated to meet contemporary realities and cultural reference points (Joseph, 2001, 331–334). Crucially, oral traditions did not disappear entirely following the introduction of Arabic and European languages, and the culture of the written word, via the holy texts of Islam and Christianity (see Chapter 7). Indeed, oral traditions continue to have a prominent position within the cultural milieu of contemporary African societies, with each country, community, and language having their own specific forms of narration and storytelling. This sub-section will not focus on African oral art, but the style, techniques, and subject matter inherent within this form of storytelling have been extremely influential to many authors who have focused on the written literary form.

How can we conceptualise contemporary African literature? The great Nigerian novelist Chinua Achebe (1965, 27) argued 'that you cannot cram African literature into a small, neat definition. I do not see African literature as one unit but as a group of associated units ... Any attempt to define African literature in terms which overlook the complexities of the

African scene at the material time is doomed to failure.' To fully appreciate these complexities and differences, and to distinguish between the various literary forms found throughout Africa, the continent must be subdivided into national and ethnic traditions, but also crucially the linguistic heritage. The continent has thousands of languages such as Yoruba, Xhosa, Afrikaans, and Gikuyu, some spoken very locally and others that span across entire regions, while simultaneously the 'official' language in most countries is historically an externally imposed one, for example Arabic, French, Portuguese, or English. An author's linguistic background will therefore influence and affect the style, form, and the audience, and consequently various African literatures have developed separately along linguistic lines.

A crucial literary debate that continues to exercise African authors and post-colonial theorists is in what language they should write. On one side of the debate, the argument holds that a true African author should reject the hegemonic languages of the coloniser and express themselves in their own tongue. Such a position was advocated by philosopher Frantz Fanon in *Black Skin, White Masks* (1967) and Kenyan novelist Ngũgĩ wa Thiong'o (1986) who argued in *Decolonising the Mind: The Politics of Language in African Literature* that by using hegemonic languages Africans were perpetuating and reinforcing imperialist tendencies, which subjugated their lived experiences to neo-colonialist pressures. In Ngũgĩ wa Thiong'o's case the only way to overcome cultural imperialism and to provide tangible expression to his surroundings was to write in Gikuyu; an example of the decision to no longer write in English was his book *Matigari ma Njirũũngi* (1986). This position was also adopted by Nigerian author Obiajunwa Wali, who believed the use of colonial languages was elitist, favouring only those who had benefited from formal education, which consequently disenfranchised the majority of Africans from engaging with literature. Furthermore, Wali (1962, 14), critical of authors such as Wole Soyinka, argued that: 'until these writers and their western midwives accept the fact that any true African literature must be written in African languages, they would be merely pursuing a dead end which can only lead to sterility, uncreativity, and frustration.' Does that mean those authors who write in hegemonic languages are not authentically African, as they have internalised the colonial mindset?

The alternative perspective asserts that rather than entirely rejecting imperial languages, African writers should use them, albeit knowingly and creatively. By using particularly French and English, it means that writing about the 'African reality' can be introduced to global audiences. In turn this could enhance understanding and knowledge about the continent far more than languages such as Igbo and Swahili could ever achieve. More importantly, through the reappropriation of language

African writers can be subversive in their efforts to achieve full decolonisation by undermining hegemonic cultures in a way that will resonate with their audience. Achebe (1965, 29–30) argued that the African writer 'should aim at fashioning out an English which is at once universal and able to carry his peculiar experience', but crucially, 'it will have to be a new English, still in full communion with its ancestral home but altered to suit its new African surroundings'. This is not to say that things should not change; writers in this theoretical camp certainly appreciate that the decolonisation process, well after political independence, is still ongoing, but they can still pursue alternative agendas and interrogate the hegemony of colonialism through the reappropriation of languages. The response is a hybridised and unconventional form of writing which continually borrows, challenges, and rephrases language, and helps to make such literature distinctly non-western. Is there a definitive answer to this debate? Not at all. African writers continue to grapple with this tricky philosophical dilemma, about authenticity, expression, voice, and marketability, which understandably influences their outputs.

Overall, based on linguistic and cultural colonial inheritances, the three main 'schools' of African literature constitute anglophone, francophone, and Maghrebi traditions. However, it must be recognised that in North Africa more so than elsewhere on the continent there is a hybridity in the style of literature, as authors are far more attuned to using a combination of French, Arabic, and Berber languages. Many Algerian authors have written primarily in French, although Rachid Boudjedra and Kateb Yacine work across the nation's linguistic boundaries, while in Tunisia, Morocco, and Libya there is a greater tendency to use Arabic, represented by writers such as Waciny Laredj, Mohamed Zafzaf, and Ibrahim al-Koni.

There is no single theme that African writers focus on, but in the colonial and post-colonial setting, as well as today, authors have utilised the power of the pen as an important political, social, and cultural weapon. Overarching similarities can be found across the three dominant literary traditions, with African authors seeking to provide a distinct 'voice' to offer alternative narratives and new non-Eurocentric perspectives. Key subjects that are prominently found in African literature often concern the recreation of specific histories and cultures, freed from external interventions; critiques of empire; the enduring and pervasive legacies of colonialism; a renewed focus on African agency and experience; the decline of the post-colonial state; social injustices; and the interactions between different cultures and religions. These main topics adopted by African authors have coincided with a change in narrative style away from narrow 'realism' to a greater experimentation with the use of imaginative storytelling techniques embracing themes of magic, surrealism, and the supernatural to convey their message, which have similarities with post-colonial authors in Latin America and Asia. Therefore literature is a site of resistance, and allows for powerful political and social interventions through popular culture. The importance and impact of literature can be demonstrated by the response of governments and organisations on the receiving end of critical comment, with many writers forced into exile such as the South African Alex La Guma and in other extreme cases murdered, as exemplified by the Algerian Tahar Djaout and the Nigerian Ken Saro-Wiwa. It is impossible to summarise African literature in its totality here, but a few important trends and authors are discussed below.

Much of the early writing on Africa was by Europeans who wrote about the continent and its people in a form that largely perpetuated negative stereotypes; novels such as Joseph Conrad's (1902) *Heart of Darkness* and Ridder Haggard's (1885) *King Solomon's Mines* are examples of this form of writing about the continent. There were a limited number of African authors who captured the attention of international audiences, including Thomas Mofolo (Lesotho) whose pioneering work *Chaka* (1925), written in Sotho, but later translated into English, was about the legendary Zulu leader and the effects of his warlike expansion (see Chapter 3). However, because of the general lack of education provided by the colonial state, few people were able to produce literary works (at least fulfilling the 'standards' of the west). Combined with a systematic indifference to African experiences, as well as racialised perceptions on the merit of particular forms of literature, consequently this meant that most authors were largely ignored by the European literary community. Therefore a significant aim for many early African authors was to redress this imbalance. However, an impediment to this goal was the paucity of publishing houses across the continent for authors to promote their work. One important initiative was the creation of the African Writers Series in 1962, published by Heinemann, which established an international platform for African writers such as Chinua Achebe, Ngũgĩ wa Thiong'o, Steve Biko, and Ama Ata Aidoo. Yet it should be noted that the number of publishing houses still continues to vary today from country to country, and can significantly inhibit literary outputs from specific locales.

In French African literature, the emergence of the Negritude movement in the 1930s was a key anti-colonial literary force. Negritude was formulated by young black writers from across the French empire who, prompted by the realities of colonial rule, rejected the concept of assimilation and European notions of 'civilisation'. They proposed an alternative philosophical and literary movement to celebrate 'blackness', while seeking to create a distinctive, shared African cultural identity, and were heavily influenced by Pan-Africanist thought (see Chapter 9). The main African proponent of Negritude was the future Senegalese president Léopold Senghor, whose poetry includes works such as *Chants d'ombre* (1945) and

Anthologie de la nouvelle poésie nègre et malgache (1948), in which he celebrated African history and glorified traditional life away from European subjugation and cultural imposition. However, the Negritude movement's construction of an unrealistic and idealised African past was highly problematic, and saw emerging francophone authors critiquing not only the effects of colonialism, but also this 'imagined' African history; this change was represented by people such as the Malian writer Yambo Ouologuem, whose *Le devoir de violence* (1968) was highly critical of African nationalism. Another author who rejected Negritude ideals was the widely acclaimed Senegalese writer and filmmaker Ousmane Sembène, whose standout novel *Les bouts de bois de Dieu* (1960) addressed the responses of Senegalese and Malian people to French colonialism during the Dakar strikes in 1947. He later published his famous book (and film) *Xala* (1973) which criticised the corruption of post-colonial elites and the rise of social injustices in Senegal as the dreams of independence were sold out.

Likewise, in the anglophone tradition authors were focusing on critiquing colonialism, the activities of political elites, and placing African themes and realities at the forefront of their writing. Early proponents included the South African writer Sol Plaatje, whose novel *Mhudi* (1930) reinterpreted South Africa's history through a non-Eurocentric perspective. As the façade of colonialism crumbled, writers such as Chinua Achebe in *Things Fall Apart* (1958) addressed the clash of traditions that emerged with the onset of British colonialism, while writing in a way that reappropriated language. The Kenyan novelist Ngũgĩ wa Thiong'o was another who reappraised colonialism through his standout work *A Grain of Wheat* (1967) set against the backdrop of the Mau Mau rebellion and the onset of independence. Other early influential anglophone writers, poets, and playwrights included the Nigerian writers Wole Soyinka and Amos Tutuola (see the *Palm-Wine Drunkard*, 1953) and the Ghanaian Ama Ata Aidoo (see *Our Sister Killjoy*, 1977), all of whom wrote critically about European colonialism and post-colonial impacts, African interactions with external subjugation, and the cultural tensions between Africa and the west.

Box 8.1 Women and literature

In traditional and socially conservative African societies, women frequently have suffered from the double oppression of colonialism and patriarchy. Significantly, literature has enabled women across the continent to develop a powerful cultural voice, as they assert their prominence in literary fields. Not only have women been able to critique some of the themes identified above such as colonial rule and western cultural values, but they have also been able to highlight their subjugated role in society, their day-to-day agency, and their lived experiences affected by male patriarchy, traditional cultures, and religious practices. Authors such as Mariama Bâ (Senegal) and Assia Djebar (Algeria) were prominent feminist writers who were able to provide a voice to women through their work. More recently, younger authors such as Chimamanda Adichie have continued to be important literary figures in promoting African literature on the global stage, but also to recount the lives and realities for women, for example in *Purple Hibiscus* (2003). Therefore, African literature offers an important cultural tool to advocate for social justice and alternative roles for women across the continent.

Modern African literature is flourishing and continues to build on African and non-African styles and influences; and through an array of languages and plot formats (covering everything from romance to science fiction) authors are examining a range of social, political, and cultural topics. While there are clearly continental similarities in terms of subject matter or cultural/linguistic heritages, individual nations such as Algeria, Senegal, and South Africa have strong literary traditions that mark them out from the rest. There are plenty of excellent authors such as Aminatta Forna (Sierra Leone), Alain Mabanckou (Republic of Congo), Maaza Mengiste (Ethiopia), and Lauren Beukes (South Africa) whose work tackles issues as diverse as environmental degradation, local and global social inequalities, HIV/AIDs, generational and cultural clashes, and migration. African literature is therefore anything but predictable, acting as an influential vehicle of popular culture.

Film

The introduction of film to the continent occurred in the early twentieth century as part of the colonial authorities' efforts to 'civilise' Africans and impart particular cultural messages about the west. With the exception of Egypt, which had a flourishing domestic film industry from the 1930s, African cinema could not fully develop until after independence, dominated as it was by European and North American productions. Most films that were shown to audiences were predominantly on non-African subjects and experiences, such as American westerns, or when the continent was portrayed it was through imagery and narratives that were far from the reality. Film was deeply embedded within the hegemonic colonial project, which only served to reinforce western domination and depicted Africa through non-African eyes; for example, *African Queen* (1951), a widely celebrated film in the west, is one which visualises many aspects of the continent in profoundly negative ways (Shaka, 2004).

The emergence of African cinema coincided with the independence era of the 1960s, as filmmakers began to use the medium as a form of political, social, and cultural resistance, while seeking to establish a new narrative for the continent. The result was that films were made to ensure African peoples and realities were placed centre stage in a way that authentically represented local experiences and stories. As a consequence, audiences could relate to the subjects, themes, languages, and the settings that reflected their environment on the screen. Moreover, film was an important opportunity to rewrite and retell history in a popular cultural format from African perspectives, so as to rectify the unbalanced and racist versions of the past told through European eyes. With these crucial objectives in mind, African directors used their films to address underlying themes of social (in)justice by examining topics such as colonial rule and its legacies; the ongoing impact and effect of neo-colonialism; questions of tradition and modernity; and post-colonial outcomes. Indeed, an important dimension of African filmmaking has been the ability to address cultural topics, one of which is the role and status of women in society. Film has provided a crucial medium to question and publicise gender norms, especially patriarchal practices, by having women starring in strong leading roles, and to give a voice to the silenced and oppressed. Indicative films include *Femmes aux yeux ouverts* (1994) which let women from across West Africa tell their individual stories of day-to-day experiences, and *Moolaadé* (2004) set in Burkina Faso which addressed the practice of female genital mutilation.

The first wave of African directors sought to establish a new form of filmmaking that entrenched the factors above while rejecting western cinematic norms. The first cinematic heavyweights of this era came from the former territories of French West Africa, represented by Ousmane Sembène (Senegal), Safi Faye (Senegal), and Oumarou Ganda (Niger) who were powerful advocates for change. Sembène is a crucial figure in the evolution of African cinema, with his first feature film *La noire de...* (1966) providing a lens on issues of race, identity, and colonial legacies through the experiences of a young Senegalese woman living in France. It was such a breakthrough that it became the first African-made film to be an internationally acclaimed hit. However, most African films remain decidedly local, rarely crossing borders.

The largest film industry on the continent is found in Nigeria, often referred to as Nollywood. In the early 1990s, Nigerians demanded films that more accurately represented their own lives and experiences; so, using home video cameras, hundreds of low-budget/low-production films were created and sold straight to tape. The innovative filming techniques and local stories addressing themes such as magic, ethnic loyalties, intergenerational tensions, and the struggles concerning tradition and modernity resonate with the audience's own experiences, which make them immensely popular. The low-budget format and the focus on stories with popular local appeal have led to spinoffs based on the Nollywood model across the continent, as directors seek to create films designed for specific audiences.

Similar to the debates found in literature (as discussed above), African directors grappled with questions over language and representation on the screen. Some directors such as the Chadian Mahamat Saleh Haroun use a mix of languages, such as Arabic and French, which ensures a more realistic portrayal of how people live and interact with one another on a daily basis. However, even though plenty of recent films use African languages such as Afrikaans (see *Skoonheid*) and Swahili (see *Nairobi Half Life*) as the basis for their narratives, plenty continue to keep colonial languages at the heart of their scripts. Although subtitling has become increasingly common for 'foreign language films' (i.e. not English), the choice of language can have an important relation on the size of audience and distribution, both locally and further afield. For example, the 2014 film *Timbuktu* demonstrated that language (the main ones spoken are Tamasheq, Bambara, and Arabic) did not have to be an impediment to critical success, receiving plenty of awards and international recognition for its compelling depiction of the Islamic invasion of northern Mali.

Box 8.2 Ousmane Sembène, the 'father of African cinema'

Sembène is often accredited as being the director who truly popularised African cinema, whose work and artistic vision pioneered new techniques and influenced generations of filmmakers. Sembène famously switched from what he regarded as the elitism of writing novels in French to filmmaking which contained characters speaking Wolof, driven by his desire to tell his stories via popular visual culture to the largely illiterate Senegalese public. In all of his films his principal audience always remained the Senegalese first and foremost, as he sought to provide a more representative version of their life on the screen. Sembène's work was highly politicised, infused with a social and political activism, in which he interrogated a range of topics including patriarchy, colonial legacies, and religion; wherever injustice was to be found, and no matter who perpetuated those abuses, he was willing to critique and publicise them in film. Sembène was a strong advocate for challenging the status quo through his films such as *Xala* (1975) that criticised post-colonial elites and *Camp de Thiaroye* (1988) which retold the 'forgotten' story of Senegalese soldiers in World War II, while condemning the hypocrisy of colonialism. The story of his life achievements was remembered and celebrated in the documentary *Sembène!* (2015) which is an excellent introduction to his films and philosophies.

One of the main challenges for African directors has been trying to establish a new style of cinema in the face of established and international networks of production that wield global influence. A global movement, referred to as Third Cinema, which originated in South America, was embraced by African filmmakers as a way of challenging hegemonic and capitalistic norms in cinema, while providing a voice to the voiceless. Yet many decades on from the foundation of this philosophy of filmmaking, the struggle for representation in film continues, with former South African president Thabo Mbeki (2001) asserting that Africans needed to 'avoid being overwhelmed by the powerful cultural imperialism that seeks to penetrate our societies through films, television, the internet and other mass media ... we have to cultivate our value systems through the production and sharing of literature [and] films ... that portray us correctly and differently from the dominant cultures.' Indeed, plenty of western-produced films continue to examine African topics, but problematically are frequently done so with white characters as the central characters in the story, exemplified by *Invictus* (2009), *Blood Diamond* (2007), *The Last King of Scotland* (2006), and *Shooting Dogs* (2005); noteworthy exceptions include *Beasts of No Nation* (2015) and *Long Walk to Freedom* (2013). An equally troubling trend has been the number of filmmakers using locations across the continent, especially big cities, to depict post-apocalyptic worlds, or hyper urban decay, most notably Johannesburg, which is clearly recognisable in releases such as *Dredd* (2012), *Avengers: Age of Ultron* (2015), and *Chappie* (2015).

There are plenty of excellent, locally produced films such as *Soleil Ô* (1967), *Tsotsi* (2005), *Daratt* (2006), *Nairobi Half-Life* (2012), and *Four Corners* (2013), but more often than not, African audiences continue to be exposed to films, ideas, and cultural norms from producers in Hollywood, the former colonial powers, and Indian Bollywood, rather than local studios. In part this is through audience choice, as foreign films have become deeply entrenched within the cinematic watching psyche, and also because the costs of making local films means it is often cheaper to buy in from abroad. An unusual example of a non-African cinematic style dominating a local market is the popularity of Bollywood films in northern Nigeria, despite having almost no Indian diaspora to speak of. The appeal of original Bollywood cinema stemmed from its focus on themes such as family values and conservative social norms, which were far more attuned to the region's predominantly Islamic audiences than those from western studios. However, with global production companies dictating funding streams, distribution networks, and promotional opportunities, it remains hard for African directors to generate audiences, with many films screened for only a limited period, if at all. One way of encouraging African filmmaking and establishing continental networks has been through film festivals, with the Pan-African FESPACO event held in Burkina Faso, first set up in 1969; only films produced by Africans, in Africa, can be screened at the festival, which offers an important way of publicising new talent and stories to a wider continental audience.

An interconnected point concerning distribution is that African societies consume films in very different ways to the rest of the world. While cinemas obviously exist across the continent, the infrastructure in rural communities is often lacking or the cost of tickets prohibitive for ordinary people. Therefore the experience of watching films can either be very recognisable from sit-down theatres (indoors and outdoors) to pop-up screens or be more unusual where in informal settings large numbers of people will gather at a small shop or bar to see a release. There is a very real demand for cinema, but communities have to be innovative to access films. Technology is driving innovation, as well as changes in viewing habits, because with the increasing availability of mobile, internet-enabled devices, more people than ever before can stream, share, and even produce their own films.

African cinema continues to grow as more films are created and distributed, aided by new technologies and a developing global interest. At film festivals the world over, the work of African directors is being recognised for its quality and innovation, as new and unfamiliar stories are told. Many films continue to critically examine issues including colonial legacies and social justice through a variety of gripping storylines such as science-fiction films like *District 9* (2009) which tackles xenophobia, violence, and apartheid. The release of Marvel's *Black Panther* (2018) offered a much needed positive, Afro-futuristic depiction of the continent, which challenged and subverted stereotypes about Africa. Therefore film is a vital dimension of popular culture across the continent; films seek to entertain audiences, but they are also there to inform, with a crucial purpose for African filmmakers being to question societal norms and challenge stereotypes.

Music

In a similar vein to film and literature, there is a rich tapestry of music across the continent, incorporating a vast array of styles and sounds, holding an important position in cultural, social, and political associations in Africa; communities have their own distinct forms of expression and sound through their music. There are clearly some similarities apparent across regions, hence why we speak of 'African music', but it is vital to recognise that musical styles differ depending on the processes and functions, and the role that musicians hold within individual societies. What must be remembered is that music is a powerful and dynamic cultural form, with the ability to cross ethnic and regional boundaries, while expressing a shared popular intercultural message (Collins & Richards, 1989, 36–37).

Traditional African music is closely linked to the continent's oral past, in which song was used as a tool for relaying societal histories, ancestral pasts, and shaping cultural affinities. There is not the space to evaluate the continental divide in the various forms of traditional African styles that can be found, but in short, North Africa and the Horn of Africa draw heavily on Arabic inspirations, while in sub-Saharan Africa it is more common to find complex, multilayered rhythms, which are often more 'open-ended' to allow for improvisation and audience participation.

Although many in the west might regard all African music as being traditional, this is far from the case. Across contemporary Africa, music has certainly not remained static or 'traditional'. Instead there is a high level of hybridity in which styles, rhythms, and sounds are continuously evolving by fusing, assimilating, and reappropriating trends from across the world, and these are sometimes shaped in response to local social and political circumstances (Lazarus, 1999, 199). For example, the first truly Pan-African sound was the Congolese rumba in the 1950s that was adapted from Afro-Cuban music, popularised in part because it had familiar 'African' rhythms and was very distinct from European music. This style later evolved into the soukous (or ndombolo) which is characterised by a much faster beat and became popular in several nations including Tanzania, due to touring Congolese bands who were encouraged by President Mobutu to spread Zairian culture (Biddle & Knights, 2007, 40–43). By the 1960s and 1970s, many musicians were increasingly influenced by Afro-American jazz and funk artists, while more recently, the global spread of American cultural norms has seen rap and hip-hop from the USA adapted and reframed into distinctly African forms by using languages such as Xhosa (see Driemanskap) or Twi (see Sarkodie). Moreover, in the mid-1990s after the fall of apartheid, South Africa saw the emergence of a popular house scene known as Kwaito pioneered by artists such as Mandoza and Zola, while more recently there is a vibrant Afro-electronica sound that has been led by people like Spoek Mathambo and DJ Mujava. Furthermore, the resurgence of religious organisations across the continent (see Chapter 7) and the prominent place music holds within such services have only reinforced its cultural capital. The outcome is that there is no single form of 'African music', but rather an eclectic mix of traditional and modern styles, which are simultaneously 'local' and 'international'.

African musicians clearly do not practice or create their music in a cultural bubble, and the internationalisation of various forms of entertainment has seen many overseas audiences seek out what is termed somewhat derogatorily as 'world music'. A number of highly successful musicians were pioneers in publicising African music on the international scene, such as Fela Kuti who popularised Afrobeat; Salif Keita; Hugh Masekela; Francis Bebey; Babatunde Olatunji; Youssou N'dour; and Miriam Makeba. Following on from these trailblazing and iconic figures, musicians such as the Songhoy Blues, Amadou & Mariam, Tinariwen, Ladysmith Black

Box 8.3 The introductory African music playlist

Rather than simply write about musical styles and musicians from across the continent, it is perhaps more effective for you to discover some of the different sounds for yourself. To give you a flavour of the different musical traditions from across the continent mentioned in this chapter, here is a list of a few artists, both old and new, to explore. A question to consider after exploring some of these tracks is why so little of this music ever reaches audiences beyond the continent?

Amadou & Mariam (Mali) – Ce n'est pas bon
Rachid Taha (Algeria) – Barra Barra
Mulatu Astatke (Ethiopia) – Yekermo Sew
Miriam Makeba (South Africa) – Pata Pata
Fela Kuti (Nigeria) – Zombie
Franco & l'OK Jazz (Zaire/DRC) – Mambu ma miondo
DJ Mujava (South Africa) – Township Funk
Diabel Cissokho (Senegal) – Boumoulendem
Tinariwen (Mali/Algeria) – Tenere Taqqim Tossam
Batida (Angola/Portugal) – Bazuka (Quem me Rusgou?)
Songhoy Blues (Mali) – Soubour
Mikael Seifu (Ethiopia) – How to Save a Life

A more extensive playlist of African music can be found at: https://open.spotify.com/user/mattgraham/playlist/3lU4V0gqPMdk K22KDo8EuT

Mambazo (who gained global attention singing on Paul Simon's album *Graceland*), Rokia Traoré, and Batida have all received international recognition for their music. However, most African music is produced and consumed very locally and 'is virtually omnipresent in the modern African city, forming the backdrop of everyday life: on the radio, the television, and in the streets ... it creates an "imagined community" of listeners providing a shared sense of cultural identity' (Biddle & Knights, 2007, 42).

Music has a powerful political and cultural role, something which was not lost on nationalist leaders or post-colonial elites, who sought to utilise it to engender popular support, communicate specific values, and to shape public opinion. The co-option of music by nationalist elites is best exemplified by President Mobutu who made use of music to try and create a distinctly Zairian culture out of this ethnically and regionally divided nation, while also seeking to cement his own dictatorial rule. Popular music in Zaire was an instrument used by institutions of state power to strengthen and maintain political legitimacy, and to promote a recognisably Zairian 'sound' which was exported around the world. The state-sponsored musicians praised Mobutu and explicitly supported the ruling establishment, most notably the legendary rumba 'king' Franco (White, 2008). Another example would be the revolutionary Burkina Faso president Thomas Sankara, a keen guitarist himself, who during his short rule (1983–87) supported musicians to spread political messages.

While political leaders realised the power of music, they also feared it. Indeed, music has continuously acted as a foci for protest and criticism against ruling elites, and enduring societal inequality. For example, throughout the anti-apartheid struggle in South Africa, music had an incredibly important role in the fight for racial justice (see the fantastic documentary *Amandla! A Revolution in Four-Part Harmony*). At domestic rallies, demonstrators frequently utilised protest songs as a tool to unify crowds against apartheid, to demand freedom from oppression, or to appeal to the exiled ANC's guerrilla fighters to liberate the country. Internationally, stars such as Miriam Makeba, Brenda Fassie, and Johnny Clegg were able to raise public awareness about the struggle abroad through their music. The Nigerian musician Fela Kuti was a vocal critic of the ruling classes, most notably in his widely acclaimed 1977 album *Zombie* which attacks the corrupt military government; Kuti later argued that 'as far as Africa is concerned music cannot be for enjoyment. Music has to be for revolution. Music is the weapon.' In 2011, music and politics intertwined in Senegal, where the Y'en a Marre (Fed up) youth movement emerged, driven largely by young hip-hop artists, who protested against political injustice and societal inequality. The popularity and 'reach' of Senegalese performers such as Keur Gui helped to mobilise youth dissatisfaction, which saw incumbent President Abdoulaye Wade lose the 2012 election, after he controversially stood for re-election.

Perhaps most appalling to all music lovers came in 2012, when the Islamist jihadist movement that had conquered two-thirds of Mali (see Chapter 6) announced that 'Satan's' music was to be totally banned in private and public spaces. For a country such as Mali where music is deeply ingrained into the cultural and social fabric, and which has produced a considerable number of world-renowned artists including Ali Farka Touré, Toumani Diabaté, Rokia Traoré, Tinariwen, and Oumou Sangaré, the jihadist decision was deeply shocking. All non-prescribed religious music was forbidden, musicians were forced into exile, and instruments were publicly destroyed, which shattered a traditional way of everyday life. The ban was eventually lifted in early 2013, after French and Malian troops liberated the country, which has since allowed for Malians to re-establish various forms of music both at home and abroad, while demonstrating the vital importance of music to their cultural life (Morgan, 2013).

Sport

Across the continent, sport has a significant social and cultural role in many people's lives. Football is by far and away the most popular pastime both in terms of a leisure activity and as a spectator event (albeit largely consumed through TV), while elsewhere on the continent, long-distance athletics is widespread in East Africa, whereas rugby (Union and 7s) and cricket are only really played in former British colonies such as South Africa and Kenya.

A sport in which African competitors dominate on the world stage is the field of long-distance running. Many of the world's most successful runners come from Kenya, Ethiopia, and Uganda. In Kenya, athletics is extremely popular because the global success of its athletes has ensured worldwide prestige for the country. Youngsters are subsequently attracted to the sport by the professionalised system of scouting and training, the international fame for the best runners, and the large economic dividends that athletes can achieve through participation in races around the world. A quick glance at marathon and Olympic results highlights the near total domination of long-distance running by East Africans (see Image 8.1). For example, by 2017, in the London marathon, every men's race since 2003 has been won by either a Kenyan (twelve) or an Ethiopian (three), and the women's race since 2010 has seen athletes from Kenya (six) and Ethiopia (two) take the title each year. Furthermore, at the time of writing, Kenyan runners hold all the world record times for men and women marathons,

Image 8.1 Kenyan athlete Ruth Chepngetich (centre) finishes first in the women's Istanbul Marathon on 12 November 2017

Source: Muhammed Enes Yildirim/Anadolu Agency/Getty Images.

and in 2017, at the Nike Breaking2 event, Eliud Kipchoge ran the fastest ever marathon clocking in at 2:00:25.

However, in Africa it is football which is the ubiquitous sport, with the ease and accessibility of the game allowing for mass participation everywhere from cities to isolated rural communities. Football was introduced to Africa through European colonialism, and was first played in ports and major urban centres by settlers, traders, and soldiers, but soon spread quickly through missionaries and colonial administrators, who utilised the sport as part of the broader imperial and 'civilising' project. At the turn of the century, football was increasingly adopted and reimagined by African communities, with the foundation of clubs becoming an important social feature that created shared networks, bonds, and cultural connections along class, ethnic, and religious identities. Many of the continent's oldest clubs, for instance Hearts of Oak (Ghana, 1911), Espérance Sportive de Tunis (Tunisia, 1919), and the Orlando Pirates (South Africa, 1937), emerged in an era of mass urbanisation in municipalities such as Accra and Soweto.

While football was a community sport, it also became a site of anti-colonial resistance and nationalist prestige. By the 1930s, some African nationalists started using football as a mechanism for mobilising people to challenge colonial rule. The most famous example where anti-colonial politics and football intertwined was Algeria's revolutionary team formed by the exiled FLN liberation movement in 1958; the very successful touring team served as a powerful symbolic tool that helped to 'internationalise' the struggle against France (see Chapter 3). After independence, football was regarded by political leaders as an 'easy' means of providing some substance to the thorny issue of 'nationhood' and belonging. To bolster national identities, new national stadiums were built across the continent, often named in honour of the heroes of the independence struggle, while the team could represent and embody the 'new' nation on the global stage.

In 1957, the Confédération Africaine de Football (CAF) was formed by Egypt, Ethiopia, Sudan, and South Africa to represent African football, as well as organise both international and club competitions. CAF is a Pan-African organisation, including North African states within its structures (see Chapter 1 for debates about conceptualisations of the continent), and continued to expand when nations gained their independence; the newest member was Zanzibar in 2017, despite not being an autonomous country. The first Africa Cup of Nations (AFCON) was held in 1957, but it demonstrated how politics and sport can be uneasy bedfellows. The South Africans refused to send a multiracial team, which prompted the other three nations to publicly criticise apartheid and ban them from participating. The decision proved to be a precursor for a series of future boycotts and suspensions of all South African sporting teams, including most significantly their rugby and cricket sides, as part of the wider anti-apartheid struggle. Since AFCON's inception, the tournament has been dominated largely by North and West African nations, with Egypt winning it a record seven times.

Although football likes to present itself as the global game of the people, the actions of former colonial powers when organising international competitions were anything but equal, openly exhibiting characteristics of racism and superiority. Egypt was the first African team to play in a World Cup in 1934, yet the continent was not represented again until 1970 because FIFA refused to offer a guaranteed place; the 1966 World Cup in England was boycotted by CAF members in protest at the intransigence, which successfully forced a change in the organisation's attitudes. From 1970, the number of guaranteed places for African nations has steadily risen, with five countries now represented at each World Cup. The first World Cup on African soil was successfully hosted by South Africa in 2010, in which Ghana narrowly missed out on reaching the semi-finals.

Box 8.4 Football and the African diaspora

A distinct feature of many of Europe's national teams is their ethnic diversity, which is represented by a large number of footballers with African heritage. This development is a legacy of former colonial powers' relationships with their imperial subjects (such as assimilation; see Chapter 3) and a product of high levels of migration and permanent settlement away from Africa (Chapter 9). At Euro 2016, half of all the competing teams had at least one player of African descent, while France, Belgium, and Portugal had many more included. An example of this development was Eusébio, who represented Portugal in the 1960s and is widely considered as one of the world's greatest ever footballers. However, Eusébio was born in Mozambique, but because the country was regarded as an extension of the metropole, he was selected to represent Portugal instead. The historical connection between Portugal and its former colonies continues to this day, with a number of high-profile players such as William Carvalho (Angola), Nani (Cape Verde), and Danilo Pereira (Guinea-Bissau) having ties to the continent. However, the diaspora has also benefited several African countries' national teams. At the 2018 FIFA World Cup in Russia, all five African nations included players from their diasporic communities, the most notable of which was the Morocco squad that included 17 players (out of 23) born abroad, which meant team talks had to be provided in Arabic, French, and English.

France has a complicated relationship with its former colonies, and debates over cultural identities and 'origin' are fought over in public, especially in relation to the make-up of its national team. The two most successful recent teams, the 1998 World Cup winners (labelled the 'black, blanc, beur'/'black, white, Arab') and the 2018 World Cup champions, were truly multicultural sides, demonstrating the integration of players with African backgrounds. Some of France's best players have parental connections to Africa, including Zinedine Zidane (Algeria), Patrick Viera (Senegal), N'Golo Kanté (Mali), and Karim Benzema (Algeria). Despite the success of the French team, there have been a series of controversies about African heritage and French nationality, such as ongoing far-right accusations that the team is underrepresented by white players; a story in 2011 that a quota system was to be introduced by the French authorities to limit the number of dual-nationality citizens from being selected; and the tendency of young players choosing to switch allegiances to represent African or North African countries, most notably exemplified by Algeria's 2014 World Cup squad, of which 16 of the 23 players were born in France.

Even though millions of Africans actively participate and engage with the sport, domestic football across the continent is in a relatively poor state, exacerbated by economic globalisation. In the late 1980s, the emergence of deregulated satellite TV helped European football clubs to become increasingly commercialised entities. The newfound wealth allowed clubs to purchase the world's finest players, which consequently created the best teams and most entertaining leagues. The perceived higher quality of European football was subsequently promoted by the TV companies, which ensured that games were showcased on a global stage. The digital TV networks began to screen large numbers of live games throughout Africa, which made major European clubs such as Manchester United, AC Milan, and Barcelona household names. The gulf in quality of the European leagues in comparison to domestic competitions was vast, which led to many people adopting an overseas club, and following their fortunes via TV or more recently, the internet and social media. If you travel anywhere on the continent you will see a plethora of replica European shirts on display, while even in some of Africa's most rural communities, people will have an in-depth knowledge of their chosen team or league. To highlight the passion and cultural significance of European football, in June 2017 a Ghanaian church held a religious service dedicated to celebrating Chelsea winning the English Premier League, coincidently led by a reverend who is an Arsenal supporter.

While there are a number of venerable and highly successful clubs that have huge support bases, such as Al Ahly and Zamalek (Egypt), Espérance de Tunis (Tunisia), TP Mazembe (DRC), and the Kaizer Chiefs and Orlando Pirates (South Africa), the consequence has been decreasing attendances at domestic football, which beyond derby matches are very low: in South Africa's Premier Soccer League, the Soweto derby will easily attract 90,000 fans, but the average league attendance is only 6,520. As fans turn away from their own leagues, the lure and wealth of overseas clubs have led to an exodus of the continent's players looking for economic gains. The migration of African players made people like George Weah (Liberia), Samuel Eto'o (Cameroon), and Didier Drogba (Côte d'Ivoire) global superstars, while thousands of others play in leagues across the world. Furthermore, to aid the migration of footballers, and so that European clubs can acquire cheap, talented players, there are a series of private and cooperative training academies across the continent designed to spot youngsters; examples include the West African Football Academy Sporting Club in Ghana, created by the Dutch team Feynoord, and Ajax Cape Town is partially owned by its namesake in Amsterdam.

However, there is an unsettling nature to these developments in African football, which are manifestly neo-colonial. The global pattern of economic inequality is replicated in football, as Europe's main teams prosper at the expense of the rest, which sees 'resources' in the form of African footballers imported to benefit overseas entities; there are plenty of examples of young players being exploited by agents and clubs, lured by the potential economic benefits on offer. While the migration of the continent's best players showcases the talent on offer to the world, it subsequently diminishes the domestic game, which reduces the ability of clubs to compete, and does little to draw crowds back to stadiums. In turn, the cultural acceptance of European football by African peoples as a superior form of the game is a paradox of globalisation (for the best study on African football which this subsection is based on see Alegi, 2010). A further example of this trend is represented by the number of non-African managers of national teams across the continent, as federations continue to employ Europeans to take charge of their squads; in 2018, 20 of the 56 nations recognised by CAF had a European as coach. Moreover, in 2017, CAF chose to alter the timing of its showpiece tournament AFCON, which was usually held in January, but under pressure from major European clubs, who objected at having their star African players missing during the middle of their domestic seasons, have since changed it to June.

This chapter has demonstrated some of the different ways in which culture manifests itself throughout the continent. There is a vibrant and lively cultural scene which provides a means of expression, societal identity, and cohesion, as well as political engagement and resistance. Many of the popular cultural activities that millions of people interact with on a daily basis are frequently ignored by external observers, yet have a vital role in daily life. Significantly, cultural activities such as literature and music can be inherently political, with ongoing resonance as a form of protest against the legacies of colonialism, neo-colonial influences, and societal inequality. When active involvement in politics is curtailed or supressed, culture provides a significant opportunity for people to resist.

Further reading

The role and impact of film across Africa are explored in Femi Shaka's (2004) *Modernity and the African Cinema*, and the recent contribution from Winston Mano, Barbara Knorpp, and Añulika Agina's (2017) *African Film Cultures*. I can only urge you to read some of the African literary authors listed in this chapter to get a true sense of the style, themes, and traditions that can be found. For studies on African music consult Eric Charry's *Hip Hop Africa: New African Music in a Globalizing World* (2012); Bob White's (2008) *Rumba Rules: The Politics of Dance Music in Mobutu's Zaire*; and Andy Morgan's (2013) *Music, Culture and Conflict in Mali*. For more information on African football a must-read is Peter Alegi's (2010) *African Soccerscapes*, while Paul Darby (2002) offers an insightful overview in *Africa, Football and FIFA: Politics, Colonialism and Resistance*.

9 AFRICA BEYOND THE NATION-STATE

The purpose of this chapter is to examine some of the main elements of contemporary Africa that can often be overlooked when examining the political and historical trajectories of the continent. The integrity of the nation-state is a fundamental concept in Africa's political thought and organisation. In 1963, the Organisation of African Unity (OAU) formally accepted the colonial boundaries, which allowed nationalist leaders to fashion 'new' nations and identities within these inherited geographic spaces. While this was extremely important to the political and social evolution of Africa, it is imperative to recognise that external influences such as Pan-Africanism and the actions of the continent's diasporic communities have played a significant role in developing and shaping perceptions and conceptualisations of 'Africa'. In turn, these philosophies have had an enormous impact on how political leaders view the continent, and the subsequent efforts to build networks and institutions of African unity. Indeed, this search for a form of African unity, based on Pan-African principles, has continued to exercise the continent, creating moments of collective harmony, yet also serious division.

This chapter will first assess the evolution of Pan-Africanist thought, and the influence this continues to have on political decision making, and the efforts to forge political, economic, and cultural unity through institutions such as the OAU and African Union (AU). It will then track the evolution of Africa's continental organisations and regional economic communities (RECs) in the search to establish collective political and economic unity, with a specific focus on how peacekeeping has become a major function in fulfilling stability and security. The chapter will then examine Africa's diaspora and the ways in which it has shaped, influenced, and worked with the continent in its different forms, and the potential these communities might have in the future. The final section will address migration, seeking to move beyond western stereotypes in order to provide a more nuanced picture of population movements, the effects these have across Africa, and the ways in which continental and international institutions have understood and responded to migration pressures.

Pan-Africanism

One of the most enduring yet nebulous ideological concepts in contemporary Africa is Pan-Africanism, an influential theoretical idea that first gained philosophical and political adherents from the early twentieth century. Colin Legum (1965, 14) observed that Pan-Africanism 'is essentially a movement of ideas and emotions; at times it achieves a synthesis; at times it remains at the level of thesis and antithesis.' What makes Pan-Africanism difficult to define is that it is a fluid ideology which has evolved and been recast over time in an effort to fulfil the aspirations of African people and their descendants, with different iterations emerging in response to changing political circumstances. At its core, Pan-Africanism is centred on recognising the shared experiences of racism, oppression, marginalisation, and (neo)colonialism, which can only be overcome through unity, solidarity, and collective action.

The Pan-African movement first originated in the African diaspora of North America and the Caribbean where black intellectuals sought to articulate their experiences, and forge a unified global racial consciousness to achieve dignity and freedom. This vision of solidarity and unity based on a common heritage and history was conceptualised through a continental rather than territorial lens, which ironically accentuated divisions across Africa when new nationalist leaders began to debate how best to practically implement its philosophical tenets. Key leaders in the diaspora that drove the earliest conceptualisations of Pan-Africanism included Trinidadian barrister Henry Sylvester-Williams and the American W.E.B. Du Bois, who convened several Pan-African Conferences, the first of which was held in London in 1900; the delegates demanded an end to racism, criticised colonialism, and asserted the need for black people to gain political rights. The core ideas behind Pan-Africanism gradually developed in the first half of the twentieth century, but it remained very much a diasporic-driven initiative. It was only in 1945, at the Fifth Pan-African Congress held in Manchester, England, that the ideology pivoted towards an African led-approach, which called for continental cooperation and unity to overthrow colonialism and achieve self-determination; this change in focus was prompted by the attendance of young, radical and militant African nationalists including future presidents Hastings Banda (Malawi), Kwame Nkrumah (Ghana), and Jomo Kenyatta (Kenya).

In the mounting anti-colonial struggles after World War II, Pan-Africanism became increasingly influential among African nationalists in the 1950s and early 1960s, who utilised the notion of unity and solidarity instilled within it to reinforce their demands for liberation (see Chapter 3). Ghana's independence in 1957, under the leadership of committed Pan-Africanist Kwame Nkrumah, accelerated the call for greater continental unity, with the ultimate goal of establishing a United States of Africa. Nkrumah quickly embarked on a charm offensive of African leaders in the period 1958–1961, in an effort to convince them of his aspirations for a unified Pan-African-inspired continent. For example, the First Conference of Independent African States was held in 1958, attended by the then eight independent nations of Egypt, Libya, Tunisia, Morocco, Sudan, Ethiopia, Liberia, and Ghana (note that Pan-Africanism did not recognise any artificial divisions of the continent, and the Arab and Islamic states were included in this vision of Africa), while a short-lived alliance known as the Union of African States was formed between Ghana, Guinea, and later Mali (1958–1963). However, it was at this stage when the theoretical ambitions of Pan-Africanism premised on continental unity clashed with the unfolding political reality. Many leaders rhetorically adhered to the principles of Pan-African unity, and recognised the need for collective solidarity to prevent neo-colonialism, the emergence of intra-African rivalry, and the 'balkanisation' of the continent. Yet the Pan-Africanist vision espoused by Nkrumah ignored not only the ethnic, religious, and cultural differences found across the continent, but also the unfolding territorial nationalism of decolonisation. Undoubtedly Pan-Africanism had political and cultural resonance, but having achieved hard-won independence, very few nationalist leaders were prepared to give up their power to the personal ambitions and self-aggrandisement of Nkrumah.

However, in spite of the practical difficulties, the Pan-African vision did not entirely disappear in the 1960s. The OAU served at various points (with varying degrees of success) as a vehicle for continental unity and common action in achieving goals such as Africa's total liberation from white minority rule. Yet the problems the OAU experienced, and the post-Cold War realities of the 1990s, saw a new-breed of African leaders envisaging a different future for the continent. Led by Thabo Mbeki (South Africa), Olusegun Obasanjo (Nigeria), and Abdelaziz Bouteflika (Algeria) they explicitly referred to the rhetorically powerful ideas of Pan-Africanism in their call for an 'African Renaissance' (Vale & Maseko, 1998) which sought to rejuvenate Africa's fortunes; redress negative perceptions of Africa in the west; overcome external interference; and promote unity to find solutions to African problems. Moreover, in 1999, Colonel Muammar Gaddafi became the unexpected heir of Nkrumah's Pan-African ideas in the OAU's reform debates, and championed continental solidarity in the shape of a United States of Africa. His proposals were unsuccessful in influencing the final direction of the AU, which was established in 2002, but he continued to keep the idea on the agenda, arguing for, among other things, a single African currency and a permanent military force, which prompted high-level debates in 2005, 2007, and 2009. The overthrow of Gaddafi in 2011 saw the concept of the United States of Africa temporarily jettisoned by African leaders, many of whom were apprehensive about Gaddafi's personal ambitions.

The Pan-African dream still remains politically relevant today and continues to serve as an influential and powerful concept behind the AU's plans for a wider continental renaissance. Theoretically, African nations appreciate the need for greater strength through collective unity to help alleviate malignant or unwelcome external interventions and economic marginalisation, while a 'single voice' is useful for campaigning internationally at institutions such as the UN and World Bank for greater recognition and input by African nations into decision making on their own future/s. In support of these aims, the AU Commission's *Agenda 2063* (2015) formulated a long-term framework rooted in the 'historical context of Pan Africanism' to achieve continental unity through greater political and economic integration. Indeed, the *Agenda* is explicit in arguing that by 2063 '[we] will have realized the fulfilment of the founders' dream or vision of a United Africa ... The political unity of Africa will be the culmination of the integration process, including the free movement of people, the establishment of continental institutions, and full economic integration.' It continues by stating: 'the fruits of the values and ideals of Pan Africanism will be manifest everywhere on the continent and beyond. The goal of the unity of the African peoples and peoples of African descent will be attained' (AU, 2015, 11, 15). A symbolic first step towards this objective occurred in 2016, when Presidents Paul Kagame (Rwanda) and Idriss Déby (Chad) launched the Pan-African passport to accelerate proposed visa free travel across the continent.

While these initiatives by the AU are laudable, there are numerous problems inherent in the current form of institutionalised Pan-Africanism. A key and enduring obstacle to unity has been the issue of national sovereignty. Political leaders across Africa have signed up to and advocated the ideological need for Pan-Africanism for decades, yet consistently, when demands are made to cede sovereignty to continental institutions, national priorities have always won out. The nationalist concerns of political elites have continued to remain intransigent to calls for deeper continental political integration. It will take a huge shift in political mindsets to fulfil the proposals.

Another major inhibitor to Pan-African ideology and its implementation is the reality that cultural and ethnic differences persist throughout Africa, with various parts of the continent having very little in common except geography. While events such as the 2010 World Cup saw Ghana emerge as 'team Africa' after progressing the furthest in the tournament, thereby generating a form of cultural solidarity, this was an isolated event rather than the norm. For example, in South Africa since 2008 the rhetoric of Pan-African solidarity has been undermined by the regular waves of serious xenophobic violence against migrants from across the continent. A question to consider is, to what extent is Pan-Africanism an elite driven, top-down concept which is out of touch with the experiences and lives of ordinary citizens? Finally, the federal vision of Pan-Africanism has little hope of succeeding if the seemingly intractable internal problems of states including the DRC, CAR, and Somalia are not resolved. Indeed, rather than seeking national unity, there has been a resurgence in the number of active secessionist movements across the continent encompassing the anglophone speakers in Cameroon, the Cabinda enclave seeking independence from Angola, and renewed calls for Biafran self-determination. The politicians in these nations have far more pressing national concerns to deal with rather than working towards grand visions of continental Pan-Africanism.

However, the importance of Pan-Africanism should be recognised as a vital and influential philosophy, which is concerned with creating an Africa free from racism, oppression, and subjugation. Through solidarity and collective action, African nations need to unite on issues of continental importance such as economic growth and environmental change, in order to achieve positive outcomes in the face of a largely unresponsive international community. Yet beyond the theoretical conceptualisations, the practical expressions of Pan-Africanism have consistently struggled to fulfil the lofty ideals, hamstrung by issues of political ambition, national sovereignty, and cultural difference.

Continental and regional integration

The search for a sense of African integration and unity emerged out of the Pan-African debates which exercised the continent's newly independent states in the early 1960s (van Walraven, 1999). The need for an institution which at its most basic level could protect and promote African interests internationally was never in question, but the form and guiding principles most certainly were. What the unfolding political debates revealed was the deep tensions and suspicions concerning alternative visions for future unity. Nkrumah's preferred idealistic conceptualisation of a truly integrated continent based on immediate and all-encompassing political unity was far from popular. In fact, the quest for African unity would stumble over the practical articulations of Pan-Africanism, and the 'ownership' of the project.

The first challenge to Nkrumah's proposition for a United States of Africa emerged in December 1960, when 12 francophone nations, known as the Brazzaville Group, rejected deep political union. To counteract this 'conservative' position, the continent's 'radical' countries spearheaded by Ghana, Mali, and Egypt convened the Casablanca Group in January 1961, demanding a rapid shift towards total integration. This was far from popular among many leaders who rhetorically supported Pan-Africanism, but wished to protect hard-won state sovereignty, and to prevent external incursions into domestic issues. In response, the Monrovia Group, including Liberia, Nigeria, Senegal, and Tunisia, was formed to prevent the project of continental unity being shaped by Nkrumah's vision of Pan-Africanism, and instead they proposed cooperation in a loose alliance. The result was that rather than generate a sense of collective unity, a continental wedge had emerged, demonstrating a significant degree of disunity, polarised on a wide range of difficult issues that included territorial federation, the Algerian Civil War, and the Congo Crisis.

However, in the early 1960s, political leaders had acknowledged the pressing need to find a mechanism to represent Africa and combat ongoing colonialism, neo-colonialism, racism, and global economic marginalisation that afflicted the continent. By 1963, a compromise was finally brokered in Ethiopia by Emperor Haile Selassie that led to the foundation of the OAU, with its principles mirroring the gradual integrationist approach favoured by the Monrovia Group. The OAU Charter (1963) pledged to promote solidarity and unity; defend sovereignty and territorial independence; eradicate colonialism; and promote international cooperation. Signed by 32 countries, the OAU conceptualised Africa as the entire geographic landmass, including the Arab nations and the island states such as Madagascar. One of the key clauses, which effectively ended Nkrumah's Pan-African ideal, was the acceptance of existing territorial borders and the principle of non-interference in domestic affairs.

The outcome of accepting the colonially constructed map of Africa was that the state was given paramount importance, and issues of self-determination represented by secessionist and irredentist movements in the Congo, Biafra, the Western Sahara, and Somalia were rejected, no matter the validity of their claims. Furthermore, the OAU's non-interference clause allowed for despotic and autocratic rulers to get away without censure from other African leaders; the popular image of the organisation in its later stages was of a self-serving 'club of dictators'. Yet the debate about whether the OAU should have sought to redraw the map of Africa to reflect the geographic realities is a moot point. Had they done so, the OAU might have seen off some of the more intractable internal problems faced by some nations as they tried to reconcile ethnic differences, most notably in the Congo, and perhaps would have allowed for Eritreans to gain their independence from Ethiopia long before 1993. But a mitigating factor for retaining the colonial borders is that immediately after achieving political independence, and with obvious examples of neo-colonialism apparent in the Congo (1960–1963), the overwhelming objective of the OAU was to secure peace and unity between states, not exacerbate conflict. While Africa's colonial inheritance was clearly flawed, the legacies of which are still felt today (see Chapters 4 and 5), it would have been unlikely that the OAU would have successfully been able to remap the continent in a peaceful and orderly fashion, in accordance with the demands of everyone. At a time of state fragility, in a hostile world, the OAU compromised the Pan-African dream for a semblance of continental unity, no matter how incomplete.

Box 9.1 Morocco and the Western Sahara

In 1976, Spain ceded control over the Western Sahara, splitting the territory between Morocco and Mauritania. Immediately, Morocco militarily occupied and 'claimed' the region despite the demands of the exiled POLISARIO Front, a Sahrawi national liberation movement, which had declared the Sahrawi Arab Democratic Republic (SADR) an independent state. Although Morocco managed to successfully halt the guerrilla fighting by the early 1980s, the extensive diplomatic efforts of POLISARIO persuaded a significant number of African nations to officially recognise the SADR as a sovereign nation. In 1982, the OAU admitted SADR into the organisation, which caused division in the membership, because the decision meant that Morocco was now officially regarded as a colonising nation. In protest at the appeasement of POLISARIO, Morocco chose to withdraw from the OAU in 1984, and instead set about reinforcing its supremacy in the Western Sahara. The OAU's Pan-African solidarity to POLISARIO, and their efforts to mediate the conflict were stonewalled by Morocco, who simply refused to acknowledge any external interventions in the territory. However, with little progress in SADR, the hopes of the nation achieving full independence suffered a setback in 2017, when Morocco was readmitted to the African Union (AU). After 33 years of exile, the AU sought to incorporate Morocco's political and economic might back into the institution, but it is a decision that essentially endorsed the country's occupation of the Western Sahara and hampers SADR's claims to self-determination. Furthermore, this could be a divisive issue because many African states have acknowledged the SADR as an independent state, still under colonial rule.

When analysing the OAU's 39-year existence, it is characterised by institutional failure, funding shortages, and an overwhelming inability to act decisively on some of Africa's most pressing problems. Although the OAU is often viewed as a failure, there were some limited successes. The one area which forged continental consensus was in the continued struggle against colonialism and apartheid, which helped create a 'single voice' in uniting disparate states. For example, the creation of the African Liberation Committee offered symbolic support, as well as sporadic funding, to liberation movements across Southern Africa including the MPLA, FRELIMO, and ANC. Other positive developments can be seen in the efforts to forge greater economic unity through policies such as the Lagos Plan of Action (OAU, 1980) which set out an agenda for economic self-reliance and development, and subsequently the Abuja Treaty which aimed to gradually establish an African Economic Community (AEC) (OAU, 1991) through RECs. These small steps, albeit limited in their scope and impact, created the foundations for the expansion of regional economic integration initiatives discussed later on in the chapter.

Yet, for the most part, the OAU was an ineffective institution, which did very little to forge any real sense of unity, or act in the interests of ordinary people. Given the OAU emerged out of compromises, few African leaders were ever fully committed to the institution, with national interests always triumphing over the rhetorical demands for unity. The OAU became an organisation where political elites could strut on an international stage and pronounce grand visions for collective action and capacity building, but always safe in the knowledge that there would be no recourse to actually fulfil the pledges. The result was that many of the policy ideas were stillborn due to a lack of political will and chronic funding shortages. The policy of non-intervention also meant the OAU was unable (even if it had been willing) to intervene in conflict mediation and peacekeeping, which effectively left the organisation as a bystander in conflicts such as Angola, Chad, and Liberia. Furthermore, poor governance and dictatorial tendencies represented by leaders such as Idi Amin and Jean-Bédel Bokassa were left unchecked, while coups were accepted as part of the general political process (see Chapter 4). The only real unity was the tacit acknowledgement that no African leader would publicly criticise another. By the mid-1990s, the OAU was in a state of inertia, unable to respond to the new post-Cold War world, nor the increased outbreaks of violence in Rwanda, Somalia, Sierra Leone, and the DRC.

As mentioned earlier in the chapter, a new set of modernising leaders led by Thabo Mbeki initiated a much needed reform process to revitalise the OAU and Pan-African aspirations, under the discourse of an African Renaissance. As a result, the AU was launched in 2002, providing a new vision for continental unity, pledging to achieve greater political and economic integration, while pursuing a more interventionist approach to secure good governance, democracy, and peace. In order to support these ambitions, the AU partially modelled on the EU set up a powerful institutional Commission to devise and implement policies; created the Pan-African Parliament as the legislative body; initiated the New Partnership for Africa's Development (NEPAD) to improve economic growth; established the African Peer Review Mechanism (APRM) to assess issues of good governance; and formed the Peace and Security Council (PSC) to work to support conflict resolution (Table 9.1). The key purpose of these wide-ranging reforms was to build an institutional framework that could strategically improve Africa's global position through shared developmental initiatives and greater self-reliance.

Table 9.1 Comparisons between AU and EU functions

AU	EU
Assembly of Heads of State and Government	The European Council (of Heads of Government/State) & Commission President
The Executive Council of the Ministries of the Ministers of Foreign Affairs	Council of the EU
The Commission of the AU	The Commission of the EU
Pan-African Parliament	European Parliament
African Court of Justice	European Court of Justice

A major change in strategic thinking institutionalised within the AU was that sovereignty no longer provided protection for dictatorial leaders, with the Constitutive Act (2000) openly declaring the 'right of the Union to intervene in a Member State pursuant to a decision of the Assembly in respect of grave circumstances, namely war crimes, genocide and crimes against humanity'. Moreover, the terms of the PSC provide the authority to arbitrate when there is a threat to peace within a member state. Therefore the AU has been successful in leading collective action in support of its activist peacekeeping role across the continent, while decisively rejecting any military coups in favour of democratic alternatives. For example, the AU has consistently stood up to coups by suspending members until power is returned to civilian rule, including Burkina Faso (2015), Egypt and CAR (2013), Mali and Guinea Bissau (2012), and Madagascar (2009). It offers a clear sign that the AU is willing to act definitively when undemocratic actions are perpetuated.

Peacekeeping is another key area in which the AU has sought to take the lead in order to secure perceptible changes in the pursuit of reforming the continent (Williams, 2007). Although the outcomes of the AU's conflict mediation and resolution efforts in settings as varied as the Comoros to Somalia have been clearly mixed, the willingness to intervene is an enormous theoretical shift from the days of the OAU. The continued outbreak of violent conflicts (see Chapter 6) remains a key impediment to Africa's search for peace, good governance, and economic development. In pursuit of the African Renaissance, the AU and Africa's eight RECs have been committed to finding African solutions to political violence. Either working alone or in partnership with the UN, African peacekeeping forces have been involved most visibly in Burundi (2003), Sudan (2004), Darfur (2007), and Somalia (2007), as well as in areas of ongoing instability including the DRC, CAR, and Mali. However, the unwillingness of belligerents to negotiate, and the AU's inability to enforce political solutions, has made the job of securing peace in these conflicts extremely challenging. For example, in Darfur, operational failures led to significant numbers of AU peacekeepers being killed, while in Mali, the French military were required to be the first responders to the Islamist invasion. Furthermore, there is an inconsistent and selective approach to security issues, with the AU failing to respond adequately to political crises in countries such as Zimbabwe (2000–2008), Burundi (2015–2016), and Republic of Congo (2015–2016). In fact, effective interventions sometimes stem from sub-regional RECs taking the lead, the most prominent of which is ECOWAS, which has been involved militarily in Liberia, Côte d'Ivoire, and most recently the Gambia.

Box 9.2 Economic Community of West African States (ECOWAS) and sub-regional peacekeeping

Reducing and managing incidents of conflict across Africa have remained high on the agenda of the AU, with a number of 'trouble spots' such as the Horn of Africa and the DRC continuing to experience political violence (see Chapter 6). However, due to the AU's budgetary issues and time lags in mobilising African troops, peacekeeping operations rely on either AU–donor partnerships (Williams & Boutellis, 2014) or sub-regional RECs to carry out conflict resolution activities. For example, in 2017, the UN (2017a) had eight peacekeeping missions operating across Africa, most of which had evolved out of the AU's initial interventions.

One of the most notable RECs involved in successful sub-regional peacekeeping and conflict mediation is ECOWAS. In West Africa, where incidents of conflict and poor governance have regularly broken out, it has been the ECOWAS Cease-fire Monitoring Group (ECOMOG), set up in 1990 in response to the Liberian civil war, which has led the efforts for securing peace. This permanent security organ of ECOWAS has conducted an active and interventionist approach to regional unrest, which has seen ECOMOG deployed in peacekeeping missions in Liberia, Sierra Leone, Guinea-Bissau, and Côte d'Ivoire. There is some debate over the successes of these missions (Gberie, 2003; Obi, 2009), but building on past experiences, its actions have steadily enshrined a greater commitment to uniting the region on security matters, while formalising the need for effective peacekeeping, conflict prevention, and good governance in West Africa. The institutionalisation of these principles was demonstrated in 2017 when ECOWAS threatened to intervene militarily in the Gambia to stop an 'unconstitutional change of government' and to prevent President Jammeh retaining power. Despite some notable problems concerning funding, mandates, and intergovernmental consensus, West Africa's security mechanism has continued to evolve, allowing ECOWAS members to demonstrate the positive role that peace and good governance have on regional development; the organisation is increasingly willing to take decisive preventative measures such as condemning coups in Niger (2009) and Côte d'Ivoire (2010), as well as intervening militarily to keep the peace where necessary.

Beyond the search for continental peace and good governance, the AU has long recognised the need for economic unity as a precursor to greater stability and development. Given the relatively small size of most African economies, combined with problematic issues concerning geographic and colonial legacies, poor infrastructure, and international marginalisation (see Chapter 5), regional unity is regarded as a crucial way to overcome some of these challenges. Building on earlier initiatives such as the Abuja Treaty, the AU's *Agenda 2063* deems RECs as the crucial mechanism to realising greater continental unity. If Pan-African objectives are to be fulfilled, then the gradual development of RECs are the most likely vehicle to ensuring future success. The AU officially recognises eight RECs (see Image 9.1), which are involved not only in economic integration activities, but also in maintaining regional peace such as efforts by the Intergovernmental Authority on Development (IGAD) in Somalia.

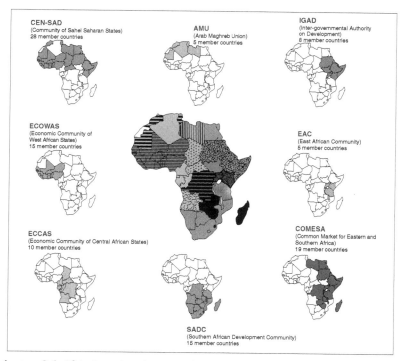

Image 9.1 Africa's regional economic communities (RECs)

Source: Created by Matthew Graham (2018) based on data in the Diplomatic Bluebook 2015 (Ministry of Foreign Affairs of Japan) (www.mofa.go.jp/policy/other/bluebook/2015/html/chapter2/c020701.html)

In terms of securing long-term economic growth and self-sufficiency for the continent, African efforts have in part been impeded by patterns of pan-continental trade. Many African nations still have economies that are not too dissimilar in structure from those inherited at independence, premised largely on the production of raw materials, and with infrastructure networks not designed for intra-continental trade, but for external export markets (see Chapter 5). This is underscored by intra-African trade consisting of only 14% of the continent's total exports (UNECA, 2015). In order to break the economic cycle of marginalisation and to develop greater regional interconnectivity, the AU has designated the eight RECs as the building blocks for enhancing international competitiveness, improving infrastructure networks, and ultimately creating a continental free trade area. A significant step forward was an agreement signed in 2015 by three RECs – COMESA, EAC, and SADC – to form TFTA. The agreement seeks to establish a substantial free trade area encompassing more than 600 million people that will maximise growth opportunities and accelerate greater integration. However, the enduring problem of attaining cohesion and integration at a continental and regional level continues to be inhibited by political considerations. For example, the TFTA has not yet materialised, with the initial deadline of 2017 for its ratification missed by all its proposed members. Furthermore, in terms of aiding regional trade, the RECs contain an array of nations at various stages of economic development, which are often dominated by one or two powerful nations such as South Africa in SADC, who regularly work in their own national interests rather than those of the region. Moreover, as Image 9.1 indicates, Africa's economic integration is stymied by an overarching lack of cohesion and standardisation; 25 nations belong to two RECs, while 17 are part of three. The result is a mix of conflicting regulations, priorities, and perspectives, which hamper rather than facilitate efforts to achieve unity.

The centrepiece of the AU's new vision for the continent was NEPAD, the Pan-African strategy adopted in October 2001 which was designed to build greater global economic and political confidence in Africa. Through sustainable growth and development projects, combined with a clear commitment to political reform, NEPAD was intended to bring about the start of the 'African Century' (see NEPAD, 2001). Initiatives such as the APRM (2003) institutionalised the commitment to good governance, and sought to generate international financial and political support. In theory, these policies were impressive, but the reality has been very different. A key point to recognise is that NEPAD did nothing to actually change Africa's marginalised economic position, as it is underpinned by western donors. NEPAD is firmly part of the neo-liberal Washington Consensus, based on market liberalisation, free trade, and liberal democracy; it has not altered the terms of engagement, but rather entrenched the status quo (Graham, 2015, 195). In fact, the model of Africa as a recipient of aid is simply perpetuated, with international institutions still able to dictate terms because they foot the bill. The extent of this dependence is underscored by the AU's budget in 2016, of which only 40% came from its member states – the rest came from donors (SAFLII, 2015). The reliance on the west for funding is accentuated by many AU members not paying their dues, with the vast majority of contributions coming from South Africa, Egypt, Nigeria, and Algeria, which only serves to inhibit the activities of the organisation. Although the AU has been relatively successful in committing to continental peacekeeping efforts, its operations are almost entirely reliant on the UN for funds. African leaders are fully aware of the need to scale back the extent of their external dependency to secure the future of the AU; for example, in 2016, reforms were proposed that would charge a 0.2% tariff on continental imports to fund peacekeeping operations. Meanwhile, the long-term future of the APRM, which emerged as a means of demonstrating a commitment to transparency and political progress, is in some doubt, with fewer countries joining the process or being reviewed; the voluntary nature of the APRM has meant that African presidents can easily refuse to participate.

Clearly the pursuit of African political and economic integration has a long history, with a series of continent-wide efforts to establish unity attempted since the early 1960s. Under the auspices of the AU, enormous strides to build greater cooperation, unity, economic development, good governance, and peace have been experienced in contemporary Africa. There are a number of positive steps being taken by the AU and its RECs, for example through condemning coups and actively intervening to maintaining peace, particularly where conflicts have a pan-regional dimension. Furthermore, the ongoing efforts to develop economic integration is a necessity for the continent to overcome some of its enduring problems, and will only serve to entrench good governance and greater development in the future.

However, the AU still has a long way to go to fulfil its Pan-Africanist objectives. An urgent imperative is for the AU to loosen its financial dependence on external donors, or it cannot possibly achieve any form of real independence. This objective is vital for the organisation's prospects, and the continent more widely; the reduction on external dependency is only gradually being addressed via much needed reforms. While the AU is a significant improvement on the OAU in terms of good governance, human rights, and democracy, there are still many concerns about the practical implementation of these goals. For example, since 2002, the revolving chairperson of the AU has included Robert Mugabe (2015),

Teodoro Obiang (2011), and Muammar Gaddafi (2009), none of whom are representative of democratic leadership. In relation to human rights, there have been disagreements concerning the ICC, which indicted Kenyan President Uhuru Kenyatta for promoting ethnic violence (a charge later dropped), and has also issued an international arrest warrant for Sudanese President al-Bashir for genocide, which has been flaunted by several nations including South Africa. In 2017, the AU threatened the mass withdrawal of its members from the ICC because of the court's African bias, although the request was not unanimously supported, with noticeable dissent from Nigeria and Senegal (HRW, 2017). Unfortunately, in making such demands the AU does not help to change the perceived notion that the continent harbours authoritarian leaders. Finally, the enduring problem of African integration revolves around the lack of political commitment and the continuing unwillingness to cede sovereignty. The AU has instigated positive progress towards building continental unity, but as long as political leaders continue to talk rather than act, then the Pan-African dream will remain as elusive as ever.

Beyond the activities of the AU and the RECs, there has been a gradual yet vitally important advance in Africa's emerging influence within global politics, allowing for the creation of common positions on pressing pan-continental issues such as climate change (Chapter 10), as well as allowing individual nations to play a greater role in multilateral organisations. Since the end of the Cold War, African diplomats and representatives have steadily ensured that the continent's perspectives are heard on the global agenda. For example, Kofi Annan was the UN Secretary General (1997–2006) who initiated the MDGs (Chapter 5), which in part sought to improve the material conditions of many African nations. Furthermore, Liberian President Ellen Johnson Sirleaf was appointed by the UN, alongside former national leaders David Cameron (UK) and Susilo Bambang Yudhoyono (Indonesia), to devise the 2030 Sustainable Development Goals (SDGs); importantly, Sirleaf's position ensured that the AU's perspectives outlined in *The Common African Position* (2014a) was incorporated into the UN's new SDGs agenda. What these brief examples demonstrate is that Africa's international position is improving.

However, the creation of institutions such as the UN and World Bank, at a time when much of Africa remained under colonial rule, has meant the historical exclusion of the continent from the main levers of financial and political power. These western-dominated institutions remain largely unreformed, and thus perpetuate traditional modes of thinking and action. This has resulted in the AU actively campaigning for wide-ranging reforms to the UN, particularly the Security Council. For example, the AU has been seeking two permanent seats with veto-wielding powers on an expanded Security Council, in order to safeguard the continent's interests. Although African nations are becoming more influential, the continent's full potential will remain limited unless there are significant changes to the international economic and political system that maintains the status quo.

The African diaspora

The diaspora most commonly refers to people of African descent who live outside the borders of the continent and share a common origin and cultural affinity to Africa. Although the phrase African diaspora is often used to describe entire groups of people, it is a contested term which is neither static nor remotely homogeneous in describing the experiences, mindsets, and realities of those of African descent. There are sizeable African diasporas found in many parts of the world, especially in North America, Latin America, the Caribbean, and Europe, yet the circumstances in which they arrived in these regions can be drastically different. For example, the forced removals during the Arab and Atlantic slave trades (see Chapter 3) displaced millions of African peoples who were subsequently united by a shared experience of racism, slavery, and marginalisation that helped inform and shape the creation of a distinct black identity, whose origins lay in Africa. It is of no surprise that the initial articulation of Pan-Africanism (discussed earlier in the chapter) came from black intellectuals in the diaspora who sought to politicise their experiences and establish a shared community based on their common ancestry from Africa. On the other side of the spectrum are the significant numbers of Africans who have migrated from the continent following independence, usually in search of employment and education opportunities, or due to socio-economic factors such as poor governance and war. The Pew Research Centre (2017) reported that 2.1 million African migrants lived in the USA alone, up from only 80,000 in 1970.

Our understanding of what actually is 'Africa' remains dependent on the context, historical time frame, and perspective, and is something that has evolved and shifted over time (see Chapter 1). With this fundamental point in mind, the problem that arises when trying to define the African diaspora is that it is comprised of several components with radically different experiences and conceptualisations of 'Africa'. One strand of the diaspora is the historically displaced populations and their descendants, largely located in North America, Latin America, and the Caribbean (Table 9.2), whose experiences are intrinsically linked to slavery, but who often regard Africa through a unitary lens. A key issue for those advocating a shared history and culture was that when these peoples were removed from the continent, African nations as we see them today did not exist, with no delineated geographic borders (see Chapter 3). Therefore, with no specific geographic anchor on the continent, and over time an increasing inability to determine ethnic lineages (the main basis of societal formation before the nineteenth century), a transnational, historically constructed narrative, based on an imagined culture, history, and identity, developed among the descendants of the coerced emigrants. The result was the articulation of a distinct black diasporic identity with its common ancestral heritage located 'in Africa', which necessarily had to transcend modern borders, history, languages, and cultures (Patterson & Kelley 2000, 15). For the historical diaspora, a mythologised yet politically motivated concept was forged to give voice to disparate groups dislocated from Africa.

Table 9.2 Largest African diasporas (historical and contemporary)

Country	Population (millions)
Brazil	56
USA	47
Haiti	8.7
Columbia	5
France	3.9
Jamaica	2.8
Venezuela	2.6
UK	2.2
Dominican Republic	2.1
Cuba	1.3

The second core strand of the African diaspora consists of the first and second generations of people that have left the continent since independence, normally through socio-economic choice, but importantly, whose realities are grounded within the concept of the nation-state. This group are definitely part of the African diaspora, but simultaneously retain distinct nationalities which inform their individual identities and interactions with the continent. For example, this group often maintains their links to their birth country through family ties, holidays, or remittance payments (see Chapter 5).

To reconcile the differences between these strands, Paul Zeleza (2008, 7) argued that 'diasporas are complex social and cultural communities created out of real and imagined genealogies and geographies (cultural, racial, ethnic, national, continental, transnational) of belonging, displacement and recreation', while Kim Butler (2000, 127) asserted that 'conceptualizations of diaspora must be able to accommodate the reality of multiple identities and phases of diasporization over time'. The key point to remember is that the African diaspora is far from monolithic, obscuring a multitude of different experiences and perceptions of the continent.

Therefore, in order to identify what the African diaspora actually constitutes, the AU (2005) after much debate decided on a broad-based definition, which asserted that 'the African Diaspora consists of peoples of African origin living outside the continent, irrespective of their citizenship and nationality and who are willing to contribute to the development of the continent and the building of the African Union'. Given the complexities in defining the African diaspora, the AU's own terminology provides sufficient vagueness and scope to encompass those whose ancestors were forcibly displaced through slavery and those that have voluntarily migrated, while also addressing issues of historical origin and shared interests, values, and cultures. Crucially, in the spirit of Pan-Africanism, the AU's definition emphasises that to be considered part of the diaspora you cannot live on the continent.

In recent decades, the importance attributed to the African diaspora has gained renewed impetus among political elites, as a potential source of financial and social capital that might assist in the general uplift of Africa. On a continental scale, the AU has sought to engage and harness the energies of the diaspora as part of the objective of enhancing the organisation, and involving them as actors in various technical fields. Almost immediately after the AU was established, the Constitutive Act (AU, 2003, 2) was amended, with specific reference in Article 3 to 'invite and encourage the full participation of the African Diaspora as an important part of our Continent, in the building of the African Union'. The political acknowledgement of the value of the diaspora prompted the AU to officially recognise the 'African Diaspora' as the so-called 'sixth region' of the continent (in addition to North, West, East, Central, and South) in an effort to engage them politically, socially, and economically. The underlying premise of the AU's conceptualisation of the diaspora is of mutual development as part of a broader 'African Renaissance' and one which unifies through collective actions. Although there was a theoretical commitment to greater participation and engagement in the functions of the AU from members of the diaspora, there was initially very little done to actively fulfil the rhetoric. However, in 2012, in an effort to provide a tangible realisation of the dream for greater cooperation, the first Global African Diaspora Summit was held in South Africa to establish an agenda for the future. The final declaration (AU, 2012) envisaged a framework that would create sustainable economic and social partnerships between the continent and the diaspora, to ensure ongoing dialogue and to strengthen Pan-African solidarity and long-term inter-governmental cooperation. In order to provide impetus to the Summit, the AU (2012, 10–11) committed itself to the adoption of five legacy projects: an African Diaspora Skills Database; an African Diaspora Volunteers Corps; the African Diaspora Investment Fund; a Development Marketplace for the Diaspora (to facilitate innovation and entrepreneurship); and the African Remittances Institute.

To support these initiatives, the Citizens and Diaspora Directorate was formed by the AU to develop partnerships between African governments, civil society, and the diaspora to ensure continued participation and representation within the organisation's structures. Furthermore, seats for diaspora representatives were provided on the Economic, Social and Cultural Council (AU, 2014b) to inform debates and decision making within the AU, while regional committees were created including Latin America and Europe. However, in spite of the political will, there has been little material progress by the AU, especially with regards to fulfilling and implementing the legacy projects; for example, after 2016, all reference to 'Legacy Projects' have been dropped from the AU's yearly handbook which outlines its ongoing activities. Moreover, the AU has not provided the necessary funds to realise many of its grand initiatives, the role of the African diaspora at a decision making level remains symbolic within the organisation, while questions concerning who actually represents the diaspora's interests and views abound. Finally, matters are further complicated by the actions of individual nations who are concurrently appealing to their own citizens abroad for social and economic assistance, who in reality are far more likely to respond to such requests from their homelands rather than the AU. The direct connection to 'home' means these diasporic communities' conceptualisations of identity are often grounded within specific territorial locales rather than on a pan-continental level.

For many governments across the continent, the contemporary African diaspora has plenty they can potentially offer in terms of social and political assistance. It must be recognised that many who reside abroad do ultimately wish to return home, albeit with significant variations in the length of their absence and the depth of their commitment to support the country of their birth. Perhaps the most important and underappreciated contribution of the African diaspora is via remittances (see Chapter 5), with the search for economic opportunity acting as an influential factor behind migration. On a local level, the vital role of remittances from the diaspora, including the large Somali and Zimbabwean populations abroad, continues to support communities across Africa, providing much needed funds for family budgets, as well as subsidising education and healthcare costs, while nationally, there is a growing tendency to provide investments as a means of supporting economic growth projects. Beyond direct financial assistance, the diaspora who have gained educational and employment opportunities abroad are also in a position to transfer skills and knowledge in a range of technical fields to aid the development of human resources in countries where these remain relatively underdeveloped. Moreover, diasporic organisations act as important civil society actors in establishing and promoting networks, as well as providing vehicles for advocacy opportunities to campaign and apply pressure on the states they reside in to take African issues more seriously. However, the success or failure of any such diaspora partnership, often rests on issues of securing funding for projects, the level of 'buy-in' from the various stakeholders involved, and the communication channels (or lack of) between the diaspora communities and home. Finally, the African diaspora holds a unique global position to change the 'story' of the 'hopeless' continent (see Chapter 1) by promoting alternative narratives, especially through social media, which can help to challenge international stereotypes of Africa.

Box 9.3 The diaspora and political activism in the Gambia

Under the autocratic and highly personalised rule of President Yahya Jammeh, the Gambia had since 1994 experienced decades of one-party governance, human rights abuses, growing poverty, and an intolerance of dissent – factors which had convinced thousands of Gambians to migrate legally and illegally to Europe and North America. For a small country, the Gambia had proportionally a very large population living outside of Africa. As Jammeh's rule became increasingly repressive, diasporic communities engaged in a range of activities in the build-up to the December 2016 elections, including highlighting human rights abuses, intensive online activism and mobilisation of Gambians around the world, and raising funds for the domestic opposition. The activities contributed to a groundswell of concerted pressure and political opposition within the country, which ultimately led to the defeat of Jammeh, who despite trying to cling to power was eventually ousted by Adama Barrow in January 2017.

While the AU and some African governments actively court the diaspora, for those countries with a democratic deficit or where power is maintained through authoritarian means, such as Eritrea and Togo, the population living abroad can be viewed as a challenge to their political authority. Utilising societal networks and their access to resources, the diaspora can become a powerful and influential force for mobilisation, advocacy, and democratic campaigning against authoritarian regimes, assisted by the proliferation of social media and internet technologies. Although it is difficult to draw a direct correlation between diasporic political activities and the undermining of undemocratic governments, their activities can certainly 'internationalise' the internal politics of specific countries and help maintain support for opposition groups.

Migration

Throughout human history, migration has been a long-standing occurrence which has contributed to the formation of cultures, identities, and nationalities globally. Indeed, Africa's history has been shaped by the regular movement of people across the continent's geographic spaces (see Chapter 3), and beyond its territorial boundaries (see diaspora). However, since the millennium, the world has experienced unprecedented levels of population mobility caused by international migration and increased forced displacement (UNHCR, 2017); the latest official statistics recorded 257 million international migrants worldwide (UN, 2018). People are persuaded to migrate due to numerous causal push and pull factors, many of which overlap, including employment, education, poverty, climate change, war, poor governance, and violence. There is no simple explanation as to why people migrate, and the phenomenon must therefore be understood as part of a complex and multifaceted trend of both forced and voluntary movements.

The recent representations of African migration in the west have typically bordered on the hysterical. If you have seen any form of western media on the issue, it is almost certainly couched in apocalyptic terms. Newspaper headlines have screamed that millions of people are heading towards Europe, while TV footage has shown people climbing the barbed wire fences of Spanish Ceuta, or trying to cross the Mediterranean in unseaworthy boats, in which thousands have drowned. This form of reporting simply reinforces the stereotypes of the 'hopeless continent', afflicted by poverty, conflict, and desperation. It is obvious that hundreds of thousands of people predominantly from West and East Africa have and continue to attempt to make the perilous journey across the Sahara in a bid to reach Europe, yet the mainstream political and media narratives do not accurately reflect the reality of migration patterns on the continent (Table 9.3).

Table 9.3 African migration destinations

Number of African migrants (millions)	Destination
16.4	Africa
4.1	Asia
9.2	Europe
0.1	Latin America
2.3	North America
0.5	Oceania
32.6	World Total

Source: Created using data from UN, Department of Economic and Social Affairs, Population Division (2016, 1), International Migration Report 2015.

Before addressing aspects of migration across Africa more fully, it is necessary to distinguish between the different forms of population movement. In the west, the prevailing public discourse employs the words 'migrant' and 'refugee' interchangeably, despite having entirely different meanings, connotations, and responsibilities for governments (UNHCR, 2016). According to the UN, refugees are people who flee their homes due to the situation being too dangerous to stay, caused by factors including hunger, political persecution, and violence. Refugees seeking asylum are afforded certain rights set out by international law, and receiving nations have a responsibility to protect them. On the other hand, migrants are characterised as those who are not forced to move because of any immediate danger, but do so out of complex choices often in search of employment, educational opportunities, or social reasons. Importantly, this group of people have to apply through specific nations' immigration laws for the legal right to settle abroad. Another term to be aware of is the concept of 'mixed migration'; several organisations, such as the International Organisation for Migration and the Regional Mixed Migration Secretariat, use it to holistically cover population movements in all its various forms, encompassing refugees, asylum seekers, economic migrants, and 'other' migrants which can also include those who are internally displaced.

Yet, in regards to African population movements, the public discourse has been intentionally skewed, and subsequently reframed in a very particular fashion to suit political, and xenophobic agendas. The term refugee or forced migrant has largely been jettisoned in favour of labelling people as 'illegal migrants' or 'failed asylum seekers', which not only criminalises them, but also absolves states of their responsibility for helping those in genuine need. For those that do embark on the hazardous trip towards Europe, the migrants might be 'pushed' through situations outside of their control, or 'pulled' by economic considerations. It can be notoriously difficult to ascertain specific categorisations, but to tarnish entire groups of people with one brush-stroke is not only misleading, it is also dangerous. To avoid the 'single story' of the continent, the causes of mass migration need to be examined beyond the simplistic and mono-causal. Moreover, the choice of language used when referring to migration is very important and can unintentionally reinforce particular agendas and perspectives about Africa.

Since the Arab Spring in 2011, and the onset of the 'migration crisis', the story fashioned through a Eurocentric lens has asserted that African population movements have been entirely tilted towards Europe. However, this is far from an accurate representation of the reality. In fact, the overwhelming majority of population movement remains within Africa and is not preoccupied with leaving the continent. The UN (2016) highlighted that 'most international migrants living in Africa, or 87 per cent of the total, originated from another country of the same region'. Moreover, those that do choose to leave Africa are almost all documented migrants, and are not just heading towards Europe, but to North America and the Gulf countries too (Bakewell & De Haas, 2007). Furthermore, of the relatively small numbers that do leave the continent, and who make up the African diaspora, 90% are economic migrants according to an IMF report (Gonzalez-Garcia et al., 2016). Of those nations that do have relatively high international out-migration, it is the North African countries, followed by South Africa, Nigeria, and Ethiopia, which have the highest proportion of citizens moving abroad. This an interesting point to highlight, because this group constitute the continent's most developed countries, which would indicate that higher, not lower socio-economic development increases the possibilities of extra-African migration (Flahaux & De Haas, 2016, 15–17). The smaller nations of Cape Verde and Mauritius should also be mentioned in terms of extra-African migration, because even though the numbers are small, they have the largest proportions of the total population living overseas.

It should be recognised that African migration is not 'exceptional' from the rest of the world, with the vast majority of people voluntarily moving for family, work, or study to neighbouring nations (Flahaux & De Haas, 2016, 2). Major 'hub nations' on the continent that are more economically developed than their neighbours draw the largest proportion of migrants, particularly from their immediate geographic regions: Côte d'Ivoire (2.3 million), South Africa (2 million), and Nigeria (0.9 million) are the top three host countries of African migrants (Gonzalez-Garcia et al., 2016). For example, South Africa's status as an economic power-house attracts significant numbers of documented African migrants for work and education, who comprise 75% of all those that arrive in the country; the neighbouring region is most prominently represented with Zimbabwe, Mozambique, Lesotho, Malawi, Swaziland, and Namibia among the top ten 'sending countries' to South Africa (Meny-Gibert & Chiumia, 2016). These 'normal' patterns of African migration constitute the overwhelming majority of population movements and need to be appreciated first in order to gain a deeper understanding of the overall situation on the continent.

While familiar forms of migration are well established, there are sig-nificant and rapidly unfolding problems of forced displacement across Africa. By the end of 2016, there were 5.5 million Africans living in 'refugee' or 'refugee like situations', of which 5.1 million were from sub-Saharan Africa (UNHCR, 2017, 14–20, 64). The epicentre of the crisis is East Africa and the Horn of Africa, which due to serious political violence in countries such as South Sudan, Sudan, and Somalia, as well as a pan-regional famine that is a human-caused disaster created by these conflicts, has led to 3.2 million refugees fleeing their homes. Further conflicts situated in the DRC, CAR, and Burundi have meant that the Central African region added a further 1.4 million people to the total number of African refugees. By the end of 2017, seven of the ten highest source countries of refugees were found in Africa. It is crucial to note that the overwhelming majority of refugees do not have the resources or capabilities to travel any further than immediate neighbouring nations. The consequence has been that the burden of supporting them has fallen on relatively undeveloped countries that do not necessarily have the means to cope with the enormous influx of people. In 2017, Uganda had accepted 1.2 million refugees and asylum seekers, of which 950,000 were from war-torn South Sudan (UN, 2017b), and housed one of the world's largest refugee camps, Bidi Bidi, which holds at least 270,000 people. Furthermore, to put the size of the infrastructure and resource strain into context Cameroon, Chad, DRC, Ethiopia, Kenya, Sudan, and Uganda hosted between them 4.9 million refugees, 28% of the global total (UNHCR, 2017, 20).

In addition to refugees, there are sizeable internally displaced popula-tions (IDPs) found throughout Africa, where people are forced to move due to political violence, conflict, and human rights violations within countries; in 2018, there were 12.5 million IDPs on the continent. People are often forced to move multiple times due to evolving states of insecu-rity and crisis, including the Lord's Resistance Army in Central Africa, the Islamist group Boko Haram in Nigeria, and the M23 rebellion in the eastern DRC. The main locations of considerable IDPs in Africa are the DRC, Sudan, and Nigeria, all of which have over 2.2 million people displaced, while South Sudan and Somalia have over 1.6 million (UNHCR, 2017, 36–37). The wide-scale internal dislocation of people in these nations creates huge domestic problems, as the forced migrants flee their homes with virtually nothing, which means the receiving areas struggle to provide adequate aid, shelter, and healthcare.

What are some of the root causes of both forced and voluntarily migration, and what effects do they have? For the vast majority of Africans, the search for a 'better life' through employment and education serves as a key underlying motivation to move within the continent. Major cities such as Cairo, Lagos, and Johannesburg have attracted significant numbers of educated migrants who are legally permitted to reside there, as urban economies diversify into more technologically focused practices. On a less formalised level, Africa's somewhat unsecured borders have allowed for the relatively easy 'irregular' movement of unskilled people in search of work in extractive industries (for example, South African mining) or in the informal economy as traders. These two sides of voluntarily migration can be beneficial in terms of developing trading networks and skill transfers, as well as the important provision of remittances. However, the negative consequences can be the significant risk of exacerbating a 'brain drain' of skilled professionals such as doctors from less developed nations, and the scapegoating of migrant communities when locals cannot find employment. It should be reiterated that the vast majority of socio-economic migration is over short distances, with the 'destination' country often having a similar linguistic and cultural heritage to the origin nation. With regards to forced migration, the causality is often tied to a range of interlinking factors that can include human rights abuses, political violence, and climate change. These are obviously highly traumatic experiences, leaving migrants with very little in terms of material resources to improve their immediate situations, as well as an uncertain future for their families in terms of long-term stability, schooling, and employment opportunities. In order to alleviate the suffering and to stem the number of refugees across the continent, urgent international action by organisations such as the AU and UN is required to mediate these conflicts, and to find political solutions to end the violence.

What has exercised the western international community most about African migration since 2011 has been the increased flows of irregular migrants seeking to enter Europe, many of whom pay people smugglers to help their journeys across the Sahara and the Mediterranean. Although constituting a relatively small proportion of Africa's total migration, there has been a surge in irregular movements, which evolved closely with the overthrow of Gaddafi in 2011, and the subsequent disintegration of law and order in Libya; the creation of ungoverned spaces facilitated the flow northwards of significant numbers of undocumented asylum seekers and economic migrants. The result was twofold: the creation of relatively unimpeded routes from West and East Africa across the Sahara into Libya, and the emergence of sophisticated and lucrative smuggling gangs operating across the Sahel in countries such as Niger. However, with the EU struggling to deal with the situation, there has been a public and political backlash against the hundreds of thousands of migrants arriving in southern Europe. The political answer has been to try and devolve the responsibility of preventing mass migration onto North African nations and the transit countries such as Sudan and Niger. Huge 'development' payments (although bribery would be a more accurate portrayal) were promised by the EU (2016) to 'partner' countries for increased border controls and the acceptance of deported migrants. The early indication from the EU (2016) was that the efforts were working, because within six months of the deal being signed in 2016, the numbers moving through Niger were reduced from 70,000 in May to around 1,500 in November of that year. However, the drawbacks of such a scheme are that the EU funds are supporting authoritarian regimes such as Eritrea and Sudan, Libya does not have a government wielding central authority to control migration or its coasts, and that border towns such as Agadez in Niger have recalibrated their economies around people smuggling, which will be extremely difficult to alter.

There are clearly different forms of migration throughout Africa, encompassing voluntary and forced movements of people. Although the majority of migration remains overwhelmingly intra-African, and for 'regular' purposes such as employment, this narrative has been subsumed by the rise in forced and 'irregular migration' that most affect the west yet are far from representative of the reality. Therefore, to truly appreciate the diversity of migration patterns in Africa, the importance of looking beyond the single story has never been so imperative.

 Further reading

A useful book from which to examine Africa beyond the nation-state is Christopher Clapham's (1996) *Africa and the International System: The Politics of State Survival*, before turning to Ulf Engel and Manuel João Ramos's (2013), *African Dynamics in a Multipolar World*. For a detailed view on the African diaspora consult Patrick Manning's (2010) *The African Diaspora: A History Through Culture*; Isidore Okpewho, Carole Boyce

Davies, and Ali Mazrui's (2001), *The African Diaspora: African Origins and New World Identities*; and Darlene Hine's (2009) *Black Europe and the African Diaspora*. For more information into the causes and patterns of African migration see Abdoulaye Kane and Todd Leedy's (2013) *African Migrations: Patterns and Perspectives*; and Alessandro Triulzi and Robert McKenzie's (2013) *Long Journeys: African Migrants on the Road*.

10 THE FUTURE OF AFRICA

What does the future hold for Africa? Is the much heralded 'Africa rising' thesis starting to gather apace, as democracy, good governance, and economic growth emerge? Is the Afro-pessimist narrative that depicted a 'hopeless' and despairing continent beginning to be rewritten? Or are the green shoots of optimism being undermined by stubborn autocratic rulers, intractable political violence, and economic stagnation? As this book has demonstrated, both narratives have grains of truth, with particular countries manifesting all the characteristics of such contradictory trends. Given that Africa is such a large and diverse continent, it is the site of multiple, coinciding, and conflicting realities: violence and peace; democracy and authoritarianism; growth and regression; domestic power and external weakness. Yet grand narratives reinforce and propagate a sweeping picture of Africa which is unfaithful to its realities, and do little to demonstrate its complexity. What this book has therefore attempted to highlight is that the one thing we can be sure of for the future is uncertainty. There have been rapid and dynamic changes in Africa's contemporary political, economic, and social trajectories, in which 'progress' and 'regression' have appeared, which makes it unwise to offer bold statements about the future.

Throughout this book, various broad areas have been examined including historical developments and legacies, political experiments and their evolution, conflict and violence, and human innovations in culture and societal organisation. However, three themes, not mentioned elsewhere, are identified in this chapter which are intrinsically related to the political, economic, and social direction of African states, and hold the potential to alter the future course of the continent, either positively or negatively. The three issues that will challenge the people and states of Africa are the rapid emergence and spread of technology, particularly mobile phones; the impact that climate change will have on human habitation across the continent; and the role of education in embedding and instigating tangible improvements for the continent. In order to effectively meet these challenges head-on, and to overcome some of the prescriptive and ongoing external interventions in the continent's affairs, the solutions must originate from African politicians and civil society.

Technology

One of the most important recent developments that has the potential to positively transform the political, social, and economic landscape for millions of people is mobile phone technology. There has been a rapid rise in the proliferation of mobile devices, and there are over 420 million unique mobile subscribers in Africa (GSMA, 2017), allowing for greater connectivity over vast geographic spaces, particularly through SMS and WhatsApp messaging. In turn, this has facilitated new forms of social inclusion, driven alternative economic opportunities, and transformed political power dynamics. A United Nations Development Programme (UNDP, 2012) report asserted that 'mobile phones can enhance pro-poor development in sectors such as health, education, agriculture, employment, crisis prevention and the environment ... that are helping to improve human development efforts around the world'. For example, there is a growing possibility (albeit with significant barriers) that educational e-resources may enhance student outcomes through digital means, overcoming the need for expensive physical infrastructure, while health-care results could be improved via distance diagnosis and treatment plans.

A continent once hamstrung by its physical infrastructure, such as poor fixed-line telephone networks, has, according to some observers, experienced a technological 'leap' through the advent of mobile data and internet connections. Improvements to signal strength and growing 4G coverage across the continent have spurred the increased usage of mobile devices. Moreover, the potential of the 'untapped' African market has encouraged technology companies to design their products to consumer needs, including the production of ever more affordable handsets. For example, Huawei sells Android phones for less than $100, while MTN Nigeria offers devices for under $50, bringing these mobiles within the reach of many. The vast majority of phones used in Africa still remain basic, non-internet enabled devices (i.e. calls and SMS), but a crucial development since 2010 has been the growing availability of smartphones, with ownership expected to reach over 550 million by 2020.

Mobile phones have helped initiate a technology 'leap'. As a result, millions of Africans previously marginalised due to poor communication infrastructure, and expensive technology such as laptops, are now connected to the wider world. In turn, there has been an upsurge in the use of social media platforms such as WhatsApp, Facebook, and Twitter, while behavioural practices including banking and political activism have been revolutionised by these new forms of communication. Information technology is rapidly changing the continent, providing opportunities for creativity, innovation, and dynamism to thrive.

The increased use of mobile technology has enormous potential to aid growth and economic development throughout Africa, not just through the ease of communication networks, but also the associated services that come with it such as airtime distributors and handset makers. Although the economic activities derived through mobile technologies and services are still in its infancy, in 2015 they 'generated 6.7% of GDP in Africa, a contribution that amounted to around $150 billion of economic value' (GSMA, 2016). At a more local level, the transformative potential of mobile technology is already having some economic impact for the continent's poorest and marginalised people. A key example of such a change is that business transactions can now be conducted through simple communication functions, which rely largely on SMS networking, rather than internet connectivity. One of the most striking cases is the way in which farmers, using SMS data platforms, can sign up for texts providing 'real-time' information on the state of the market, and the fluctuations in prices. For rural famers, many of whom are forced to travel long distances, using poor and costly transport infrastructure to sell their produce in markets, the information gained through SMS empowers them to make informed business choices (Acker & Mbiti, 2010). For subsistence farmers using SMS updates in Niger, their knowledge of grain prices resulted in a 29% rise in profits (Acker & Mbiti, 2010, 218). This basic information provides rural communities with greater knowledge about the markets they operate within, while improved product prices help stimulate poverty reduction and transform lives.

However, the most innovative and well-known African technological solution that has revolutionised the economic landscape has been mobile money transfer platforms. As recently as 2012, only 23% of Africans held an account at a formal financial institution, a statistic which obscured the reality that most were held in southern Africa; as a consequence, the overwhelming majority of African society remained disenfranchised from the formal economic system (AfDB, 2013). The increased prevalence of mobile phones was a catalyst for finding a practical and simple technological solution to the problem of money transfers, payments, and savings, without the need for having a bank branch or ATM. A consumer-friendly, needs-driven platform was devised that allowed millions of people to access and utilise financial services which were previously unattainable, simply by using a phone and SMS code. Consumers set up free mobile bank accounts, and for a small charge by the specific provider make financial transactions for goods and services, including paying for items such as taxi fares (well before Uber was even conceptualised in the west), swiftly, easily, and entirely by SMS. This form of mobile money transfer was a pragmatic and innovative African solution to meet the basic problem of access and inclusivity. The outcome

Box 10.1 M-Pesa

The earliest pioneer of mobile money transfer was M-Pesa in Kenya. In 2007, Safaricom launched M-Pesa (Swahili for money), which enabled users to deposit, withdraw, and transfer money securely via a unique SMS code. The lack of physical banking infrastructure had been an inhibitor to accessing the formal economic sector for the majority of Kenyans. To overcome this problem, Safaricom licensed a network of 120,000 M-Pesa agents across Kenya who, working out of pre-existing kiosks, petrol stations, and shops, sold airtime credit and enabled users to withdraw funds (Image 10.1). The technology was easy to use, intuitive, and operated effectively; it is safe to say that M-Pesa has had an enormous impact on Kenyan society. In 2016, after ten years in existence, 'mobile money is ubiquitous in Kenya [and] is used by at least one individual in 96% of Kenyan households' (Suri & Jack, 2016). Similar m-banking platforms have subsequently proliferated across the continent, such as Etisalat's introduction of the GTEasySavers account in Nigeria and Econet's EcoCash system in Zimbabwe. These mobile money systems have had a profound effect within the countries that operate such platforms, with one long-term study in Kenya estimating that use of M-Pesa had helped lift 194,000 households out of poverty, enabled greater occupational choices for women, while enhancing financial resilience and saving (Suri & Jack, 2016). The change in economic behaviour and practice that this technology has engendered in such a short time is remarkable.

Image 10.1 M-Pesa

Source: Trevor Snapp/Bloomberg via Getty Images.

has had enormous socio-economic benefits across the continent, and Africa is the world leader in this form of mobile money transfer technology.

Moreover, the economic potential from mobile technology, especially the internet, has facilitated the emergence of a series of 'tech hubs', such as 'Silicon Savannah' in Kenya, supported by government and civil society funding (Table 10.1). These hubs are designed to kick-start the tech industry in various African countries, which bring together entrepreneurs, stimulate creative and innovative ideas, start businesses, and hopefully create employment opportunities (Adesina et al., 2016). There are over 310 such hubs located in many of Africa's major cities such as Lagos and Johannesburg, although they are unevenly distributed across the continent, with the majority centred in just five countries: South Africa, Kenya, Nigeria, Egypt, and Ghana (CMAS, 2016). The importance of technology has prompted some countries to invest in sustained and growing ICT infrastructure, particularly in Rwanda, whose president Paul Kagame declared that 'the internet is a needed public utility as much as water and electricity' (Ben-Ari, 2014); Rwanda has subsequently implemented initiatives to improve health and education through internet provision. The ever growing number of mobile devices owned across Africa, and the search for alternative solutions to local problems, has also seen a rapid rise in technologically focused businesses; there are apps for almost everything including religious services, investing in livestock, and getting

Table 10.1 Differences in internet penetration across Africa

Country	Penetration (percentage of population)	Internet users (millions)
Kenya	81.8	39.64
Mauritius	62.7	0.83
South Africa	51.6	28.58
Nigeria	48.8	95.39
Egypt	36.5	34.8
Cameroon	20	4.9
Djibouti	16.5	0.15
Ethiopia	11.1	11.53
Togo	7.1	0.54
Sierra Leone	4.6	0.31
Guinea-Bissau	4.3	0.08
Niger	2	0.43
Eritrea	1.3	0.07

Source: Created using data from Internet World Stats, www.internetworldstats.com/stats1.htm

medical advice. The economic dividends established through technology businesses can certainly help to generate growth, develop human capital and skills, and improve service delivery in many African countries (World Bank, 2016a). On the face of it, these economic transformations nourish the 'Africa rising' narrative.

The potential political ramifications derived from mobile technology in Africa could be dramatic for ordinary citizens across the continent. Mobiles are increasingly regarded as a tool both for political mobilisation, as demonstrated by the use of social media during the Arab Spring in 2011, and to hold elites to account through the spread of information on themes such as good governance, corruption, and violence. The proliferation of mobile phones has broken the monopoly on information, once the sole preserve of the state-run media, making it easier for malpractice by elites to be monitored, criticised, and publicised to a far wider audience, while offering alternative sources of news. For example, in Zimbabwean elections, camera phones are used to monitor the democratic process by photographing the results at individual polling stations, which are sent to activists at the central counting office, to prevent blatant rigging and ballot box stuffing, practices all previously employed by ZANU-PF to manipulate the outcome. Another excellent example of technologically driven political activism was the creation of *Ushahidi* (witness) an open-source, geo-tagging platform that used Google Maps to pinpoint and report on voting fraud and ethnic violence in the aftermath of Kenya's 2008 election. Kenyans could text or email incidents of local violence, which were then recorded and collated to provide an overarching picture of incidents of unrest across the country. The software has since been exported and used across the world including disaster relief efforts in the USA, Chile, and Russia. Technologically driven activism is also having an important impact in Egypt, where 'HarassMap' serves as a tool for women to report on sexual harassment, which seeks to encourage collective action against the perpetrators and to facilitate an end to gender-based violence in the country.

The rising use of social media among Africa's ever growing youth population has played a part in supporting various forms of activism, popular mobilisation, and political awareness. Across North Africa, protesters utilised Facebook and Twitter effectively to coordinate and direct street protests against authoritarian regimes in 2011, while in South Africa the #RhodesMustFall campaigns (2015–2016) were utilised by university students to organise mass demonstrations across the country demanding the decolonisation of higher education.

Although it is only right to praise the changes that have been facilitated by mobile technology, it alone cannot possibly be a panacea for the continent's problems. A key issue is that the developments are far from comprehensive nor evenly spread, even within countries. Technology can somewhat diminish the socio-economic gaps, but it can also accentuate the distance between the haves and have nots. For example, the creation of new digital infrastructure does not come cheaply, and governments and mobile companies are highly unlikely to prioritise the spread of wireless networks to rural communities, which will only disenfranchise these regions further when compared to urban areas. The continental divisions are apparent too with the faster internet connections found only in the coastal nations due to the underwater cables laid around Africa in 2009; it means that landlocked countries still struggle to experience the digital benefits because of their geographic distance from the landing terminals (World Bank, 2016a, 212).

In fact, as Juma (2017) has argued, the optimism in the mobile revolution might be misplaced, because a modern economy cannot be achieved without an industrialisation strategy and sufficient infrastructural investment to support it. Although mobile technology has allowed for the 'leapfrogging' of some infrastructure such as landlines, African countries cannot 'leap' the process of industrial development. Juma's argument is accentuated by inadequate energy supplies experienced in many nations. To facilitate this technology, a consistent energy supply is vital, yet millions of people remain unconnected to the electricity grid; for example, only 32% of people in Angola, 7% in Burundi, and 4.5% in South Sudan have access (World Bank, 2017). Africa's digital economy will not be realised unless regular and comprehensive supplies of energy are provided to its citizens. It should also be noted that those who do work within the tech industry are often highly skilled and educated in comparison to their counterparts, which means the much heralded digital economy still has a long way to go due to discrepancies in access to services and jobs. Moreover, by 2020, 60% of Africa's population will still not have internet access (GSMA, 2016); this is a huge barrier for socio-economic development, especially when internet penetration in Latin America and Asia has been increasing much more rapidly. There are also further issues such as the affordability of devices ($50 is expensive if you are living on $1.50/day) and the cost of reliable data and internet packages, which unless they fall significantly will inhibit greater uptake. Finally, big international companies such as Amazon and Facebook have begun to muscle into African markets, which may stymie some local innovations. It must be recognised that the grand narrative concerning the transformative powers of mobile technology fails to consider whether the consumption of these services in Africa is actually regenerating local and regional economies, or if the profits are being outsourced to multinational companies.

The potential political power of technology might be enormous, but it alone will not overthrow autocratic leaders. In fact authoritarian regimes are all too aware of the power of technology, and have increasingly begun to restrict its use. In recently disputed elections including in Uganda, Gabon, Chad, Burundi, and Congo-Brazzaville, or where there is civil unrest, for example in Cameroon and Ethiopia, governments have all shut down the internet to prevent the spread of information and to impede the mobilisation of public protest through social media. Furthermore, throughout Africa, authorities in countries including South Africa, Ethiopia, Nigeria, Angola, and Zimbabwe have all imposed new laws which restrict citizens' online freedoms, while allowing government access to their social media profiles. All too regularly activists and opposition politicians from countries such as Egypt, Mozambique, and Zambia have been arrested for 'defamatory' or 'hate' speech, usually directed towards the ruling elite.

The positive aspects of mobile technology across Africa are clear, and must be recognised for the changes that they are inducing for millions of people. For those that do gain access to the opportunities outlined above then their experiences are rapidly evolving and provide important and positive steps forward. However, the all-encompassing transformative gains hailed by some of the 'Africa rising' protagonists do need to be tempered by a more sober and realistic perspective that the socio-economic or political dividends are far from universal, nor as far-reaching as previously believed.

Climate change

The severe impact of climate change across Africa is very much a reality, and through its geographical setting the effects of these environmental fluctuations are only expected to worsen through rising temperature levels at a rate 1.5 times faster than the global average, decreased and erratic rainfall, and rising sea levels (IPCC, 2014). In the last few years alone, there have been intense droughts in eastern and southern Africa, serious flooding in West Africa, and rapidly evolving desertification throughout the Sahel region. According to the Climate Change Vulnerability Index (2016), Africa is the most susceptible continent to climate change, accounting for four of the five world's most at risk countries, with a total of 27 African nations identified as being 'extremely' vulnerable. For example, by 2020, between 75 million and 250 million people will live in areas which have little or no water due to climate change. The result of these climatic changes will be diminishing agricultural yields and productivity of arable land and increased insecurity over access to food supplies and water, which in turn will negatively influence livelihoods, economic activity, and political stability. The very socio-economic fabric of the continent is at risk due to climate change.

Climate change usually refers to significant alterations to weather patterns that affect 'normal', long-term conditions such as average temperatures and anticipated rainfalls, as well as increasing the frequency of major environmental disasters such as flooding. Climate change is not a new phenomenon, but through increasing global temperatures over the last century, especially via human activity, and the erratic nature of rainfall (either too little or too much), the impacts are becoming far more noticeable and sustained. For example, the environmental changes in East Africa have contributed to a prolonged drought that has put 13 million people at risk of famine (Oxfam, 2017). For Africa, time is of the essence, because even though the continent has done the least to contribute to climate change, accounting for only 3.8% of global greenhouse gas emissions, the region will bear the brunt of it (Africa Progress Report, 2015). To emphasise the contrast between the rest of the world and the continent in terms of emissions, it takes a Tanzanian '8 years to consume as much electricity as an American consumes in one month' (Africa Progress Report, 2015, 41).

The serious impact of environmental change will be felt by millions of Africans, most noticeably those involved in agriculture. As discussed in Chapter 5, the continent still relies heavily upon the agricultural sector, accounting for 65% of all employment, while there is an estimated 50 million pastoralists on the continent who require grazing grounds for their cattle (World Bank, 2016b, 24); their livelihoods are under unprecedented pressure. Climate change has exacerbated extreme 'drought like conditions' in many regions of Africa. If the rain does not fall, it is impossible to grow arable crops or find sufficient grasslands for cattle, which can result in famine (IPCC, 2014). Elsewhere, the higher temperatures mean that precipitation rapidly evaporates, which reduces the water content in the soil and significantly diminishes agricultural yields. These climatic changes when combined with unsustainable farming practices on already overworked and increasingly stressed land further accelerate soil erosion and desertification. Moreover, due to poor energy infrastructure, many people are without regular access to electricity, forcing people to cut down trees for fuel which only worsens the precarious state of the ecosystem.

The seriousness of the situation was outlined by the UN Food and Agriculture Organization (FAO) which estimated that by 2030 the continent will have lost two-thirds of its arable land to desertification. If global temperatures rise by even 2 degrees Celsius, then by 2050, many of the factors outlined above will be manifest throughout Africa, with disastrous consequences for ecosystems and human existence if urgent action is not taken. The outcome for human habitation is poverty, malnutrition and hunger, increased mortality, political instability (for example, Darfur; see Chapter 6), and migration as people are forced to flee (see Chapter 9).

It is not just rural areas that are affected by the impact of climate change, but Africa's growing cities too. Large coastal cities such as Durban (South Africa), Abidjan (Côte d'Ivoire), and Dar es Salaam (Tanzania) are all susceptible to flooding due to erosion, rising sea levels, and overpopulation on flood plains. Moreover, African cities will be affected not only by the reduced agricultural productivity from rural regions, impacting upon the ability to feed large urban populations, but also by the availability of drinking water. The consequence of decreased rainfall and more droughts is a reduction in the extent of secure and regular water supplies; in early 2018, the city of Cape Town announced a state of emergency as its network of dams had less than 100 days left of water available, with the city rapidly approaching 'Day Zero' when supplies ran out. In fact, the struggle over securing access to water has taken on pan-regional significance in East Africa, as Egypt, Sudan, and Ethiopia are locked in a diplomatic dispute over the construction of the Grand Ethiopian Renaissance Dam (see Chapter 2). Egypt and Sudan are concerned about the potential reduction in water flow of the Nile River, which will impact upon industrial activity, agriculture, and the availability of drinking water downstream. It is also important not to forget Africa's small island nations, including Seychelles and Mauritius, which are particularly vulnerable to flooding through rising sea levels.

While the environmental picture may seem unremittingly bleak, there are some developments that offer cautious grounds for optimism. In Chapter 9, the various challenges that had inhibited African nations' attempts at collaboration on issues of continental importance were outlined. Yet it was the severity of the environmental threat that recognises no territorial borders that prompted African leaders to cooperate as a unified block at the Paris Climate Summit in 2015. Not only did African nations achieve continental consensus through the negotiations, but they also effectively influenced the international community to accept the ambitious proposals tabled. African interests were firmly enshrined in the Paris Agreement (UN, 2015), which saw a deal signed to keep global temperature rises below 2 degrees Celsius, as well as outlining clear plans for international financial support to react and respond to environmental change. However, in 2017, US President Donald Trump sought to withdraw America from the Paris Climate deal, which places some of the financial commitments required to fulfil the environmental projects in doubt.

Box 10.2 The great green wall

One innovative initiative that has been introduced in a bid to mitigate and slow the effects of climate change and desertification is the so-called 'Great Green Wall'. Started in 2007, the ambitious internationally funded project is aiming to plant an 8,000 km long forest of trees, and vegetable gardens across the Sahel, stretching from

Senegal to Djibouti. Through the mass planting of indigenous trees and the careful management of the 'wall', the aim is to block the encroachment of the Sahara Desert, replant the region, repopulate the natural ecosystem, and provide jobs and livelihoods. The Great Green Wall is a long-term vision, which seeks through training, environmental education, and employment to tackle climate change and its associated problems such as famine, drought, and instability.

A final potentially positive development is the emergence of a pan-continental green economy based on renewable energies, which could alleviate the economic reliance on raw materials; reduce the pollution caused by fossil fuels; expand the availability of clean energy to those currently disenfranchised from access to electricity supplies; and stimulate new employment opportunities. Many countries already utilise hydroelectric power, but the continent has the ability to exploit various other clean energy sources, particularly solar and wind power; for example, it has been estimated that Africa could generate 1,100 GW of solar capacity, which would far exceed continental demand (Mo Ibrahim Foundation, 2017, 230). African nations have begun to appreciate the potential this technology holds, and are increasingly investing in renewable energy, with projects such as Morocco's solar power plant in Ouarzazate, while Kenya is constructing the continent's largest wind farm at Lake Turkana, which has 365 turbines. If politicians are strategic and far-sighted, then African states could begin to invest in the manufacturing processes of the components for solar panels and wind turbines to create jobs and skills, rather than relying on imports. However, vast sums of money are required to make the initial investment into the required technology and infrastructure, and it should be noted that the potential to utilise renewable energy sources such as wind is not available uniformly, requiring collaboration and partnerships across the continent to maximise the prospective green energy boom.

As this section has demonstrated, climate change could have untold environmental and human consequences if global measures to tackle it are not implemented very soon. If climate change is left unchecked, then famine, agricultural degradation, poverty, and mass migration are far more likely to occur throughout Africa as people and nations struggle to access and secure limited resources. Yet if strategic measures are enacted to temper some of the worst-case scenarios, then African nations might just benefit from a green revolution in jobs and energy.

Education

In order for the African continent to fulfil its future economic, political, and social potential, the provision of and access to high-quality education will be crucial. The benefits of education are clear in that it can provide the underlying platform for improving a number of societal indicators including employment, poverty reduction, health, and a commitment to democracy (Harber, 2017). Many of the themes previously discussed in the book including good governance, economic growth, and the techno-logical 'revolution' are all things that the continent is aspiring towards, but cannot possibly be achieved without overcoming some of the ongo-ing barriers which prevent millions of young Africans from receiving a good education. Without an immediate political commitment to the roll-out of widespread and strategically targeted investment in education and skills, the continent will continue to lag behind the rest of the world in its educational outcomes, and Africa's expanding youth population will remain marginalised in an age of globalisation. It is difficult to envisage Africa collectively moving away from poverty if its population continues to be deprived of an education that adequately prepares them for the future.

When we consider that the UN regards education as a basic human right, the overarching picture of educational attainment across the con-tinent is far from encouraging. On a basic statistical level, Africa's adult literacy rates (aged 15 and above) remain among the lowest globally, with the continental average at only 64.3% (UNDP, 2016, 233). However, this headline figure obscures some enormous discrepancies. At the high-est end of the scale, countries such as Mauritius, Seychelles, and South Africa all perform well with adult literacy rates of over 90%, and oth-ers such as Botswana, Tunisia, and Zimbabwe are not far behind with levels above 80%. Yet at the very bottom, Niger's literacy rate is below 20%, while CAR, Burkina Faso, Guinea, and Mali are all under 40%. The UNESCO (2015, 231–233) Education for All Development Index, which examined various strands of educational data over a 15-year period (2000–15), ranked 16 African nations in the worst 20 worldwide, while the highest placed African country was Mauritius (55th), and the best performing sub-Saharan nation was Ghana (89th).

To provide a sense of why there is such low educational attainment on the continent, the levels of student enrolment across primary, secondary, and tertiary education offers a serious cause for concern (Table 10.2). First of all, it should be noted that there has been a sustained effort over the last few decades to tackle student participation, with African governments achieving tangible improvements in primary enrolment which has risen substantially from 59% in 1999 to 79% in 2012 (UNESCO, 2015, 6). However, this does still mean that 21% (or 34 million) of sub-Saharan

African children never go to primary school, the highest proportion in the world. Moreover, a significant number of children do not go on to fully complete primary school, with an average dropout rate of 41.7% (UNDP, 2016, 232–233) and some countries exhibiting alarming levels of non-completion including Ethiopia (63.4%), Mozambique (69.3%), and Uganda (75.2%). The further up the educational level you move, there is a dramatic decrease in student enrolment, with the continental average for secondary education at 43%, and by the tertiary stage it is only 8% (UNDP, 2016, 232–233). In simple terms, more than half of all Africans do not gain a secondary education or the requisite skills needed for future employment and possible poverty alleviation.

The key question is what are the barriers to accessing a better quality of education in Africa? Statistics always hide a multitude of variations, and the data on literacy and attainment should be viewed with scepticism, but, as Harber (2017) asserts, 'there are inequalities in outcomes from education, as well as access to education, and the quality of education provided'. The historical inequalities perpetuated by colonial education provision (or lack of) certainly meant that many African governments were playing catch-up at independence, and despite some impressive initial improvements, the onset of the economic crisis in the 1980s saw education budgets slashed during structural adjustment. Furthermore, educational systems throughout Africa are still influenced by the former metropole in many respects, including teaching in the colonial language, which might be the second or third language for the pupils and teachers. Therefore a range of historical and contemporary socio-economic and political factors must be considered as to why educational outcomes remain weak.

One crucial factor is poverty, as there is a direct correlation between growing wealth and increased educational participation (UNESCO, 2012, 13). For example, family poverty is a barrier to a child's education, as the cost of school fees, as well as associated add-on charges such as uniforms, means that for the poor they simply cannot afford to send their children to school. In turn, for poorer families, there is a greater likelihood that children will be required to be in paid employment to make ends meet, which either means no or reduced attendance at school; in countries such as Cameroon, Malawi, and Senegal, a large proportion of children work. For example, in 2011, just under 70% of Cameroonian children aged 12–14 were in employment (UNESCO, 2015, 117–118). Furthermore, location continues to have an impact on access, with rural communities often overrepresented in underattainment statistics in comparison to urban areas, as they are usually hamstrung by the large distances to the nearest schools, which are frequently underequipped; in Mali, there was nearly a 30% differential in attendance at lower secondary schools between urban and rural children (UNESCO, 2015, 117). A final socio-economic

Table 10.2 Educational achievements

Country	Adult literacy rates (percentage aged over 15)	Population with at least some secondary education (percentage aged 25 and over)
South Africa	94.3	74.9
Mauritius	90.6	59.7
Botswana	88.5	85.9
Algeria	80.2	34.9
Kenya	78	32
Egypt	75.2	61.4
Zambia	63.4	51.8
Mozambique	58.8	5.2
the Gambia	55.5	31.9
Mauritania	52.1	17.3
Mali	38.7	11.5
Benin	38.4	23.3
Guinea	30.4	n/a
Niger	19.1	6.1

Source: Created using data from UNDP, 2016, 230–233.

issue is gender; patriarchal societies will frequently prevent girls from attending school, as they will be expected to help the family instead of learning, which, as a consequence, results in greater illiteracy among adult women. To reinforce this point, a startling report found that in South Sudan on the eve of independence in 2011, a 'girl is more likely to die in childbirth than to learn to read and write' (*The Economist*, 2011a).

Another key factor is the political will and ability to invest in education, and again there are major differences recorded across Africa. For some countries, investing in education is a national priority. Namibia and Swaziland both have state expenditure on education at over 8% of GDP, but at the bottom of the scale Guinea-Bissau, South Sudan, and the DRC record spending at under 2% (UNDP, 2016, 232–233). Other governments have sought to achieve universal primary education by abolishing school fees, such as Ghana, Kenya, Mozambique, and Tanzania. This is an important first step in widening access, but alone it is not enough to improve education outcomes. It is all well and good getting people into a school, but if there are insufficient teaching resources and facilities – for example in Chad, Côte d'Ivoire, Equatorial Guinea, Madagascar, and Niger at least 60% of schools are without toilets (UIS, 2012, 6) – it negatively impacts upon the quality of the education provided, and ultimately pupil attainment. The inability to expand resources and infrastructure to match demand for schools has seen class sizes increase. Average single class sizes can differ drastically across Africa, with some countries having well over 50 pupils per class such as Chad (68), Republic of Congo (69), and Mali (57), while Cape Verde (28) is more in line with international norms (UIS, 2012, 3). This is a pressing dilemma for policy makers as Africa's school-aged population is set to rise from 444 million in 2010 to 552 million by 2020 (UNESCO, 2012, 12). The result of large classes and poor facilities is for teachers to focus on rote learning, which does little to facilitate critical understanding or independent thinking. Even Africa's richest nations such as South Africa are affected by budgetary concerns and misspending, exemplified by the Limpopo textbook scandal (2012–2013), where students did not receive the necessary resources due to political mismanagement. A final problem is the quality of teaching itself. Many teachers do admirable jobs in challenging circumstances; however, with so few African students ever reaching tertiary level education – for most countries it is under 10%, well below the global average of 35% (UNDP, 2016) – it means that those who do graduate from university are less likely to be enticed into the poorly paid teaching profession. The outcome is that schools are often forced to employ poorly trained and undereducated teachers who are unable to drastically alter the quality of education.

The overarching consequence is that a series of interlinking issues including poverty, infrastructure, societal attitudes, resources, finances, and political will have for the majority of African nations led to comparatively poorer outcomes in terms of knowledge, understanding, and skills. Every nation globally that has experienced economic and political development has had to focus upon improving educational attainment. For the continent as a whole, there has to be a renewed focus on the quality of outcomes. While primary education is now free at the point of access for the majority of African pupils, there will have to be a concurrent commitment first to secondary and then to tertiary education to reinforce the gains made at the lower levels. Moreover, there will have to be greater investment into resources and infrastructure, including the reduction of class sizes and providing facilities which create positive learning environments that motivate students to learn (Image 10.2). The provision of resources through technology has the potential to overcome some of the barriers to access, including textbooks, but this in turn

Image 10.2 Senegalese primary school children in class

Source: SEYLLOU/AFP/Getty Images.

requires mass investment, whether this comes from the state or increasingly private sources, as well as long-term strategic planning. Finally, the issue of the quality of teacher training and the remuneration of the profession will be important areas that have to be addressed in order to attract good-quality candidates that can improve teaching standards. These are not insurmountable issues, but they do require a commitment to improving education so that Africa's potential can be fully realised in the future.

Final thoughts

To sum up, this book has highlighted various dimensions concerning contemporary Africa's evolution, examining the positive and negative aspects of the continent. The underlying theme of diversity is a crucial point to bear in mind as there is clearly no 'single' African story, with the 55 nations each having their own specific histories and contemporary developments. However, for such a diverse continent many patterns of similarity can still be identified to make instructive and effective comparisons. This may appear at first glance to be a contradictory statement, but as has been demonstrated there are multiple experiences and realities throughout Africa. Furthermore, the book has emphasised the intersections between the past and present, as well as the significant changes experienced throughout the continent over the last century through external and internal actions, which are very much apparent across contemporary African societies. These developments continue to influence the continent's varied, conflicting, and uncertain future. The hope is that this introduction to contemporary Africa will enthuse you to further explore the many and intriguing narratives, and to provide a platform for future research about this exciting, dynamic, complex, and welcoming continent.

BIBLIOGRAPHY

Achebe, C. (1965), 'English and the African writer', *Transition*, 18, pp. 27–30.

ACLED (2017), *Conflict Trends (no. 55). Real-time Analysis of African Political Violence*, February 2017, https://reliefweb.int/sites/reliefweb.int/files/resources/ACLED_Conflict-Trends-Report-No.55-February-2017-pdf.pdf (accessed 13 August 2018).

Adams, W., Goudie, A. & Orme, A. (eds) (1999), *The Physical Geography of Africa* (Oxford: Oxford University Press).

Adesina, O. et al. (eds) (2016), *Innovation Africa: Emerging Hubs of Excellence* (Bingley: Emerald Group Publishing).

Adibe, J. (2009), *Who is an African? Identity, Citizenship and the Making of the Africa-Nation* (London: Adonis & Abbey Publishers).

Adichie, C. (2009), *The danger of a single story, TED Talk*, https://www.ted.com/talks/chimamanda_adichie_the_danger_of_a_single_story (accessed 13 August 2018).

AfDB (2011), *African economic outlook 2011: Africa and its emerging partners*, www.afdb.org/fileadmin/uploads/afdb/Documents/Generic-Documents/Media_Embargoed_Content/EN-AEO_2011_embargo%206%206%20Juin.pdf (accessed 29 June 2016).

AfDB (2012), *African economic outlook 2012: Promoting youth employment in Africa*, www.africaneconomicoutlook.org/sites/default/files/content-pdf/AEO2012_EN.pdf (accessed 3 July 2016).

AfDB (2013), *Financial inclusion in Africa*. https://www.afdb.org/fileadmin/uploads/afdb/Documents/Project-and-Operations/Financial_Inclusion_in_Africa.pdf (accessed 13 August 2018).

AfDB (2014), *Tracking Africa's Progress in Figures*, www.afdb.org/fileadmin/uploads/afdb/Documents/Publications/Tracking_Africa%E2%80%99s_Progress_in_Figures.pdf (accessed 16 July 2016).

AfDB (2015), *African Economic Outlook 2015: Regional Development and Spatial Inclusion*, www.africaneconomicoutlook.org/en/telechargements (accessed 6 July 2016).

AfDB (2016), *African Economic Outlook 2016: Sustainable Cities and Structural Transformation*, www.africaneconomicoutlook.org/en/ (accessed 17 July 2016).

Africa Centre for Security Studies (2016), 'Overlapping effects of autocracy and conflict in Africa', Africa Center for Strategic Studies, https://africacenter.org/spotlight/autocracy-conflict-africa/ (accessed 30 June 2017).

African Economic Outlook (2015), *Regional Development and Spatial Inclusion*, www.africaneconomicoutlook.org/fileadmin/uploads/aeo/2015/PDF_Chapters/Overview_AEO2015_EN-web.pdf (accessed 27 July 2017).

African Economic Outlook (2017), *Entrepreneurship and Industrialisation*, www.africaneconomicoutlook.org/en (accessed 27 July 2017).

Africa Progress Report (2015), *Power, People, Planet: Seizing Africa's Energy and Climate Opportunities*.

Afrobarometer (2016), *Do Africans Still Want Democracy?*, http://globalreleases. afrobarometer.org/global-release/pp36-do-africans-still-want-democracy (accessed on 27 July 2017).

Afrobarometer (2016a), *Do Trustworthy Institutions Matter for Development? Corruption, Trust, and Government Performance in Africa*, http://afrobarometer. org/sites/default/files/publications/Dispatches/ab_r6_dispatchno112_trustwor-thy_institutions_and_development_in_africa.pdf (accessed 27 July 2017).

Aker, J. & Mbiti, I. (2010), 'Mobile phones and economic development in Africa', *Journal of Economic Perspectives*, 24, 3, pp. 207–232.

Alegi, P. (2010), *African Soccerscapes* (Athens: Ohio University Press).

Alesina, A., Easterly, W. & Matuszeski, J. (2011), 'Artificial states', *Journal of the European Economic Association*, 9, 2, pp. 246–277.

Amin, S. (1973), *Neo-colonialism in West Africa* (London: Penguin African Library).

Anderson, D. (2006), *Histories of the Hanged: Britain's Dirty War in Kenya and the End of Empire* (London: Weidenfeld & Nicolson).

Anderson, D. & McKnight, J. (2015), 'Kenya at war: Al-Shabaab and its enemies in Eastern Africa', *African Affairs*, 114, 454, pp. 1–27.

Asante, M. (2015), *The History of Africa: The Quest for Eternal Harmony* (Abingdon: Routledge).

AU (2000), *Constitutive Act of the African Union*. https://au.int/sites/default/files/pages/ 32020-file-constitutiveact_en.pdf

AU (2003), *Protocol on the Amendments to the Constitutive Act of the African Union*, https://www.au.int/web/sites/default/files/treaties/7785-file-protocol_amend-ments_constitutive_act_of_the_african_union.pdf

AU (2005), *Meeting of Experts on the Definition of the African Diaspora*, https://au.int/ sites/default/files/treaties/7785-treaty-0025_-_protocol_on_the_amendments_ to_the_constitutive_act_of_the_african_union_e.pdf (accessed 13 August 2018).

AU (2012), *Declaration of the Global African Diaspora Summit*, https://au.int/sites/ default/files/treaties/7785-treaty-0025_-_protocol_on_the_amendments_to_the_ constitutive_act_of_the_african_union_e.pdf (accessed 13 August 2018).

AU (2014a), *The Common African Position*, https://au.int/sites/default/files/docu-ments/32848-doc-common_african_position.pdf

AU (2014b), *African Union Handbook 2014*, www.un.org/en/africa/osaa/pdf/au/ au-handbook-2014.pdf

AU (2017), *African Union Handbook 2017*, https://www.au.int/web/sites/default/ files/pages/31829-file-african-union-handbook-2017-edited.pdf

AU Commission (2015), *Agenda 2063 Framework Document: 'The Africa we want,'* www.un.org/en/africa/osaa/pdf/au/agenda2063-framework.pdf

Baker & McKenzie (2015), *Spanning Africa's Infrastructural Gap: How Development Capital Is Transforming Africa's Project Build-out*, The Economist Corporate Network, http://ftp01.economist.com.hk/ECN_papers/Infrastructure-Africa

Bakewell, O. & De Haas, H. (2007), 'African Migrations: Continuities, discontinuities and recent transformations', in L. de Haan, U. Engel. & P. Chabal (eds), *African Alternatives* (Leiden: Brill).

BarbieSaviour, www.barbiesavior.com/ (accessed 13 August 2018).

Barrow, O. & Jennings, M. (2001), *The Charitable Impulse: NGOs & Development in East and North-East Africa* (Oxford: James Currey).

Bates, R. (1981), *Markets and States in Tropical Africa: The Political Basis of Agricultural Policies* (Berkeley, CA: University of California Press).

Ben-Ari, N. (2014), *Big dreams for Rwanda's ICT sector*, www.un.org/africarenewal/magazine/april-2014/big-dreams-rwanda%E2%80%99s-ict-sector (accessed 30 June 2017).

Berg, E. (1981), *Accelerated Development in Southern Africa: An Agenda for Africa* (Washington, DC: World Bank).

Biddle, I. & Knights, V. (2007), *Music, Identity and the Politics of Location: Between the Global and the Local* (Aldershot: Ashgate).

Blas, J. (2014), 'Equatorial Guinea: Squandered riches', *The Financial Times*, 3 February.

Bøås, M. & Dunn, K. (2007), *African Guerrillas Raging Against the Machine* (Boulder, CO: Rienner).

Boni, S. (1999), 'Striving for Resources or Connecting People? Transportation in Sefwi (Ghana)', *The International Journal of African Historical Studies*, 32, 1, pp. 49–70.

Braathen, E., Bøås, M., Sæther, G. (eds) (2000), *Ethnicity Kills?: The Politics of War, Peace and Ethnicity in Sub-Saharan Africa* (London: Palgrave Macmillan).

Brautigam, D. (2009), *The Dragon's Gift: The Real Story of China in Africa* (Oxford: Oxford University Press).

Brautigam, D. (2015), '5 myths about Chinese investment in Africa', *Foreign Policy*, http://foreignpolicy.com/2015/12/04/5-myths-about-chinese-investment-in-africa/ (accessed 17 June 2016).

Brendon, P. (2008), *The Decline and Fall of the British Empire, 1781–1997* (New York: Alfred A. Knopf).

Brenner, L. (1993), *Muslim Identity and Social Change in Sub-Saharan Africa* (Bloomington, IN: Indiana University Press).

Burke, J. (2017), 'Witnesses say dozens killed in al-Shabaab attack on Kenyan troops', *Guardian*, 27 January.

Butler, K. (2000), 'From black history to diasporan history: Brazilian abolition in Afro-Atlantic context', *African Studies Review*, 43, 1, pp. 125–139.

Cain, P. & Hopkins, A. (2002), *British Imperialism, 1688–2000* (Harlow: Longman).

Cederman, L., Wimmer, A. & Min, B. (2010), 'Why do ethnic groups rebel? New data and analysis', *World Politics*, 62, 1, pp. 97–119.

Chamberlain, M. (2010) *The Scramble for Africa* (Harlow: Longman).

Chabal, P. & Daloz, J. (1999), *Africa Works: Disorder as Political Instrument* (Oxford: James Currey).

Charry, E. (2012), *Hip Hop Africa: New African Music in a Globalizing World* (Bloomington, IN: Indiana University Press).

Chazan, N. (1999), *Politics and Society in Contemporary Africa* (Boulder, CO: Lynne Rienner Publishers).

Cheeseman, N. (2010), 'African elections as vehicles for change', *Journal of Democracy*, 21, 4, pp. 139–153.

Cheeseman, N., Anderson, D. & Scheibler, A. (2014), *Routledge Handbook of African Politics* (London: Routledge).

China Statistical Yearbook, 2000–2015, www.stats.gov.cn/english/statisticaldata/AnnualData/ and www.stats.gov.cn/tjsj/ndsj/2015/indexeh.htm (17 June 2016).

Cilliers, J. and Schünemann, J. (2013), 'The future of intrastate conflict in Africa: More violence or greater peace?, ISS Paper No. 246.

Clapham, C. (1996), *Africa and the International System: The Politics of State Survival* (Cambridge: Cambridge University Press).

Clapham, C. (1998), *African Guerrillas* (Oxford: James Currey).

Climate Change Vulnerability Index (2016), *Climate Change Vulnerability Index 2017,* http://reliefweb.int/report/world/climate-change-vulnerability-index-2017 (accessed 5 August 2017).

Cohen, A. (2017), *The Politics and Economics of Decolonization in Africa: The Failed Experiment of the Central African Federation* (London: I.B.Tauris).

Collier, P. (2008), *The Bottom Billion: Why the Poorest Countries Are Failing and What Can be Done About It* (Oxford: Oxford University Press).

Collier, P. & Gunning, J. (1999), 'Why has Africa grown slowly?', *The Journal of Economic Perspectives*, 13, 3, pp. 3–22.

Collier, P. & Hoeffler, A. (2004), 'Greed and grievance in civil war', *Oxford Economic Papers*, 56, 4, pp. 563–595.

Collins, J. & Richards, P. (1989), 'Popular music in West Africa', in Frith, S. (ed) *World Music, Politics and Social Change* (Manchester: Manchester University Press).

Cooper, F. (1996a), *Decolonization and African Society: The Labor Question in French and British Africa* (Cambridge: Cambridge University Press).

Cooper, F. (1996b), '"Our strike": Equality, anticolonial politics and the 1947–48 railway strike in French West Africa', *The Journal of African History*, 37, pp. 81–118.

Cooper, F. (2002), *Africa Since 1940: The Past of the Present* (Cambridge: Cambridge University Press).

Cooper, F. (2005), *Colonialism in Question: Theory, Knowledge, History* (Berkeley, CA: University of California Press).

Curtin, P. (1971), 'Jihad in West Africa: Early phases and inter-relations in Mauritania and Senegal', *The Journal of African History*, 12, pp. 11–24.

Darby, P. (2002), *Africa Football and FIFA: Politics, Colonialism and Resistance* (London: Frank Cass).

Darwin, J. (1997), 'Imperialism and the Victorians: The dynamics of territorial expansion', *English Historical Review*, 112, 447, pp. 614–642.

Davidson, B. (1992), *The Black Man's Burden: Africa and the Curse of the Nation State* (London: James Currey).

Davis, N. (1978), 'The Angolan Decision of 1975: A personal memoir', *Foreign Affairs*, 57, 1, pp. 109–124.

de Waal, A. (2004), 'Counterinsurgency on the cheap', *London Review of Books*, 26, 15, pp. 25–27.

de Waal, A. & Abdel Salam, A. (2004), 'Islamism, state power, and jihad in Sudan', in A. de Waal (ed), *Islamism and its Enemies in the Horn of Africa* (Bloomington, IN: Indiana University Press).

de Waal, A. & Ibreck, R. (2013), 'Hybrid social movements in Africa', *Journal of Contemporary African Studies*, 31, 2, pp. 303–324.

de Witte, L. (2002), *The Assassination of Lumumba* (London: Verso).

Decalo, S. (1990), *Coups and Army Rule in Africa* (New Haven, CT: Yale University Press).

Des Forges, A. (1999), *'Leave None To Tell The Story': Genocide in Rwanda* (New York: Human Rights Watch).

Diamond, L. (1997), *The Prospects for Democratic Development in Africa* (Stanford, CA: Hoover Institution on War and Peace).

Dike, K. (1956), *Trade and Politics in the Niger Delta, 1830–1885; An Introduction to the Economic and Political History of Nigeria* (Oxford: Clarendon Press).

Dowd, C. & Raleigh, C. (2013), 'Briefing: The myth of global Islamic terrorism and local conflict in Mali and the Sahel', *African Affairs*, 112, 488, pp. 498–509.

Dwyer, M. (2017), *Soldiers in Revolt: Army Mutinies in Africa* (London: Hurst & Co.).

Dwyer, P. & Zeilig, L. (2012), *African Struggles Today: Social Movements Since Independence* (Chicago: Haymarket Books).

Economist Intelligence Unit (2017), *Democracy Index 2016: Revenge of the 'Deplorables'*.

Ehret, C. (2016), *The Civilizations of Africa: A History to 1800* (Charlottesville, VA: University of Virginia Press).

El Din, A. (2007), 'Islam and Islamism in Darfur', in A. de Waal (ed), *War in Darfur and the Search for Peace* (London: Justice Africa).

Ellis, S. (1999), *The Mask of Anarchy: The Destruction of Liberia and the Religious Dimensions of an African War* (London: C. Hurst).

Ellis, S. (2002), 'Writing histories of contemporary Africa', *The Journal of African History*, 43, 1, pp. 1–26.

Ellis, S. & ter Haar, G. (1998), 'Religion and politics in sub-Saharan Africa', *The Journal of Modern African Studies*, 36, 2, pp. 175–201.

Ellis, S. & van Kessel, I. (2009), *Movers and Shakers: Social Movements in Africa* (Leiden: Brill).

Engel, U. & Ramos, M. (2013), *African Dynamics in a Multipolar World* (Leiden: Brill).

Englebert, P. & Ron, J. (2004), 'Primary commodities and war: Congo-Brazzaville's ambivalent resource curse', *Comparative Politics*, 37, 1, pp. 61–81.

Englebert, P., Tarango, S. & Carter, M. (2002), 'Dismemberment and suffocation: A contribution to the debate on African boundaries'. *Comparative Political Studies*, 35, 10, pp. 1093–1118.

EU (2016), *Second Progress Report: First Deliverables on the Partnership Framework with third countries under the European Agenda on Migration*, https://eeas.europa.eu/sites/eeas/files/second-progress-report-1_en_act_part1_v11.pdf (20 July 2017).

Fage, J. (1969), 'Slavery and the slave trade in the context of West African history', *The Journal of African History*, 10, 3, pp. 393–404.

Falola, T. (2008), *Key Events in African History* (Westport, CT: Greenwood Press).

Fanon, F. (1967), *Black Skin, White Masks* (New York: Grove Press).

Fanon, F. (2001), *Wretched of the Earth* (London: Penguin Books).

FAO, IFAD and WFP (2015), *The State of Food Insecurity in the World 2015: Meeting the 2015 international hunger targets: Taking stock of uneven progress*, www.fao.org/3/a-i4646e.pdf (accessed 13 August 2018).

Faris, S. (2007), 'The real roots of Darfur', *The Atlantic*, www.theatlantic.com/magazine/archive/2007/04/the-real-roots-of-darfur/305701/ (accessed 20 June 2017).

Ferguson, J. (1994), *Anti-Politics Machine* (Minneapolis, MN: University of Minnesota Press).

Ferguson, N. (2004), *Empire: How Britain Made the Modern World* (London: Allen Lane).

Fieldhouse, D. (1973), *Economics and Empire, 1830–1914* (Ithaca, NY: Cornell University Press).

Fieldhouse, D. (1986), *Black Africa: Economic Decolonisation and Arrested Development* (London: Allen & Unwin).

Flahaux, M. & De Haas, H. (2016), 'African migration: Trends, patterns, drivers', *Comparative Migration Studies*, 4, 1, pp. 1–25.

Flint, J. (1983), 'Planned decolonization and its failure in British Africa', *African Affairs*, 82, 328, pp. 389–411.

Flint, J. (1999), 'Britain and the scramble for Africa', in Winks, R. (ed), *The Oxford History of the British Empire: Vol. 5* (Oxford: Oxford University Press).

Flint, J. & de Waal, A. (2005), *Darfur: A Short History of a Long War* (London: Zed Books).

Frankema, E. (2012), 'The origins of formal education in sub-Saharan Africa: Was British rule more benign?' *European Review of Economic History*, 16, pp. 335–355.

Freedom House (2018), *Freedom in the World 2018*, https://freedomhouse.org/report/freedom-world-2018-table-country-scores (accessed 13 August 2018).

Freund, B. (2007), *The African City: A History* (Cambridge: Cambridge University Press).

Foster, V. & Briceño-Garmendia, C. (2009), *Africa's Infrastructure: A Time for Transformation* (Washington, DC: World Bank).

Fuest, V. (2009), 'Liberia's women acting for peace: Collective action in a war-effected country', in Ellis, S. & van Kessel, I. (eds), *Movers and Shakers: Social Movements in Africa* (Leiden: Brill).

Gberie, L. (2003), 'ECOMOG: The story of an heroic failure', *African Affairs*, 102, 406, pp. 147–154.

Gberie, L. (2009), 'African civil society, "blood diamonds" and the Kimberley Process', in Ellis, S. & van Kessel, I. (eds), *Movers and Shakers: Social Movements in Africa* (Leiden: Brill).

Gerhart, G. & Glaser C. (2010), *From Protest to Challenge: Vol. 6 [Challenge and Victory, 1980–1990]* (Bloomington, IN: Indiana University Press).

Gleijeses, P. (2002), *Conflicting Missions: Havana, Washington, and Africa, 1959–1976*, (Berkeley, CA: University of North Carolina Press).

Global Witness (1998), 'A rough trade', https://www.globalwitness.org/en-gb/archive/rough-trade/ (accessed 26 June 2017).

Gonzalez-Garcia, J., Hitaj, E., Mlachila, M., Viseth, A. & Yenice, M. (2016) *Sub-Saharan African Migration: Patterns and Spillovers* (Washington, DC: IMF).

Gould, J. (2005), 'Conclusion: The politics of consultation', in Gould, J. (ed), *The New Conditionality. The Politics of Poverty Reduction Strategies* (London: Zed Books).

Graham, M. (2011), 'Covert collusion? American and South African relations in the Angolan Civil War, 1974–1976', *African Historical Review*, 43, 1, pp. 28–47.

Graham, M. (2015), *The Crisis of South African Foreign Policy* (London: I.B.Tauris).

Great Green Wall (2017), http://www.greatgreenwall.org/about-great-great-wall (accessed 13 August 2018).

Grossman, H. (1999), 'Kleptocracy and revolutions', *Oxford Economic Papers*, 51, 2, pp. 267–283.

Groth, H. & May, J. (2017), *Africa's Population: In Search of a Demographic Dividend* (Springer International).

Grove, A. (1993), *The Changing Geography of Africa* (Oxford: Oxford University Press).

GSMA (2016), *The Mobile Economy: Africa 2016*. https://www.gsma.com/mobileeconomy/africa/

GSMA (2017), *The Mobile Economy: Sub-Saharan Africa 2017*. https://www.gsmaintelligence.com/research/?file=7bf3592e6d750144e58d9dcfac6adfab&download (accessed 13 August 2018).

Gyimah-Boadi, E. (2015), 'Africa's Waning democratic commitment', *Journal of Democracy*, 26, 1, 101–113.

Harber, C. (2017), *Schooling in Sub-Saharan Africa: Policy, Practice and Patterns* (London: Palgrave Macmillan).

Hargreaves, J. (1988), *Decolonization in Africa* (London: Longman).

Hanlon, J. (1986), *Beggar Your Neighbours: Apartheid Power in Southern Africa* (Bloomington, IN: Indiana University Press).

Herbst, J. (2000), *States and Power in Africa* (Princeton, NJ: Princeton University Press).

Hershey, M. (2013), 'Explaining the non-governmental organisation (NGO) boom: The case of HIV/AIDS NGOs in Kenya', *Journal of Eastern African Studies*, 7, 4, pp. 671–690.

Hine, D., Keaton, T. & Small, S. (2009), *Black Europe and the African Diaspora* (Urbana, IL: University of Illinois Press).

Hintjens, H. (1999), 'Explaining the 1994 genocide in Rwanda', *The Journal of Modern African Studies*, 37, 2, pp. 241–286.

Hirsch, J. (2001), *Sierra Leone: Diamonds and the Struggle for Democracy* (London: Lynne Rienner Publishers).

Hobson. J. (1902), *Imperialism: A Study* (London: George Allen & Unwin).

Hodgkin, T. (1956), *Nationalism in Colonial Africa* (London: Frederick Muller).

Howard, A.M. (2010) 'Actors, places, regions, and global forces: An essay on the spatial history of Africa since 1700', in U. Engel and P. Nugent (eds), *Respacing Africa* (Leiden: Brill).

Howe, H. (1998), 'Private security forces and African stability: The case of executive outcomes', *The Journal of Modern African Studies*, 36, 2, pp. 307–331.

HRW (2015), *Equatorial Guinea*, https://www.hrw.org/africa/equatorial-guinea (accessed 7 May 2017).

HRW (2017), *AU's 'ICC Withdrawal Strategy' Less than Meets the Eye*, https://www.hrw.org/news/2017/02/01/aus-icc-withdrawal-strategy-less-meets-eye (accessed 24 July 2017).

Hubbell, A. (2001), 'A view of the slave trade from the margin: Souroudougou in the late nineteenth-century slave trade of the Niger Bend', *The Journal of African History*, 42, 1, pp. 25–47.

Huntington, S. (1991), *The Third Wave: Democratization in the Late Twentieth Century* (Oklahoma, OK: Oklahoma University Press).

Hyden, G. (2000), 'The governance challenge in Africa', in Hyden, G. (ed), *African Perspectives on Governance* (Trenton, NJ: Africa World Press).

Iliffe, J. (1995), *Africans: History of a Continent* (Cambridge: Cambridge University Press).

IMF (2014) *Africa Rising: Building to the Future Conference*, Maputo, Mozambique 29–30 May, www.africa-rising.org/ (accessed 20 April 2016).

IMF (2015), *Press Release: IMF Approves US$918 Million ECF Arrangement to Help Ghana Boost Growth, Jobs and Stability*, https://www.imf.org/external/np/sec/pr/2015/pr15159.htm (accessed 17 June 2016).

IMF (2016), *Regional Economic Outlook: Sub-Saharan Africa, Time for a Policy Reset* (Washington, DC: IMF).

IMF (2018), *Heavily Indebted Poor Countries (HIPC) initiative and Multilateral Debt Relief Initiative (MDRI): Statistical update*, www.worldbank.org/en/topic/debt/brief/hipc (accessed 12 June 2018).

Inikori, J. (1994) 'Ideology versus the tyranny of paradigm: Historians and the impact of the Atlantic slave trade on African societies', *African Economic History*, 22, pp. 37–58.

Inter-Parliamentary Union (2018), *Women in National Parliaments: 2018*, http://archive.ipu.org/wmn-e/classif.htm (accessed 12 June 2018).

IPCC (2014), *Climate Change 2014: Synthesis Report*. https://www.ipcc.ch/pdf/assessment-report/ar5/syr/SYR_AR5_FINAL_full_wcover.pdf (accessed 6 July 2017).

Jackson, R. (1993) *Quasi-States: Sovereignty, International Relations, and the Third World* (Cambridge: Cambridge University Press).

Jackson, R. & Rosberg, C. (1982a), *Personal Rule in Black Africa* (Berkeley: University of California Press).

Jackson, R. & Rosberg, C. (1982b), 'Why Africa's weak states persist: The empirical and the judicial in statehood', *World Politics*, 35, 1, 1–24.

Jackson, R. & Rosberg, C. (1984), 'Personal rule: Theory and practice in Africa', *Comparative Politics*, 16, 4, 421–442.

Jackson, S. (1995), 'China's Third World Foreign Policy', *The China Quarterly*, 142, pp. 388–422.

Jennings, M. (2013) 'NGOS', in Cheeseman, N., Anderson, D. & Scheibler, A. (eds), *Routledge Handbook of African Politics* (London: Routledge).

Jerven, M. (2013a), *Poor Numbers: How We Are Misled by African Development Statistics and What to Do About It* (Ithaca, NY: Cornell University Press).

Jerven, M. (2013b), 'For richer, for poorer: GDP revisions and Africa's statistical tragedy'. *African Affairs*, 112, 446, pp. 138–147.

Jerven, M. (2015), *Africa: Why Economists Get It Wrong* (London: Zed Books).

Joseph, G. (2001) 'African literature', in Gordon A. & Gordon, D. (eds), *Understanding Contemporary Africa* (Boulder, CO: Lynne Rienner).

Joseph, R. (1999), *State, Conflict and Democracy in Africa* (Boulder, CO: Rienner).

Judd, D. (2013), *The Boer War* (London: I.B.Tauris).

Juma, C. (2017), 'Leapfrogging progress: The misplaced promise of Africa's mobile revolution', *The Breakthrough*, 7, https://thebreakthrough.org/index.php/journal/issue-7/

Kane, A. & Leedy, T. (2013), *African Migrations: Patterns and Perspectives* (Bloomington, IN: Indiana University Press).

Kaplan, R. (1994), 'The coming anarchy', *Atlantic Monthly*, www.theatlantic.com/magazine/archive/1994/02/the-coming-anarchy/304670/ (accessed 15 February 2015).

Kapuscinski, R. (2003), *Gazeta Wyborcza*, 23 August.

Kaunda, K. (1974), *Humanism in Zambia and a Guide to its Implementation* (Lusaka: Division of National Guidance).

Keen, D. (1998), *The Economic Functions of Violence in Civil Wars* (Oxford: Oxford University Press).

Killingray, D. & Plaut, M. (2012), *Fighting for Britain: African Soldiers in the Second World War* (Woodbridge, ON: James Currey).

Klein, M. (1992), 'The slave trade in the western Sudan during the nineteenth century', in Savage, E. (eds), *The Human Commodity: Perspectives on the Trans-Saharan Slave Trade* (London: F. Cass).

Lafi, N. (2017), 'The "Arab Spring" in global perspective: Social movements, changing contexts and political transitions in the Arab world (2010–2014)', in Berger, S. & Nehring, H. (eds), *The History of Social Movements in Global Perspectives* (London: Palgrave Macmillan).

Larmer, M. (2010), 'Social movement struggles in Africa', *ROAPE*, 37, 125, pp. 251–262.

Lazarus, N. (1999), *Nationalism and Cultural Practice in the Postcolonial World* (Cambridge: Cambridge University Press).

Legacies of British Slave-ownership database, https://www.ucl.ac.uk/lbs/.

Legum, C. (1965), *Pan-Africanism: A Short Political Guide* (New York: Frederick A. Praeger, Inc.).

Legum, C. (1975), 'The organisation of African unity - success or failure?' *International Affairs*, 51, 2, pp. 208–219.

Liebau, H. (2010), *The World in World Wars: Experiences, Perceptions and Perspectives from Africa and Asia* (Leiden: Brill),

Lindberg, S. (2006), *Democracy and Elections in Africa* (Baltimore, MD: Johns Hopkins University Press).

Louw-Vaudran, L. (2016), *Super Power or Neo-colonialist: South Africa in Africa* (Cape Town: Tafelberg).

Lovejoy, P. (2012), *Transformations in Slavery: A History of Slavery in Africa* (Cambridge: Cambridge University Press).

Lovejoy, P. & Richardson, D. (2002), 'The initial "crisis of adaptation": The impact of British abolition on the Atlantic Slave trade in West Africa, 1808–1820', in Law, R. (ed), *From Slave Trade to 'Legitimate' Commerce: The Commercial Transition in Nineteenth-Century West Africa* (Cambridge: Cambridge University Press).

Lunn, J. (1999), *Memoirs of the Maelstrom: A Senegalese Oral History of the First World War* (Portsmouth: Heinemann).

Mahajan, V. (2008) *Africa Rising: How 900 Million African Consumers Offer More than You Think* (Upper Saddle River, NJ: Wharton School Pub).

Maltz, G. (2007), 'The case for presidential term limits', *Journal of Democracy*, 18, 1, pp. 128–142.

Mamdani, M. (2001), *When Victims Become Killers: Colonialism, Nativism, and the Genocide in Rwanda* (Princeton, NJ: Princeton University Press).

Manning, P. (1983), 'Contours of slavery and social change in Africa', *The American Historical Review*, 88, 4, pp. 835–857.

Manning, P. (2010), *The African Diaspora: A History Through Culture* (New York: Columbia University Press).

Mano, W., Knorpp, B. & Agina, A. (2017), *African Film Cultures: Contexts of Creation and Circulation* (Newcastle: Cambridge Scholars Publishing).

Marshall, R. (2009), *Political Spiritualities: The Pentecostal Revolution in Nigeria* (Chicago, IL: The University of Chicago Press).

Martinez, M. & Mlachila, M. (2013), *IMF Working Paper 13/53: The Quality of the Recent High-Growth Episode in Sub-Saharan Africa*, https://www.imf.org/external/pubs/ft/wp/2013/wp1353.pdf (accessed 3 March 2016).

Mazrui, A. (1969), 'European exploration and Africa's self-discovery', *The Journal of Modern African Studies*, 7, 4, pp. 661–676.

Mazrui, A. (2005), 'The re-invention of Africa: Edward said, V. Y. Mudimbe, and Beyond', *Research in African Literatures*, 36, 3, pp. 68–82.

Mazrui, A. (2009), 'Preface: Comparative Africanity – blood, soil and ancestry' in Adibe, J. (ed), *Who is an African? Identity, Citizenship and the Making of the Africa-Nation* (London: Adonis & Abbey Publishers).

Mazrui, A. & Tidy, M. (1984), *Nationalism and New States in Africa* (London: Heinemann Educational).

Mbeki, T. (2001), 'The African Renaissance: Africans defining themselves', speech at the University of Havana, Cuba, 27 March, www.sahistory.org.za/archive/address-president-thabo-mbeki-university-havana-cuba-27-march-2001 (accessed 14 June 2017).

McGowan, P. (2003), 'African military coups d'état, 1956–2001: Frequency, trends and distribution', *The Journal of Modern African Studies*, 41, 3, pp. 339–370.

Meade, J. (1961), *The Economic and Social Structure of Mauritius: Report to the Governor of Mauritius* (London: Methuen).

Meny-Gibert, S. & Chiumia, S. (2016), *Where do South Africa's international migrants come from?*, https://africacheck.org/factsheets/geography-migration/

Meredith, M. (2005), *The State of Africa: A History of the Continent Since Independence* (London: Free Press).

Meredith, M. (2006), *The Fate of Africa: From the Hopes of Freedom to the Heart of Despair* (New York: Public Affairs).

Meredith, M. (2007), *Diamonds, Gold and War: The Making of South Africa* (London: Pocket).

Ministry of Foreign Affairs, Japan (2015), *Diplomatic Bluebook 2015*, www.mofa. go.jp/policy/other/bluebook/2015/html/chapter2/c020701.html (accessed 23 July 2017).

Mkandawire, T. & Soludo, C. (1999) *Our Continent, Our Future: African Perspectives on Structural Adjustment* (Ottawa, CA: Council for the Development of Social Science Research in Africa).

Mo Ibrahim Foundation (2016), *2016 Mo Ibrahim Index of good governance: A decade of African governance 2006–2015*, http://mo.ibrahim.foundation/iiag/downloads/ (accessed 14 August 2018).

Mo Ibrahim Foundation (2017), *Africa at a tipping point. 2017 forum report.*http:// s.mo.ibrahim.foundation/u/2017/11/21165610/2017-IIAG-Report.pdf

Moghalu, K. (2014), *Emerging Africa: How the Global Economy's 'Last Frontier' Can Prosper and Matter* (London: Penguin Books).

Mohan, G. (2000), *Structural Adjustment: Theory, Practice and Impacts* (New York: Routledge).

Morgan, A. (2013), *Music, Culture and Conflict in Mali* (Copenhagen: Freemuse).

Moyo, A. (2001), 'Religion in Africa', in Gordon, A. & Gordon, D. (eds), *Understanding Contemporary Africa* (Boulder, CO: Lynne Rienner).

MSF (2014), *Pushed to the limit and beyond*, https://www.msf.org.uk/sites/uk/files/ ebola_-_pushed_to_the_limit_and_beyond.pdf (accessed 3 July 2017).

Mudimbe, V. (1988), *The invention of Africa: Gnosis, Philosophy, and the Idea of Knowledge* (Bloomington, IN: Indiana University Press).

Mueller, J. (2000), 'The banality of "ethnic war"', *International Security*, 25, 1, pp. 42–70.

Nasson, B. (2011), *The Boer War: The Struggle for South Africa* (Stroud: History Press).

Ndegwa, S. (1996), *The Two Faces of Civil Society: NGOs and Politics in Africa* (West Hartford, CT: Kumarian Press).

Nellis, J. (1986), *Public Enterprises in Sub-Saharan Africa* (Washington, DC: World Bank).

NEPAD (2001), *The New Partnership for Africa's Development*.

NEPAD (2003), *The African Peer Review Mechanism: Base Document*.

Neslen, A. (2015), 'Morocco poised to become a solar superpower with launch of desert mega-structure', *The Guardian*, 26 October.

New York Times (2013), 'China finds resistance to oil deals in Africa', 17 September.

Ngũgĩ wa Thiong'o (1986), *Decolonising the Mind: The Politics of Language in African Literature* (London: Heinemann Educational).

Nkrumah, K. (1965), *Neo-colonialism: The Last Stage of Imperialism* (London: Panaf LTD).

Nugent, P. (2012), *Africa Since Independence* (Basingstoke: Palgrave Macmillan).

Nunn, N. (2008), 'The long-term effects of Africa's slave trades', *The Quarterly Journal of Economics*, 123, 1, pp. 139–176.

Nyerere, J. (1968), *Ujamaa: Essays on Socialism* (Dar es Salaam: Oxford University Press).

OAU (1963), *OAU Charter*.

OAU (1980), *Lagos Plan of Action*.

OAU (1991), *Abuja Treaty*.

Obi, C. (2009), 'Economic community of West African states on the ground: Comparing peacekeeping in Liberia, Sierra Leone, Guinea Bissau, and Côte d'Ivoire', *African Security*, 2, pp. 119–135.

OECD (2016), *Youth unemployment rate*, https://data.oecd.org/unemp/youth-unemployment-rate.htm (accessed 6 June 2017).

Okpewho, I., Boyce Davies, C. & Mazrui, A. (2001), *The African Diaspora: African Origins and New World Identities* (Bloomington, IN: Indiana University Press).

Oliver, R. (2001), *Medieval Africa, 1250–1800* (Cambridge: Cambridge University Press).

Oliver, R. & Sanderson, G. (eds) (1985), *Cambridge History of Africa, Vol. 6: From 1870 to 1905* (Cambridge: Cambridge University Press).

Olsen, G. (1998), 'Europe and the promotion of democracy in post-Cold War Africa: How serious is Europe and for what reason?', *African Affairs*, 97, pp. 343–67.

O'Toole, T. (1986), *The Central African Republic: The Continent's Hidden Heart* (Boulder, CO: Westview Press).

Oxfam (2013), *Make Poverty History, and G8 Promises – Was It All Really Worth It?*

Oxfam (2017), *A climate in crisis: How climate change is making drought and humanitarian disaster worse in East Africa.*

Parnell, S. & Pieterse, E. (2014), *Africa's Urban Revolution* (London: Zed Books).

Patterson, T. & Kelley, R. (2000), 'Unfinished migrations: Reflections on the African Diaspora and the making of the modern world', *African Studies Review*, 43, 1, pp. 11–45.

Pearce, R. (1984), 'The colonial office and planned decolonization in Africa', *African Affairs*, 83, 330, pp. 77–93.

Pew Research Centre (2017), *African immigrant population in US steadily climbs*, www.pewresearch.org/fact-tank/2017/02/14/african-immigrant-population-in-u-s-steadily-climbs/ (accessed 21 June 2018).

Pitsiladis, Y., Bale, J., Sharp, C. & Noakes, T. (eds) (2007), *East African Running: Toward a Cross-Disciplinary Perspective* (Abingdon: Routledge).

Posner, D. & Young, D. (2007), 'The institutionalization of political power in Africa', *Journal of Democracy*, 18, 3, pp. 126–140.

Prunier, G. (2005a), *The Rwanda Crisis: History of a Genocide* (London: Hurst).

Prunier, G. (2005b), *Darfur: The Ambiguous Genocide* (London: Hurst).

Prunier, G. (2009), *Africa's World War: Congo, the Rwandan Genocide, and the Making of a Continental Catastrophe* (Oxford: Oxford University Press).

PWC (2015), *From fragile to agile. Africa oil & gas review. Report on current developments in the oil & gas industry in Africa*, https://www.pwc.co.za/en/assets/pdf/oil-and-gas-review-2015.pdf

Radelet, S. (2010), *Emerging Africa: How 17 Countries Are Leading the Way* (Baltimore, MD: Center for Global Development).

Radi-Aid, www.rustyradiator.com/

Raleigh, C. (2014), 'Political hierarchies and landscapes of conflict across Africa', *Political Geography*, 42, pp. 92–103.

Raleigh, C. (2016), 'Pragmatic and promiscuous: Explaining the rise of competitive political militias across Africa', *Journal of Conflict Resolution*, 60, 2, pp. 283–310.

Randall, V. & Svåsand, L. (2002), 'Political parties and democratic consolidation in Africa', *Democratization*, 9, 3, pp. 30–52.

Ranger, T. (1993), 'The invention of tradition in colonial Africa', in Hobsbawm, E. & Ranger, T. (eds) *The Invention of Tradition* (Cambridge: Cambridge University Press).

Reed, W. (1998), 'Guerrillas in the midst: The former government of Congo-Zaire', in Clapham, C. (ed), *African Guerrillas* (Oxford: James Currey).

Reno, W. (1998), *Warlord Politics and African States* (London: Lynne Rienner Publishers).

Reno, W. (2007), 'Patronage politics and the behaviour of armed groups', *Civil Wars*, 9, 4, pp. 324–342.

Reyntjens, F. (2009), *The Great African War: Congo and Regional Geopolitics, 1996–2006* (Cambridge: CUP).

Reyntjens, F. (2016), 'The struggle over term limits in Africa: A new look at the evidence', *Journal of Democracy*, 27, 3, pp. 61–68.

Robertson, C. & Okonjo-Iweala, N. (2012), *The Fastest Billion: The Story Behind Africa's Economic Revolution* (London: Renaissance Capital).

Robinson, R. & Gallagher, J. (1961), *Africa and the Victorians: The Official Mind of Imperialism* (London: Macmillan).

Rodney, W. (1966), 'African slavery and other forms of social oppression on the upper guinea coast in the context of the Atlantic slave-trade', *The Journal of African History*, 7, 3, pp. 431–443.

Rodney, W. (1972), *How Europe Underdeveloped Africa* (Washington, DC: Howard University Press).

Ross, M. (1999), 'The political economy of the resource curse', *World Politics*, 51, 2, pp. 297–322.

Rotberg, R. (2013), *Africa Emerges* (Cambridge: Polity Press).

SAFLII (2015), *Budget of the African Union for the 2016 Financial Year*, www.saflii.org/au/AUDECISIONS/2015/19.pdf (accessed 24 July 2017).

Samson, A. (2012), *World War I in Africa : The Forgotten Conflict among the European Powers* (London: I.B.Tauris).

Sanderson, G., N. (1985), 'The European partition of Africa: Origins and dynamics', Roland O. & Sanderson, G. (eds), *The Cambridge History of Africa. Volume 6 – From 1870 to 1905.* (Cambridge: Cambridge University Press).

Sardar, Z. (1999), 'Development and the locations of Eurocentrism', in Munck, R. & O'Hearn, P. (eds), *Critical Development Theory: Contributions to a New Paradigm* (London: Zed Books).

Sarkin, J. (2011), *Germany's Genocide of the Herero: Kaiser Wilhelm II, His General, His Settlers, His Soldiers* (Cape Town: University of Cape Town Press).

Schumacher, E. (1975), *Politics, Bureaucracy, and Rural Development in Senegal* (Berkeley, CA: University of California Press).

Scott, S. (2004), 'How many perpetrators were there in the Rwandan genocide? An estimate', *Journal of Genocide Research*, 6, 1, pp. 85–98.

Shaka. F. (2004), *Modernity and the African Cinema* (Trenton, NJ: Africa World Press).

Shepard, T. (2006), *The Invention of Decolonization: The Algerian War and the Remaking of France* (Ithaca, NY: Cornell University Press).

Shivji, I. (2007), *Silences in NGO Discourse: The role and Future of NGOs in Africa* (Nairobi: Fahamu).

Shipway, M. (2007), *Decolonization and its Impact: A Comparative Approach to the End of the Colonial Empires* (Oxford: Blackwell).

Shillington, K. (2012), *History of Africa* (Palgrave Macmillan).

Shubin, V. (2008), *The Hot 'Cold War': The USSR in Southern Africa* (London: Pluto Press).

Soares, B. (2009), 'An Islamic social movement in contemporary West Africa: NASFAT of Nigeria', in Ellis, S. & van Kessel, I. (eds) *Movers and Shakers: Social Movements in Africa* (Leiden: Brill).

Stockwell, J. (1979), *In Search of Enemies* (London: Futura Publications).

Stoecker, H. (1986), *German Imperialism in Africa* (London: C. Hurst).

Storey, A. (2009), 'Measuring Human Development' in McCann, G. & McCloskey, S. (eds), *From the Local to the Global: Key Issues in Development Studies* (London: Pluto).

Strachan, H. (2004), *The First World War in Africa* (Oxford: Oxford University Press).

Straus, S. (2004), 'How many perpetrators were there in the Rwandan genocide? An estimate', *Journal of Genocide Research*, 6, 1, pp. 85–98.

Stuart, L. (2013), T*he South African Non-profit Sector: Struggling to Survive, Needing to Thrive*, www.ngopulse.org/article/south-african-nonprofit-sector-struggling-survive-needing-thrive, (accessed 7 June 2017).

Sun, Yun (2014), *Africa in China's Foreign Policy*, www.brookings.edu/~/media/Research/Files/Papers/2014/04/africa-china-policy-sun/Africa-in-China-web_CMG7.pdf?la=en (accessed 14 May 2017).

Suri, T. & William, J. (2016), 'The long-run poverty and gender impacts of mobile money', *Science*, 354, 6317, pp. 1288–1292.

The Economist (2000), 'Hopeless Africa', 11 May.

The Economist (2011), 'The hopeful continent: Africa rising', 3 December.

The Economist (2011a), 'Now for the hard part', 3 February.

The Economist (2013), 'Lurching ahead', 13 April.

The Lancet (2014), 'Global, regional, and national prevalence of overweight and obesity in children and adults during 1980–2013: A systematic analysis for the Global Burden of Disease Study 2013' Volume 384, Issue 9945, pp. 766–781, August 30, 2014.

Thomas, M., Butler, L. & Moore, B. (2015), *Crises of Empire: Decolonization and Europe's Imperial States* (London: Bloomsbury).

Thompson, A. (2007), *The Media and the Rwanda Genocide* (London: Pluto Press).

Thompson, V. (1964), 'The Ivory Coast', in Carter, G. (ed), *African One-Party States* (New York: Cornell University Press).

Thornton, J. (1998), *Africa and Africans in the Making of the Atlantic World, 1400–1800* (Cambridge: Cambridge University Press).

Time Magazine (1994), 'Descent into Mayhem', 18 April.

Trans-Atlantic Slave Trade Database, www.slavevoyages.org/tast/index.faces.

Trevor-Roper, H. (1964), *Rise of Christian Europe* (New York: Harcourt, Brace & World).

Triulzi, A. & McKenzie, R. (2013), *Long Journeys. African Migrants on the Road* (Leiden: Brill).

Turner, T. (2007), *The Congo Wars: Conflict, Myth and Reality* (London: Zed Books).

UIS (2012), 'School and teaching resources in Sub-Saharan Africa', *UIS Information Bulletin*, no.9.

UN (2002), '*Final Report of the Panel of Experts on the Illegal Exploitation of Natural Resources and Other Forms of Wealth of the Democratic Republic of the Congo*'.

UN (2015), *Framework for Climate Change: Adoption of the Paris Agreement*.

UN (2016), 'World Population Prospects: The 2015 Revision', Department of Economic and Social Affairs, Population Division, https://esa.un.org/unpd/wpp/DataQuery/ (accessed 3 July 2016).

UN (2017), *Department of Economic and Social Affairs, Population Division*, 'World Population Prospects: The 2017 Revision'.

UN (2017a), *Peacekeeping Fact Sheet*, www.un.org/en/peacekeeping/resources/statistics/factsheet.shtml (accessed 24 July 2017).

UN (2017b), *More than $350 million pledged for refugees in Uganda*, https://www.un.org/apps/news/story.asp?NewsID=57050#.WXcJEoTyupr (accessed 12 July 2017).

UN (2018), *International Migration Stock: 2017 Revision*.

UNAIDS (2016), *Global Aids Update*.

UNCTAD (2015), *Building the African Continental Free Trade Area* (New York: United Nations).

UNCTAD (2016), *Handbook of Statistics 2016* (New York: United Nations).

UNECA (1989), *Economic Report on Africa, 1989* (Addis Ababa: Economic Commission for Africa).

UNECA (2015), *Intra-African Trade and Africa Regional Integration Index*, https://www.uneca.org/sites/default/files/uploaded-documents/RITD/2015/

CRCI-Oct2015/intra-african_trade_and_africa_regional_integration_index.pdf (accessed 15 June 2017).

UNECA (2016), *Transformative Industrial Policy for Africa* (Addis Ababa: Economic Commission for Africa).

UNESCO (2012), *World Atlas of Gender Equality in Education.*

UNESCO (2015), *Education for All 2000–2015: Achievements and Challenges.*

UNHCR (2016), *'Refugee' or 'migrant' – Which is right?*, www.unhcr.org/uk/news/latest/2016/7/55df0e556/unhcr-viewpoint-refugee-migrant-right.html

UNHCR (2017), *Global Trends: Forced displacement in 2016*, www.unhcr.org/uk/statistics/unhcrstats/5943e8a34/global-trends-forced-displacement-2016.html

UNHDR (2015), *Human Development Report*, http://report.hdr.undp.org/

UNDP (2012), *Mobile technologies and empowerment: Enhancing human development through participation and innovation*, www.undp.org/content/undp/en/home/librarypage/democratic-governance/access_to_informationande-governance/mobiletechnologiesprimer.html

UNDP (2015), *The Millennium Development Goals Report 2015*, www.un.org/millenniumgoals/2015_MDG_Report/pdf/MDG%202015%20rev%20(July%201).pdf (accessed 9 July 16).

UNDP (2016), *Human Development Report 2016. Human Development for Everyone.*

UN-Habitat (2010), *The State of African Cities 2010: Governance, Inequalities and Urban Land Markets.*

United Nations University (2016), *'Like it or not, poor countries are increasingly dependent on mining and oil & gas'*, https://www.wider.unu.edu/publication/it-or-not-poor-countries-are-increasingly-dependent-mining-and-oil-gas

Uvin, P. (1997), 'Prejudice, Crisis, and Genocide in Rwanda', *African Studies Review*, 40, 2, pp. 91–115.

Vale, P. & Maseko, S. (1998), 'South Africa and the African Renaissance', *International Affairs*, 74, 2, pp. 271–287.

van de Walle, N. (2001), *African Economies and the Politics of Permanent Crisis, 1979–1999* (Cambridge: Cambridge University Press).

Vandervort, B. (1998), *Wars of Imperial Conquest in Africa, 1830-1914* (Bloomington, IN: Indiana University Press).

van Dijk, M.P. (2009), *The New Presence of China in Africa* (Amsterdam: Amsterdam University Press).

Vansina, J. (1990), *Paths in the Rainforests: Toward a History of Political Tradition in Equatorial Africa* (Madison, WI: University of Wisconsin Press).

van Walraven, K. (1999), *Dreams of Power: The Role of the Organization of African Unity in the Politics of Africa, 1963–1993* (Aldershot: Ashgate).

Vencovsky, D. (2007), 'Presidential term limits in Africa', *Conflict Trends*, 2, pp. 15–21.

Wali, O. (1963), 'The Dead End of African Literature?', *Transition*, 10, pp. 13–15.

Westad, O. (2007), *The Global Cold War: Third World Interventions and the Making of Our Times* (Cambridge: Cambridge University Press).

White, B. (2008), *Rumba Rules: The Politics of Dance Music in Mobutu's Zaire* (London: Duke University Press).

WHO (2014a), *World Malaria Report 2014*.

WHO (2014b), *Statement on the 1st meeting of the IHR Emergency Committee on the 2014 Ebola outbreak in West Africa*, www.who.int/mediacentre/news/statements/2014/ebola-20140808/en/

WHO (2016a), *World Malaria Report 2016*.

WHO (2016b), *Ebola data and statistics*, 11 May 2016, http://apps.who.int/gho/data/view.ebola-sitrep.ebola-summary-latest?lang=en

Widner, J. (1992), *The Rise of a Party-State in Kenya: From 'Harambee!' to 'Nyayo!'* (Berkeley: University of California Press).

Williams, D. & Young, T. (2012), 'Civil society and the liberal project in Ghana and Sierra Leone', *Journal of Intervention and State Building*, 6, 1, pp. 7–22.

Williams, G. (1994), 'Why structural adjustment is necessary and why it doesn't work', *ROAPE*, 21, 60, pp. 214–225.

Williams, P. (2007), 'From non-intervention to non-indifference: The origins and development of the African Union's security culture', *African Affairs*, 106, 423, pp. 253–279.

Williams, P. (2016), *War and Conflict in Africa* (Cambridge: Polity).

Williams, P. & Boutellis, A. (2014), 'Partnership peacekeeping: Challenges and opportunities in the United Nations–African Union Relationship', *African Affairs*, 113, 451, pp. 254–278.

World Bank (1980), *World Bank Development Report 1980* (Washington, DC: World Bank).

World Bank (1984), *World Bank Development Report: Recovery or Relapse in the World Economy?* (Washington, DC: Oxford University Press).

World Bank (1989), *Sub-Saharan Africa: From Crisis to Sustainable Growth: A Long-Term Perspective Study* (Washington, DC: World Bank).

World Bank (1990), *World Development Report: Poverty* (New York: Oxford University Press).

World Bank (1994), *Adjustment in Africa: Reforms, Results, and the Road Ahead* (Washington, DC: World Bank).

World Bank (2000), *African Development Indicators* (Washington, DC: World Bank).

World Bank (2008), *Improving Trade and Transport for Landlocked Developing Countries* (Washington, DC: World Bank).

World Bank (2015), *Development Indicators*, http://data.worldbank.org/data-catalog/world-development-indicators (accessed 5 May 2015).

World Bank (2016a), *Digital Dividends 2016 Report* (Washington, DC: World Bank).

World Bank (2016b), *Annual Report, 2016* (Washington, DC: World Bank).

World Bank (2017), Access to electricity (% of population), https://data.worldbank.org/indicator/EG.ELC.ACCS.ZS?page=5

Young, C. (1982), *Ideology and Development in Africa* (New Haven, CT: Yale University Press).

Young, C. (1988), 'The African colonial state and its political legacy' in Rothchild, D. & Chazan, N. (eds), *The Precarious Balance: State and Society in Africa* (Boulder, CO: Westview).

Young, C. (1994), *The African Colonial State: In Comparative Perspective* (New Haven, CT: Yale University Press).

Young, C. (2012), *The Postcolonial State in Africa: Fifty Years of Independence, 1960–2010* (Madison: University of Wisconsin Press).

Zeilig, L., Larmer, M. & Dwyer, P. (2012), 'An epoch of uprisings: Social movements in post-colonial Africa, 1945–98', *Socialist History*, 40, pp.1–24.

Zeleza, P. (2008), 'The challenges of studying the African diasporas', *African Sociological Review*, 12, 2, pp. 4–21.

Zimmerer, J. & Zeller, J. (eds) (2008), *Genocide in German South-West Africa: The Colonial War (1904–1908) in Namibia and its Aftermath* (Monmouth: Merlin Press).

Zimmerman, A. (2001), *Anthropology and Antihumanism in Imperial Germany* (Chicago, IL: Chicago University Press).

Zghal, A. (1995), 'The "bread riot" and the crisis of the one-party system in Tunisia', in Mamdani, M. & Wamba-dia-Wamba, E. (eds), *African Studies in Social Movements and Democracy* (Dakar: CODSRIA).

Zolberg, A. (1966), *Creating Political Order: The Party-States of West Africa* (Chicago: Chicago University Press).

INDEX

In this index *c* represents chart, *f* represents figure, *i* represents image, *m* represents map, and *t* represents table.

Made in the USA
Columbia, SC
17 July 2020

14070188R00167